EDUCATION AND EVOLUTION

School Instruction and the Human Future

Charles R. Reid

University Press of America,® Inc.
Lanham • New York • Oxford

Copyright © 2000 by
University Press of America,® Inc.
4720 Boston Way
Lanham, Maryland 20706

12 Hid's Copse Rd.
Cumnor Hill, Oxford OX2 9JJ

Library of Congress Cataloging-in-Publication Data

Reid, Charles R.
Education and evolution : school instruction and the human future /
Charles R. Reid.
p.   cm.
Includes bibliographical references.
1.   Education—Social aspects—United States. 2. Education—Aims and
objectives—United States. I. Title.
LC191.4.R43   2000   370'.973—dc21   99-056969 CIP

ISBN 0-7618-1595-3 (cloth: alk. ppr.)

♾™ The paper used in this publication meets the minimum
requirements of American National Standard for Information
Sciences—Permanence of Paper for Printed Library Materials,
ANSI Z39.48—1984

"Quickness of understanding is a mental faculty, but right doing
requires the practice of a lifetime."

Goethe

To the memory of my mother and father

and for

Mia, aide, counselor, friend

TABLE OF CONTENTS

Acknowledgments

The author expresses his thanks for her superb work in transcribing his original script to Ms. Eleene Kraft, and also to former teaching colleagues: Trudy Weyzen, Barton Stillman, Larry Weiner, and Denis Bettencourt for their encouragement and sustained interest in his topic and in its development.

INTRODUCTION

Is American Education Different?

"Only in America"—in a post-Cold War world where the US is left as the single superpower, this evocative phrase resonates with as great a credibility as ever. The global imagination, perhaps today more than at any point in the industrial past, recognizes the centrality of the American experience. True, the long-evolving capitalist civilization of Western Europe controlled until fairly recent times the main threads of world development. But only in modern America have both the triumphs and failures of human experience, personal as well as social, been so categorically "of the age." Only there have so many reached for the maximum in human attainment—or been able to.

In worldwide popular thinking, as carefully listening travelers soon learn, this perception of American uniqueness comes down to more than just an appreciation of the achievements of a few US historical leaders in political life and industry. It is more than solely an admission that the US is militarily or economically powerful. It credits the US with an unfailing strength in every realm of human activity, even the most essential economic, political, and cultural processes requiring mass interest and participation. American uniqueness thus also translates into a kind of automatic "consensus ability," a built-in mechanism by which great undertakings are moved forward irrespective of how or why the process is being carried out. The average person, native or foreigner, thus has a tendency to confuse US (as indeed he does world) process with progress, even with change itself—an error which distorts the reality, as perceived, of various major domains of human activity.

Some American institutions, certain popular patterns of behavior, even whole sequences of historical events in the US, do seem uniquely the product of this nation; they could be established or occur nowhere else. They fit the American social psyche. It is also likely that in many respects the US anticipates world change far more effectively than most other industrial societies which can only, given their situations, imitate and play catch-up in the headlong race to adapt to a post-Soviet world capitalist economy. With its history, its size, its appetite for novelty and tolerance for the bizarre, and its free market preferences, the US often sets the pace of world change, or at least as much as do smaller, older, and in fact less dynamic (though often cited) nations such as Sweden.

But there is a down as well as an upside in all social development, in whatever nation. In addition, the tendency exists to overlook the significance of basic routine in many important social processes. A case in point in both these contexts is education, which after all is an undertaking that undergirds a society's entire effort at progress over the generations. Change can be occurring in a negative far more than in a positive direction in this vital realm, even while a nation stands preeminent before the world for its accomplishments in many spheres, both in the present and over past adult generations.

Beyond even this, it is undeniable that some processes are more socially salient than others. Education is the most self-evident proof of this truth, literally a process on which all others depend. One may with considerable justification assert that the process of education is not only critical in the overall directions change will take for a nation; because it occupies this special position in the hierarchy of *all* processes, it must also support change in a positive direction, and do so by employing a rationale which renders the routine of process more effective. Educational outcomes (to use a favored item of professional jargon) should be the result of routines which derive from this rationale.

In the second half of the twentieth century, it is generally agreed, whatever other successes the US can claim, its educational accomplishments have been neither exceptional nor unique. Some more unhappy critics even insist that, in effect, only in America has mass formal education proven so categorically a "bad process"—meaning that, if examined closely, it can provide the world with a serious model of what *not* to do. The fact is that US academics (though by no means a majority) were complaining of the process and its outcomes as early as the 1960s. But only with passing time did "the system" gradually become a source of growing knowledge and concern, even embarrassment, to the country at large.

The slow slide into "bad process" did not fail to merit attention abroad. By the 1980s various foreign critics too were joining in with calls for "reform." America itself was still unique in many eyes, but its educational institutions, especially over the K-12 grade span, seemed to pass one nadir point after another, and the problems were becoming too obvious to be ignored. By the 1990s, some formal indicators of school achievement in this country reflected apparent improvement. But they were few and unconvincing. In spite of the most extensive financial support ever accorded such an enterprise in the history of man, critics keep asking: How is US education either different or unique, except in its failure to produce the very minimum results even its most ardent would-be vindicators desire?

***   ***   ***

Historically viewed, fundamental criticisms of a US seemingly no longer willing or able to prepare its children or youth for a difficult future took firm hold in the decade of the 1980s. For the special issue of *Time* of June, 1986, dedicated to an examination of the USA and what it stands for, foreign notables contributed a double page of commentary on America in the contemporary world. Amid the many often politically slanted statements of a kind so familiar in the emotionally charged atmosphere of the 1980s, the remarks of French intellectual J. J. Servan-Schreiber were striking in their pointed simplicity. His words were of small comfort to anyone seriously concerned with American education and, indeed, the entire future of American society:

> ...today the US faces a crisis in education. The level of primary and secondary education is well below the worldwide average. Young Americans entering college can hardly write a decent one-page text. They take little time and no pleasure in reading. They ignore that there is a world of human beings outside the borders of the US.[1]

For once the foreigner saw little reason to use carefully toned-down language in criticizing a public undertaking in the world's richest, most powerful democracy. Americans themselves have preferred indirection, speaking in the more politically acceptable jargon of a "nation at risk." But, if true, does choice of words matter? However the situation is stated, the future is left distinctly clouded by the failure of a mass education system of which Americans could once be reasonably proud. What is being done, or could be done, that might make a difference? How does anyone make headway against the barriers to drastic substantive reform? The questions are easily put. Answers are remarkably hard to come by.

At the peak of every pyramid-type organization, solutions are conceived in bureaucratic context. The top dictates, the bottom obeys. Thus the Carnegie Commission and like-minded bodies have categorically placed the main burden of proof on teachers and teacher preparation programs. Both must be upgraded. (A second motif in some reform scenarios may call for a corresponding downgrading of the administrative role.) If teachers are to be given real responsibility for what goes on in the instructional area, such is the reasoning, they must be both independent and accountable; self-determining teachers in their instructional fiefdoms will require teacher aides of various kinds and clerical help, but hardly more. Wherever teaching is carried on, teachers should be given broader powers in the instructional sphere and in school operations generally; yet overall, as an organized unit each school must be governed on-site by principals with skill and authority. Such is, relatively, the underlying contemporary American wisdom of school as a functioning entity.

For those in a more liberal tradition, teachers also should be better rewarded financially, not paid off at a level equivalent to that of household servants of a few generations ago, so that now their standard of living rates below that of garbage collectors and hod carriers. The result of such changes and others could be a turnaround in what has been a shockingly downhill progress of American mass education over five-plus postwar decades. Yet such proposals remain fundamentally administrative nostrums, not directly aimed at altering the negative psychological aspects of instruction for either students or teachers. Few critics, even those favorably disposed, see reason to claim that the result of these shifts in school modes of operation and teacher compensation will be a real turnaround in educational outcomes.

As with so many well-intentioned approaches to the education problem in America at the millennium, there surfaces in all this top-down theorizing a decided touch of old-line managerial utopianism, one phenomenon that seems by now excessively déjà vu. Consider the central assumption that the teacher ought to have an enhanced role in both instruction and management aspects of school operation. Why or how should this yield better results, even if it can be implemented in a forceful way? Even if teacher preparation programs are improved significantly, does this not leave the lockstep of the school schedule still to confront, to say nothing of the standard textbook, the limited repertory of instructional techniques, and the drawbacks for individual students of state or district mandated curriculum programs? In short, will "empowerment" of teachers really mean anything, however it is realized?

Change, then, is more easily talked about than actually brought into being. As Bernard Gifford, then Dean of Education at the University of California, Berkeley, once expressed it in referring to a Carnegie Commission plan for teacher empowerment, "it stands a high chance of ending up in the dust bin of history because it challenges the status quo...and in education there are so many entrenched interests with veto power."[2] This less-than-positive view of any far-reaching scheme of planned change has been regularly echoed not only by such entrenched interests within education as the AFT and National Education Association but also by leaders in business, industry, and the media.

Indeed, there are some grounds for contending that *any* "teacher-empowerment" scheme could in many ways worsen, rather than improve, the instructional climate, notwithstanding the factor of increased teacher prestige and income. One has the impression that a new psychological gap could readily be created between elitist, highly paid teachers and often defiant and uninterested masses of students who remain victims of mandatory attendance laws. The net effect would likely be to expend additional billions to support technological baubles, an unjustified increase in adult personnel (aides to perform duties of a semi-instructional or non-instructional nature), and teachers' salaries soon enough in the six-figure range while, at the same time, leaving essentially unchanged the instructional situation itself—thereby, once again, despite all the added expense and buildup of public expectation, failing to come to grips with the school's age-old basic problem, that of instruction suited to the individual learner's needs. As with so many "magic formulas" dredged up in the past by committees of reformers, plans of this kind now as before are only too likely to bring about not so much planned effective change as merely "more of the same."

The opportunities for meaningful action do not boil down simply to an upgrading of responsibilities and status for those whose primary duties involve the planning and delivery of instruction. The nature of each individual student continues to present a prior variable which somehow has to be taken into account before across-the-board changes are forced upon the educational enterprise. The teacher in tomorrow's school, as in today's, will still face the individual learner across a gulf of years and experience. She cannot somehow miraculously reinvent the little red schoolhouse of a century ago with the expectation that her students will oblige by acting the parts of those presumably ingenuous, well-mannered, automatically thoughtful and reserved pupils of the 1890s. More than ever in the more distant past, the learner presents a psychological challenge, a chameleon-like antagonist operating to one degree or another in disharmony with the prescribed "rules of the game" as perceived by adults. We cannot wish away this hard reality, this child raised as much on television and peer group influences as by parental nurture.

Oversize classes are only one (though admittedly an important) aspect of the problem. The teacher today has an implicit mandate to "reach" the individual. Yet few are the teachers who can carry on their work, like the doctor or lawyer, in a one-to-one fashion with the student. Teachers, in the main, work in group settings. They teach, in a typical instance, between twenty and forty children at any one time. The search for some psychological means of "reaching" every individual within a classroom milieu, therefore, is a daunting and never-completed task. The teacher, like a businessman or economist continually trying to "calculate the market," obliges himself to be forever on the lookout for a "master explanation," some generic psychological code which, while employed with groups, will somehow fit each individual, will unlock the secret chamber of each child-mind with equal effect. The hunt is always on for that unique holistic formula which, as a kind of educational equivalent of Einstein's mass-energy equation in physics, will explain why something must happen in a certain way in the teaching-learning situation at hand—and thus provide the needed clues for advance planning.

Yet never does such a magic formula quite materialize. Tantalizing theories emerge from psychological laboratories and university graduate schools, only to prove as often as not inapplicable to the needs of a given local situation. This does not bring the search to an end, however. If anything, it increases the pressure for generic "solutions." Teachers and administrators in city and rural districts alike look with panic and mounting concern to the domain of the learned for new keys by which to resolve their problems. Piaget and other contemporary authorities from abroad are made the basis of a huge literature of second-hand thinking vaguely directed at the task of providing new insights. Dewey and other native writers on pedagogy are interpreted and then reinterpreted in the same cause. Professional researchers pour out studies and pamphlets, all purporting to deal with the issues and reveal new knowledge pertinent to them. The resources of an entire spectrum of the emerging Information Society seem devoted in one way or another to an explication of the enigma of instruction.

Nothing helps. The circle of dependencies grows larger, yet the results sought are not forthcoming. It makes no sense to suggest that all the activities of research organizations, university scholars, school district personnel, school boards, and the many other interested parties do not add to the knowledge society itself can use to make decisions about education. But all the research to date, the endless conferences, seminars, debates, and brainstorming sessions devoted to "how to do it," while illuminating in an abstract sense, have not brought consensus about what to do in concrete real life situations. Indeed, in some cases scholarly input and popular opinion on the subject alike have only served to muddy waters further.

Meantime the school as a provider of essential experiences and knowledge for the millions of children and youth who will inherit the duties and burdens of citizenship a short generation hence goes its own way—and not a very satisfactory way by any standards. One recalls Paul Goodman's description of the schools of the 1960s; they provide a "universal trap," and are not geared any longer even to the middle class values on which they were thought to be based. "The schools less and less represent any human values, but simply adjustment to a mechanism."[3]

Mass schooling in America in the 1980s and 1990s did not improve on mass schooling in the 1960s, clearly, but matters continue bad enough so that gradually the rest of the world joins in our worries. The Servan-Schreibers of the fin de siècle and beyond must continue to labor the obvious: the US, once the global leader in mass education, can no longer guarantee either the process or the product. We are, in fact, "educating" one age cohort after another at a progressively lower absolute standard. It may rightly be asked if, after enough time has passed, we can be said to be educating at all any longer.

***   ***   ***

Few social scientists fail to accept the large role education will have to play in preparing masses of citizens for participation in the society of the future. The same may be said for informed adults in general, though they are a distinct minority of the population. The broader public itself as yet provides no significant input to the problem. It awaits some new kind of consensus from experts and politicians on actions to be taken—not willing to admit, as yet, its own unavoidable role in decision-making. A consensus of sorts long ago emerged that "something is wrong," however, and this has been fully grasped by the politicians. As for what can possibly be done to improve matters, the prospect unavoidably is for more, rather than less, conflict among those must make the real political decisions.

The element of conflict slowly becomes more pronounced with time. The periodic US Governors Conferences on Education provide an eloquent example of the extent of differences between political perceptions of the "education problem" and traditional establishment views. While still wedded to the concept of an organizationally manipulated "solution," the governors usually see nothing but more trouble arising from continued absolute dependence on existing modes of instruction and administration. They tend to ask fundamental questions about change in the system: Should parents have a choice as to which schools their children attend? Shall schools function on a year-around basis? Should children of the poor or culturally disadvantaged be given special help at one or more stages of the educational ladder? Can merit pay for "superior teaching" be introduced as standard practice everywhere? Can students themselves actually be held responsible for meeting the tougher requirements called for if US schools are to become competitive with better foreign ones? Can local school systems be held accountable for specific achievement levels which students there will be expected to meet? Will high school "leaving exams" make more trouble than they will do good?

These are hard questions and they are not easily answered in a context of "business as usual." Nor are they being answered simply by the imposition of stiffer curriculum and attendance standards, heavier course requirements in teacher preparation programs, and the like. For while these seem the only appropriate first steps politicians, as themselves dedicated administrators, feel competent to demand of school systems at this point, they are inadequate to the situation. Still, governors and other leading elements within the spectrum of US politics have certainly valid reasons for complaint as they view the state of American education from the relatively well-informed centers of statehouse or local administrative management.

A glance at economic reportage in any metropolitan US newspaper over a few days or weeks makes clear why politicians continue taking the education crisis ever more seriously. Presently stable state economies could face a doubtful future; there is lack of both corporate and worker "competitive skills." Things may be going well now, but what lies ahead? It takes no unusual exercise of the imagination to foresee what can and likely will happen over succeeding decades if the entire American economy, agriculture perhaps excepted, goes the way of, say, the US garment industry. The depressing example of Europe's seemingly permanent high unemployment rates provides an unappetizing preview of what may well lie over the horizon in our medium-term future. The problem has both an educational cause and a result which bespeaks a further educational dilemma. Economist J. K. Galbraith touched on the central aspect of this problem a few decades ago in his *New Industrial State*:

> (While) the unemployed are reduced in number, they come to consist more and more of those, primarily the uneducated, who are unemployable in the industrial system. The counterpart of this resistant core is a growing number of vacancies for highly qualified workers and a strong bargaining position for those who are employed.[4]

Then what can be done? What should be done? These are indeed difficult questions, not least for the layman. Yet for those already fairly knowledgeable of the subject, two rather less obvious prior issues rise to the surface: these are the social and individual purposes of learning, on one hand, and on the other the psychological aspect of instruction. Of the first no one can pronounce with finality, for society's own wishes play so important a role in the making of major decisions, and while one may have personal preferences it remains for an expression of popular will to validate changes in the goals of popular education.

Yet the second issue, that of learning and instruction in their psychological aspect, offers a unique entree to resolution of society's larger quandary over general directions to be taken. By seeking and, to a degree finding, answers to the main question of pedagogy—What are the essential process elements in an instructional system which leads to optimum learning for a given individual?—the community of education professionals could in fact do better in guiding society in general to an improved understanding of why there must be changes in the instructional process itself.

Margaret Mead spoke of the need for "a new kind of teaching altogether," for "a teaching of a readiness to use unknown ways to solve unknown problems."[5] This expresses something of the nature of the instructional problem of the future, if not so much in its depth then at least in its breadth. But teaching, even of the best type, will hardly succeed without the receptivity of an interested learner. Young minds a thousand miles away, lost in dreams of escape from the prison of self and circumstance, are no more easily reached than are adult minds already too aware of the limitations of self and circumstance, and expending all available energy resisting those limitations. This state of affairs, seemingly, has already been realized in the US school system to an unprecedented extent.

***   ***   ***

America's educational problems, it will be argued, are unique to that society and culture, and the rest of the world has little to learn from its travail. This at best can be no more than half-truth. World education as a system cannot be reduced to a single seamless web, for every culture matures under different circumstances and at different rates of speed. Yet historical experience in all the advanced nations strongly suggests, I believe, a clear commonality of process in development of formal education structures—from initial concept through the various phases of system rationalization, and adaptation to phenomena of change in both incremental and fundamental aspects.

Germany and Japan, today's leading competitive nation-states, like the US have had universal free and compulsory education systems for a long time. In both cases their educational history reveals a slow development through trial and error, with alternating cycles of systematization and breakdown, and through it all a continuous trend to increased control over all aspects of system performance from the center—a growing dependence over several centuries on hierarchy and standardization of process. That these two civilized countries, with their enormous reservoirs of intellectual talent, their history of creative thought and artistic and technological achievement, could become the twentieth-century's fascist nightmares is an historical fact the proper interpretation of which, in light of their advancements in education, remains to be provided.

Perhaps the only thing safely to be said is that the failure of democracy in two such advanced nations taught the Germans and Japanese a lesson that others have yet to learn—that mass literacy attained through a universal system of school instruction is not in itself a complete answer to the problems of nationhood or national adaptation in a world of uncompromising evolutionary pressures. But if utilizing education as a hierarchical sorting process for adult life was a danger, it was also a necessity in a universally competitive international environment. The net effect, then, in these nations, was simply to reinforce popular postwar insistence on a traditional process of instruction, in which the burden of proof for learning rested finally and exclusively with child and parents. The system of formal education itself dared not change, for any deeply fundamental change could bring on an uncertainty over society's own longer-range future more fearsome than anything known before.

This explanation may not be proven wholly plausible by history, yet there can be little question that the national soul-search forced upon both Germans and Japanese after the greatest of all human wars has had the effect of blunting not merely a return of ideology but also of reinforcing the significance of tried and true (even if not innovative) social processes. Thus the Japanese and Germans are today succeeding by looking backwards through time and cultivating dependence on methods still in a measure valid—in *their* cultures—and which "work" because in one degree or another historical memory acts to restrain in those nations the growth of radical and individualistic defiance of instructional conventions so evident elsewhere.

In North America the social psychological conditions left over in the major losers of World War Two obtained little, and in the US the wave of educational challenge sure to beset the world in general later on made its appearance early, beginning with small negative effects in the immediate postwar decades, and then hitting with more general and devastating effects during the "mad" decade of the 1960s, and since. The whole "process of instruction of the young" has by now in a great number of US schools become an issue seemingly defying any human logic. The *method of instruction*, for a mass of disaffected school learners, indeed, which more and more people recognize cannot be dealt with by resort to a dependence on incremental, politically and culturally convenient changes alone, is a topic which by the 1990s had begun to irk adult Americans beyond all reason. The theme of "instructional reform" is thus characteristically ubiquitous in adult conversation. It has also characteristically become a staple of every politician's program for maintaining social and economic progress.

Then will Japanese or German models for mass education become the world norm? Should it be simply taken for granted that America—and after it the world at large—will follow the lead of these seemingly more "successful" educational systems, facing backward through time, imitating that same inflexible posture? Will the whole world then see progress on the educational front solely in terms of an insistence on firmer adherence to nothing more than established international educational practice—which individualistic Americans already find so confining and irksome?[6] I believe that this interpretation fails entirely in its appreciation of the scope of the coming century's global problem of school instruction—indeed, of education as the most vital process of future world society itself.

It is much more likely that America, as it struggles against the shackles of a centuries-old traditional method of school instruction— one, incidentally, in a shorter national history never fully assimilated to the powerful and distinct national tradition of individualism per se—must forge ahead of all others against the universal pressures of a twenty-first-century crisis of "information overflow." The contradictions and contractions of a coming century of universal limits, in brief, are being faced first and most sharply by a nation which in the past two centuries faced the least such limits. It should not seem strange in historical context, then, that greater difficulties and disappointments should initially visit—and in their most perplexing forms—a people whose initial outlook was least conditioned by negative experience of a constricting socio-cultural or economic environment.

In the chapters that follow I try to provide one observer's view of the larger dimensions of our shared problems in the world education enterprise, with a distinct emphasis on the American experience. Inevitably such a task involves an effort to bring to fuller light of day those aspects of mass schooling systems I regard as critical to their success in the difficult decades ahead. These factors fall mainly under the single rubric of instruction, but also include its "secondary" administrative, psychological, technological, and general social contexts.

Indeed, I see these secondary aspects as critical for two reasons: First, because while admitted by all to be an influence in instruction they elude the exclusively linear, cause-effect reasoning typical of management-oriented analysis (so that they are then wrongly ignored in standard institutional studies); second, because they often tend to suggest new or diverse possibilities for action—and these possibilities are not in every case readily obvious (or as yet perhaps even acceptable) to either the professional educational establishment or the broader adult public.

I submit, finally, that an Information Society cannot avoid certain self-examination procedures and that these must begin with the unhampered insights of experienced individuals. Social self-examination is, of course, as yet only an idea and not a fact, a concept whose time can only come in a deep future context. It would seem to have little significance in a world still drawn to the psychological over-simplifications of Enlightenment-era optimism or the unworkable social dynamics preached more recently by Marx and Lenin. But perhaps we are already approaching a time in human social evolution when men in greater numbers will work harder to achieve an understanding of (rather than merely continue to avoid thinking about) the central issues of their time. One of these issues, perhaps the most central of all, must surely be that of an education for the masses of children and youth consistent with the problems they are certain to meet in the century to come.

With these hesitant thoughts I invite the reader to share with me some speculations on the longer-term future of public education in the democratic tradition. The only logical point of beginning must be not some vague, utopian dream of perfection a hundred years hence, with no hints as to how such a state of perfection can possibly be attained and which skips conveniently over what is sure to prove an overwhelmingly difficult, if not indeed an outright chaotic intervening period; the only rational starting-point must be what has properly been described as "the real world of institutional breakdown" in contemporary mass education systems.

Such systems, though they still seem to us today strikingly different in aims and organization, are alike in the nature of the challenges they meet.   Inevitably, the world of tomorrow will be one with commonalities of outlook for education far outpacing old differences of perspective associated with separate national cultures.   Perhaps Bertrand Russell best summed up the expectations a civilized "city of the nations" should look to in his anti-war tract of 1917:

> What is to be desired (of citizens everywhere) is not cosmopolitanism, not the absence of all national characteristics that one associates with couriers, *wagon-lit* attendants, and others, who have had everything distinctive obliterated by multiple and trivial contacts with men of every civilized country.... The international spirit...will be something added to love of country, not something taken away.[7]

PART ONE

TODAY'S SCHOOL
AND ITS PROBLEMS

THE GLOBAL PICTURE

Chapter 1

An American View of Mass Education and the Information Age

Perhaps the term "Information Age," as cynics claim, is overblown. It already universalizes a too-little-appreciated phenomenon: the gradual but inescapable encroachment of ever-enlarging bodies of information, either in "raw" form or as pre-digested and interpreted by cultural entities, upon individual consciousness. The implication of such a term is largely negative; it suggests a steady increase in personal psychological burdens, making it contrary to the bent of human nature and something to be resisted, even if necessary by an act of individual will.

But what does an Information Age mean for education? Since information is the single most essential element in education, any answer here must be ambiguous. One can honestly view education as a social exercise in interpretation of information, an investment of time, energy, and money by both collective and individual, to provide both with a higher yield from a universal flood with which all must cope. Yet to many adults any effort either to prepare for an information-rich future or even to use information to meet the challenges of childhood and youth today, asks more than children should have to endure. Education should not "force" anything on anyone. It should deal with information, yes, but not in ways that increase any child's psychological burdens. Let the child live as a child, such people have been saying for centuries, and not be rushed into the troubled waters of adulthood. And such an outlook is by no means limited to parents who are uneducated or economically and culturally disadvantaged.

This much admitted, it remains only too evident that a reckoning with the Information Society or an Information Age is inevitable. The world more and more runs on information, and those who manage and manipulate it are contemptuous of and indeed will take advantage of those who lack the skill or motivation to process it. At the same time the extent and depth of ignorance in the world has never been greater. Modern life is not synonymous with uniformities of progress. The informed dictate to the uninformed, just as in ages past. This imbalance is inconsistent with democracy and even the implicit meanings of the term "Information Society" itself.

Japan, it is claimed, has already become an Information Society. How the availability of ever-more burdensome mountains of information has actually made life any easier for the average Japanese would be hard to see, however. Nor are the US and most other developed nations beneficiaries in any wholly positive sense of the Information Age. A cogent argument can in fact be made that ignorance really retains the whip hand, forcing decisions of major social import, in both advanced and developing societies.

Men of all shades of political opinion are rightfully disturbed by the prevalence of ignorance, and by its implications for mankind's long-term progress. As Michael Marien, editor of the US publication *Future Survey* and a commentator perhaps more forthright than many others of the American intelligentsia, has put it: "We must recognize that we live in an Age of Ignorance, where the "learning needs of all age groups are out-racing their attainments. Our nation is indeed at risk."[1]

In one respect, however, America's mass education system differs from the majority of others in the contemporary world: both in theory and operationally it is oriented to primarily local standards and goals. As a matter of historical development and national preference, in global context this tendency can be overstated. Centrally dictated practices only too readily become the norm wherever adequate local initiative is lacking, traditional rhetoric notwithstanding. Even so, this commitment to localism has a far more respectable standing in the US than in almost any other industrial country, and in a degree it was an important factor in building American power in the world.

This was a phenomenon that did not go unnoticed. The relative success in the past of America's system of local control has both

impressed and puzzled outsiders. As Columbia University Professor
Freeman Butts states it:

> The mass participation of citizens in American public educational affairs
> has always bewildered Europeans accustomed to centralized authority in
> education. The US was able to modernize its education from below,
> because the incentive to produce education on a large scale was widely
> dispersed throughout the population who saw its value for economic,
> social, political, and cultural advancement.[2]

In fact, the world trend in general has been away from local initiative
and direction. Whether one looks at developed modern nation states or
at underdeveloped societies still emerging from a tribal past, the
centralizing tendency dominates. America stands out as different not
so much in its preference for local control as in the evident willingness
of its citizens on occasion to act on local views in the governance of
mass education. That willingness has a long-term significance which
could well be pondered by other societies, underdeveloped and
advanced. But the value of this phenomenon of decentralization as a
factor in mass education has yet to be demonstrated under
circumstances other than the North American.

The extent to which local control exists in fact as well as in theory
can have a direct bearing on both ends and means in education, of
course. But the survival over centuries of a will to exercise local self-
management means little in and of itself. World modes of
administration generally stress a philosophy of decentralization on the
verbal level, while at the same time enforcing an ever more ironclad
rule from the center. Hierarchy in the American setting can thus differ
only in degree from what—in a global modus operandi responding to
needs for order regardless of the result—is the single and universal
norm of functioning in the realm of instruction.

Still, to assert this and no more ignores the as-yet uncertain
capabilities of world society as a whole to coexist with and adapt to
future pressures common to all evolving hierarchical systems. There
are definite limits to any trend moving exclusively in just one neat
channel, toward excessive centralization on one hand or too much
decentralization on the other, toward absolute restriction or absolute
freedom. History seldom offers humanity clear-cut choices on such a
universal issue, and educational history is no exception to the rule.

Educational Technology's Current Limits

If the tendency to hierarchic centralization is important, so too is technology in the processes of social development. Almost needless to state, tomorrow's education will have to come to grips in a much more forcible way with the optimum role of technology in school instruction. The huge expense of formal education alone mandates increased deployment of machines to aid learning. This need not be looked at as a retrogression or negative solution (because it removes students from the constant control of human professionals). Professor Christopher Dede of Houston University explains that

> In fact, properly done and applied to appropriate content, teaching devices can be more interesting and motivating than the typical teacher; young children will require some amount of adult attention, older students relatively little. Some learners—either because of emotional problems or idiosyncratic learning styles—will require a traditional classroom context, but most students could readily and profitably adapt to a mixture of machine and human instruction.[3]

Yet as a highly traditional, labor-intensive activity, education has never appeared to move very well with the times where technology is concerned. The ancient saying, "The more things change, the more they remain the same," reflects the brute truth of matters. Philip H. Coombs, a well-known specialist in international education, sums up the historical gist of it:

> Traditionally, and up to the present, education has been the last in line to adopt promising new technologies—including even the book (which even the great Socrates disdained on the grounds that a student could not talk back to a book, ask it questions, and have an enlightening dialogue). Yet the book finally made it.[4]

Still, given the difficulties confronting modern mass education, it seems unwise to underestimate the influence any of the newly developing technologies might come to have. Technology possesses an unknown potential for determining both shape and scope of all future social and psychological processes. Looking at it in a patronizing way hardly fits with a truly global and modern view of world development in the coming century.

The thing most needing to be said of technology, perhaps, is that we need to be careful not to lose sight of it. Those societies which make the optimum use of technology will fare best in a high tech future. This is widely understood, fortunately. In those countries where economic development and the unfettered movement of information are accepted universally as system "basics," the US and Japan being prime examples, pressures both for and against introduction of more advanced technologies into traditional social processes (formal education among them) have become acute. In most cases, so far, restraint appears to overbear innovation. In education the deadweight of traditional practice is hard to cast aside. But public awareness of the possibilities of technology in the realm of instruction and learning is growing.

Today's laser disk technology provides an example of the contradictions posed by advanced technology in education. This technology, usually referred to as CD-ROM, allows the contents of whole encyclopedias to be impressed on just one disk the size of a small household plate. It permits a user instant access to virtually every field of formal learning and, in theory, could come to replace libraries in toto. Yet no one, least of all students themselves, seems in any hurry to see this system brought universally on line. Indeed, there are good reasons for thinking that CD-ROM will not go very far at all in impacting the information-recovery market, which includes in theory all institutions of formal education. There may be no reasonable route by which the mass of potential users can ever, by themselves, be driven to employ it. The slower lookup process afforded in traditional libraries thus far has continued as the preferred mode of information search.

One must always, it seems, keep in mind the extreme limits of the human being as an energy system. No human can process and interpret information at more than a certain maximum speed and a given level of efficiency. As with other, presumably promising high tech products (in Coombs' words, "gadgets...expected to perform educational miracles"[5]), the high-capacity laser storage disk can do little more for an ordinary user at this stage than the old-fashioned book or magazine itself. And why? Because every learner or user is after all no more than a biologically limited processing system, a being subject to ennui, fatigue, loss of interest in one topic or stimulus and buildup of interest in another, plus a host of "back-of-the-mind" psychological images often creating countervailing pressures to divergent thinking far greater than the momentary possession of a novel lookup device can combat.

A CD data base has value, then, over and above that of a standard encyclopedia or library, only insofar as it better matches some learner's or user's capabilities and needs as an information consumer. Beyond this its rationale is unclear. Miracles of technology yield no corresponding human miracle when the humans who might use the technology recognize no opportunity for individual fulfillment as they experience it. In the world of schooling, this is an old story. Like the horse which is not thirsty, children can be led to the fountain of learning, but they may still refuse to drink.

Information Explosion and Human Processing Abilities

It is of just such conundrums that today's educational struggle consists. Meantime, around the world education systems continue to waver between two archetypes, the elitist, hierarchical one of European tradition on one hand and the more populist American one on the other. So far the European version seems the favorite. If anything, Asian, African, and Latin American systems in the latter half of the twentieth century, perhaps thanks as much to their lack of, or misallocation of, resources as much as to their colonial heritage, have drifted toward even greater selectivity and elitism than have their European models, which have themselves been plagued with resource and excess-demand problems. In any case, world education is by now uniformly grounded in a Western secular and scientific orientation, as to both curriculum and modes of management. Whether or not such emphasis on elitism and rational science, in either subject matter or management, works to the common advantage remains an open question.

Technological breakthroughs are universally awaited; they are seen as the only answer to the problems of education, whether in the domain of mass access, of financing, or of instruction itself. Some futurists believe in the certainty not just of such breakthroughs but of their preordained success as well. Servan-Schreiber, for example, sees the microprocessor as the ultimate godsend; it will give every Third World peasant what he could never have had before: an information-producing and processing machine that will free him from the millennia of ignorance to which his ancestors were condemned, a form of technology that will yield him a power over his environment comparable to that already attained by citizens of any advanced Western society.[6]

Yet the likelihood of such a dramatic development seems as remote as ever. It is even questionable how many of the Third World's millions of peasants could be made to see the value of a machine that processes information in the first place. Worldwide ignorance is still pervasive. Too often it is a culturally approved ignorance, which deadens individual motivation. Hence the mere spread of Western concepts, with or without accompanying technological miracles, raises a difficult question of the absorptive powers of peasant cultures. Though Western beliefs and the Western outlook are paramount among those already educated, will the masses eventually accept or reject such an orientation? Educational historian Butts poses the question thus:

> Here is the challenge to the education of the West in the future. Can it enable the learners of the world—and their teachers—to study and understand the world as a whole and to take their part in it?[7]

Clearly information technology has a central place in the unavoidable effort to meet this challenge. Yet by itself information remains as inert as the physical matter of rocks or steel. It has to be made part of the human experience. And education, to be effective, demands more than the mere blind use of technical gimmicks for pouring out information on students; those who make policy as well as those who implement it need to grasp the "why" and "how" of human information processing.

It was the mathematician and intellectual father of cybernetics, Norbert Wiener, who pointed out a singular fact about the human use of information, that "it is more a matter of process than of storage."[8] Wherever we look in today's chiaroscuro world, we witness the value of individual processing power applied to bulk information. That intelligence which knows how to select, ponder, and finally use information as a primary resource will be able to achieve command over an environment while others merely interact with it. The intelligence which, though blessed with potential, sits by passively, waiting for some other intelligence or a technological miracle to give it access on the cheap to the effective meaning piled up in millions of bits on compact disks or in a computer's memory, or even in a newspaper column, relapses ultimately into a state of dependence. It falls into a permanent habit of "letting the other chap do it." Such an intelligence, committed by habit to passivity, has no claim of entree to a community of decision makers, who must wrestle with information in all its vagueness and profundity.

It is easy to say then that education can make all the difference. That statement, nonetheless, oversimplifies. Education is a process which succeeds or fails in a context of mass consciousness and adult norms of expectation. Consensus on what education should achieve is a tenuous thing at best, often expressed in implicit but never explained agreements only about what should not be achieved. Beyond this, it must be conceded that learners are, after all, first and foremost, individuals. Both children and adults learn as persons, not simply as cogs in some grand machine containing units which are all alike. Education has to mean something for the *individual* before it has meaning for his society. Information can enslave as well as liberate.

Issues of Information Control in Education

But will not an Information Society have resolved dilemmas like these? Clearly not, unless such a society is defined by its participants as something in which artificial restriction of personal growth and development is deemed more important than any other social good—an unlikely prospect. It is unfortunate that even many well-informed people today view information as the substance of a new world religion and the Information Society as a millennial realization on earth of that religion. Information, in fact, since it constantly expands, tends rather to create more new problems and leave old ones even less resolved. An Information Society cannot be a utopia of any kind, at least not in the early stages. It may lead in that direction eventually, but everything depends on the extent of human psychic malleability—or, to be more precise, of human learning possibilities. Thus schools are sites of permanent conflict whose substance is information—a conflict both internal (i.e., psychological, affecting learners and managers of learning) and external (i.e., involving society).

Within adult social cultures information content in flow can never be wholly free of controls. In every society certain groups seek to impose their preferred forms of information. For education, since the young require familiarization with a range of adult thought, rather than inculcation of a single dominant mode, the practical solution may at times seem clear enough. Today's smorgasbord curriculum, for instance, is currently thought to be the "solution." Yet this issue of control of information content in education is never quite so cut and dried. We can still ask in every specific instance: Who controls information substance here, and with what motives? Organized education must always possess some element of "cultural persuasion," it seems. But who determines the source of this element?

Can we really identify something called the "mainstream" and simply assume this to be a sufficient provider of wisdom as to what information shall be conveyed to the as yet untutored child? Is not this mainstream itself a mere subset of some larger whole—if in fact any public rationale of choice and a selection of information suitable for purposes of school instruction can even be brought into existence in the first place?

But perhaps the graver question is that of self-convinced subgroups whose views run counter to the prevailing general mores. So-called fundamental values are clearly losing ground in US society, and what remains of the mainstream, where formal education is concerned, has in effect given up hope of using the schools to restore such values. Not so various religious sects with deep roots in the past, however. Even so, there are practical limits facing such sects in maintaining private schools of their own. Children from such sects must still, in many cases, attend public schools, even in those few areas where they dominate the population numerically. The question is of more than passing interest: How will situations of this kind affect education, and in particular the information content of instruction?

Could a religious sect, say the Catholics, Amish, or Mormons in the spheres where they are powerful, then legitimately substitute the primary ethical values in their subcultures for those abandoned by the mainstream in education? If not, what are the limits on mainstream interposition in schools where these sects prevail culturally? The child is by definition an impressionable consumer of information. When textbooks as well as teachers already represent fairly extreme aspects of cultural persuasion, should other elements in conflict with those aspects be eliminated or reinforced? Is there a middle-of-the-road line that must always be adhered to whenever conflict over essential information uses in some education setting arises?

No questions of this kind can be answered by merely claiming that education must downgrade indoctrination and elevate free inquiry. It has become well-nigh impossible to separate authoritarian from non-authoritarian factors in a learning environment so rent by conflicting

influences as the US school. Falling back on simple categories of
fundamental opposition (e.g., "liberal" vs. "conservative" types of
information control) helps very little. Nothing about instructional
policy can be so reduced to ideology, unless we are to go forward in the
simplistic and for practical purposes unuseful terms of an "ideology of
the individual child." The contradictions of adult thinking on education
only mount; but there is no choice: Given what we know of universal
social and economic trends and the nature of individual development,
we have to give more direct thought to what the goals of education in
an Information Society might really have to be.

Difficulties of Consensus on Educational Purposes

People used to avoiding thought about educational goals may be
surprised to learn how constant throughout history are the definitions of
goals, as well as the implicit assumptions about human nature in those
definitions. In both East and West, seers from Confucius and Plato
onwards patiently remind us of certain abiding verities. Even a brief
glance at the literature leaves no doubt about the kind of individual and
the kind of society education is expected to produce.

Yet are classic educational objectives really relevant to late modern
life? One might better ask: How can they not be? That a few hours
spent in the slum schools of a large US city today would make the
statements of every thinker on the subject down through the ages
appear at first glance slightly ridiculous cannot alter the validity of
those statements historically, or even in an evolutionary sense. Certain
elemental facts remain. Man cannot retrogress to an animal state in his
mental operations if he is to survive as a species. He is obliged as a
social being to develop certain qualities, attain a certain state of
knowledge.

Centuries ago Aristotle in his *Politics*, anticipating Ben Franklin,
dithered over whether the young should be trained primarily by contact
with "things useful in life" or with "things conducive to virtue." But he
also acknowledged as a practical matter much of what today we regard
as the standard curriculum: "Roughly, four things are generally taught
to children, (a) reading and writing, (b) physical training, (c) music, and
(d) not always included, drawing."[9]

Further, it is clear "that there should be laws laid down about
education, and that education itself must be made a public concern."[10]
Beyond this, "there are some useful things, too, in which the young

must be educated, not only because they are useful (for example, they must learn reading and writing), but also because they are often the means to learning yet further subjects."[11] Words like these are millennia on in time still regularly echoed by not just every aspiring politician but by all who see in effective school learning the only route by which the mass of men can move forward into a better ordered world society. The ancients' wisdom, in short, still has a bearing in a modern Information Society.

Indeed, more knowledgeable parents and citizens in any country share a largely common view as to what the education of the young ought to accomplish. Updating Aristotle's categories, they expect that youth learn reasonably well in school at least the basic skills of communication (an ability to read and write, to express oneself adequately for any interpersonal situation in the native language); skills of number, so as to have know-how in the manipulation of numeric symbols (especially in the public marketplace); the minimum social competencies, those elemental graces one associates with life in any civilized society.

These are goals so general, so basic, that they merit adult acceptance everywhere. People become understandably uncomfortable—as now, in the 2000s—when evidence accumulating over decades demonstrates that, to an increasing extent, even the most rock-bottom standards of school attainment are routinely impossible to meet. Why should a majority of American high school graduates not know who was the author of *Leaves of Grass*? Or the country in which Shakespeare lived? Yet endless polls and surveys continually reveal new depths of non-attainment in even the most basic areas of knowledge. College-level instruction itself, in the realm of undergraduate work, notably in North America, has had to undergo serious restructuring in light of lower school failures in such critical areas of basic knowledge as elementary math and reading/writing.[12]

Accustomed to thinking in terms of statistics and large populations, we easily disregard underlying cultural and psychological blocks which turn large numbers of otherwise potential achievers in the enterprise of formal education into below-minimum performers. We fall back on cliches, demanding better instruction in "the basics" or "competency learning" or whatever the latest fad or catchword may appear to prescribe. There is a harsh reality about all problems of school instruction we find extraordinarily difficult to face: The human animal whose performance we find it convenient to measure according to this or that established norm of achievement remains an individual; he retains his own power of self-direction in an environment which can do only so much to restrict his exercise of free will. In the classroom, as a citizen of a modern democracy, he can do as he is bidden—or not. We define goals for the overall enterprise, and these invariably direct students to accomplishment of standard subject-matter objectives, the curriculum of Aristotle in some updated form. But this hardly binds the individual learner. He still has to be motivated to pursue his own goal, and pursue it as an individual.

Professor Robert Gagné, in his now-classic text in educational psychology, states it this way: "It has frequently been said that motivating the student is one of the most important jobs the teacher can do...motivating should probably be considered the primary task of the teacher.... Learning itself takes place within the learner, largely as a result of his activity. But something must drive this activity, and direct it toward the goal of achieving objectives."[13]

Something in any case drives all individual energy placement. The application of energy can be constructive or destructive, advantageous or disadvantageous to society. But these terms have meaning only in the minds of individuals. What adult society may see as a constructive activity may to some neophyte within that society seem quite the opposite. Why is it that in so great a number of instances the individual—often even an individual who possesses good potential—"turns off" from formal learning? Educational psychologists have tried for generations to get at the principles that explain how negative motivation actually develops in these cases and how it can be contained—without, so far, much success.

Something of the problem, this seemingly universal "retreat from learning," may, of course, be explainable only in terms of the effects of a global "entertainment culture" itself, since the average child or youth cannot escape the influences of that culture. But if true, this interpretation hardly provides clues for those responsible for the improvement of instruction. Education, unfortunately, at this stage remains more a game of chance than a science.

None of this augurs well for countries already feeling the advance burden of a twenty-first-century Information Age. The society of three or four decades on in time will reward men and nations in a manner different from anything known in the past. It will have left far less room than yesterday for a "non-thinking" mass of drones. It will be based more than ever on brains and not brawn. Imagined, abstract "orders of things," rather than mere immediately perceivable environments and matter-of-fact sensory impressions, are the stuff with which every intelligence will have to wrestle, and on an incremental scale, in the information-rich world of deeper tomorrow. But too many of our children, at least for now, are retreating from this challenge rather than embracing it. The Age of Information has already proven too much for them.

Ambivalence of Consensus

It is no exaggeration to say that there is a problem of social consciousness involved in the provision of education for an Information Society. Mankind in general has yet to come abreast of the continuing significance of individual mind in maintaining momentum in social and economic development. What the term "individual" means in practical terms is understood neither by the masses nor by their appointed administrators. In education as elsewhere a gross tendency exists to submerge the person in the mass, to prevent him from moving beyond restrictive norms, to deny him an "educational individuality," largely on grounds of the necessity for equality (and as a means of reducing the complexities of management). This view is quickly conveyed from the adult generation to its children. But can such an essentially negative approach to the great and overriding need for individual learning lead to lasting beneficial results?

Given the enveloping "bigness" of mass life, with its conflicting cultural compulsions, an understandable confusion does arise about the role of the individual in all social processes. As long ago as the 1950s US sociologist David Riesman brooded over the problem. What, he asked, should be the real limits of collective power over the person? Do groups have a tendency, ever present, to destroy individualistic drives that are in fact socially necessary for progress? These were for Riesman then, and for many sociologists now, serious as well as formidably abstract issues.

The judgment was that, one way or the other, no conclusive proofs are available. Nor does it matter, Riesman decided, how much pressure is exerted on individuals to conform to patently non-democratic group decisions, so long as the individual retains an inalienable right to veto a decision, is left in the position of being able to retreat into apathetic disinterest, can manifest a lack of agreement by withdrawing from the group, and so on. "No ideology, however noble, can justify the sacrifice of an individual to the needs of the group."[14] In short, it is the tradition of independent-minded individualism which allows, indeed forces, mass life to move forward with some degree of meaning. Riesman's argument, in essence: "We depend for advance, in morals no less than in physical science, on individuals who have developed their individuality to a notable degree."[15]

But one must first become sufficiently mature to cast a veto knowledgeably. In the learning years the tradition of individual freedom has its greatest practical value, before the restricting limits of adult life take hold. Yet what can the neophyte accomplish if he cannot learn effectively? Through all the centuries of man's history, often under the most negative conditions, a familiar youthful groping after individuality specifically through learning has gone on. Even so, if the individual's desire to learn is to bear fruit, enabling conditions must exist. Though these conditions are nearly impossible to define in practical language, society rightly attempts to provide them through publicly supported education. Within the precincts of too many modern schools, however, both individuality and the desire that should go with it for learning are all too often absent. The Age of Information has caught up with a system of instructional management no longer flexible enough to serve.

Then is there literally "no way out"? Does inflexible tradition have to hamstring instruction forever? Traditions indeed are valuable when kept in proper perspective. But many societies seem to have acquiesced in a policy of preserving those elements of school tradition which are the least subject to wide-scale argument, yet are also the ones least conducive to more effective instruction and learning. Others of more potential value, often too full of political dynamite, are pointedly ignored. Caught in a quagmire of rigidities of management thinking, men have assumed that the school's modus operandi has reached a stage at which fundamental experiment is no longer necessary, whereas just the opposite is the case. Logically, in a social evolutionary sense, matters cannot continue indefinitely as they are, in a sad limbo between mediocrity and outright failure. The operations and output of schools will either become more consistently degraded or they will improve. The question is: How can anyone go about trying to insure the latter?

Schools in any event will not disappear; they serve too important a purpose. And most children will have no choice other than to attend government-sponsored common schools. That familiar blanket denunciation which says "the schools are hopeless" resolves nothing. Schools are a fundamental problem in every society, and one that does not go away by being ignored. Decisions will have to be taken about improving them. And the public cannot depend on experts for all the right decisions. The public itself is involved, willingly or not.

The willingness of some and the unwillingness of others to think about educational issues contribute in equal measure to our increasing controversy over schools. Education has willy-nilly become a subject of enormous contention. Every critique, every study or report on the subject receives media coverage. Private groups form and reform to deal with issues. We even see changes in the laws regarding education. (Several US states have taken actions, in a few cases drastic, to create new requirements or enlarge the scope of old ones, in curriculum, teacher education, personnel licensing, administrative practices, and other areas of education amenable to quantitative alterations.) Political leaders and constituencies, along with special interest groups, are more than ever involved in making or encouraging educational policy. Yet the extent of progress achieved through these actions becomes increasingly difficult to determine. Even more difficult to judge at this stage is whether or not the existing public concern for education can be translated into support for genuine (as against cosmetic) experiment—something now needed more than ever and just as hard to bring about as at any time in the past.

As education writer Herbert Kohl despairingly put it a few years ago:

> The schools are being criticized from many different perspectives. Is there a common core of sense in the criticisms leveled by conservative members of the Council on Basic Education, progressives who consider themselves members of the alternative school movement, and just plain frustrated parents? Why is it that all of the innovations and experiments of the last twenty years have led to frustration?[16]

Kohl's question is fundamental to debate, and unanswerable for now. Then are the pessimists right in writing off mass education in free common schools, especially those serving the average and below-average child? Has universal formal education for the young reached a point of no return, a drowned state induced through the lure of media entertainments and mass adult confusions of mind, from which no effort at reform or retrenchment can lever it back on course? Is the concept of an optimum education for all just the idle dream the nay-sayers have been for such a long time insisting it was?

I believe that the role of the common school as a necessary catalyst in the process of mass learning has not been exhausted, and that people in all the developed countries will have to gain a new perspective on its possibilities rather than give up on it. But this will hardly be a "business as usual" perspective. Unless people are willing to extend their thinking beyond standard issues of managerial legerdemain to "get at" education in its basic evolutionary and social functions, they run a serious risk of seeing only the trees and never the forest—addressing problems in their external guise only while passing over, to everyone's detriment, their internal substance.

And further difficulties lie beyond the immediate horizon of us who live in the few rich nations. What is the advanced country's need today becomes that of the less-advanced tomorrow. Global evolutionary trends cannot be ignored; the few developed nations are already experiencing—though at differential rates, to be sure—certain universal forces of evolution sooner or later to be felt by the rest of humanity as well. Education is a tangible, as well as an intangible, good, required by all. The world's ignorant masses outside the orbit of developed nations will be demanding their fair share of educational riches in due time, even as they now demand a fairer share of the planet's physical wealth, and the level of world conflict will thereby be heightened yet once more.

Education may not be a universal cure-all, but it is already recognized everywhere as the major means of access to that better life the industrial age promotes. But how to get it? How make it available to all who seek it? Innovation in education is not an option for the poor nations. Yet even the rich to this point resist radical change in education—though it can only be to their ultimate advantage to embrace it. Conscious experiment, evidently, is always frightening, to any society at any level of advancement. Yet it becomes a clear necessity in the global scheme of social evolution, nonetheless. The question is simply posed: Can informed trial and error in education be evaded over the longer-term future, regardless of the degree of continuing stasis we are sure to confront in the next decade or two?

Chapter 2

Current Response and Future
Realities in Reform of School Instruction

The world is awash in a flood of magic formulas for educational reform. Every educator or journalist, (to say nothing of lawmakers) has his scheme for "making schools work again." In North America since the early 1980s, when the concept of "a nation at risk" finally penetrated public consciousness, myriad theories for improving instruction have surfaced, some with strongly ideological overtones (e. g., vouchers). To grasp why so many of these proposals seem always to generate more smoke than fire, changing nothing in the instructional impasse, one must ask: What do all these ideas, whether liberal or conservative in origin, whether coming from educators directly or from the public at large, have in common?

This is by any measure a reasonable question whose answer can be provided: These proposals, nearly without exception, are exclusively *administrative* in character; that is, they aim to engineer change through administrative manipulations alone. Nonetheless, say their supporters, they will "work," not just in the practical sense of school management but in a pedagogical sense as well, meaning they will lead to better *individual* learning and the "hard" evidence to prove it—higher test scores en masse.

The term *experimental* is of course applied in all such contexts. But when we examine any one of these cases with care, the same fact emerges: the "experiment" in question invariably involves situations where it is *group* instructional arrangements or oversight being manipulated. Individual learners succeed (when they do) because they supposedly "fit in" with the group mode of learning. But does this happen with any degree of frequency? Does this fundamental assumption of classroom management and that mode of management *alone*—on which all administrative "experiment" rests—accord with psychological reality? Does a costly pro forma provision of personal counseling for that small proportion of learners seen as "having difficulties" go very far in closing the gaps? We are forced on to a further basic question: In what way are any administrative schemes for change indeed *pedagogically experimental*?

No one questions the need, in a mass society and an Information Age, for children to learn and gain experience as individuals participating in meaningful group activity. The question raised by exclusive dependence on the classroom environment in any culture, however, has precisely to do with the matter of what is also meaningful in management of the instructional process. We can say that a single human teacher in charge of a class of forty schoolchildren today functions at least in an overseer's role. But we are overstating the case entirely when we aver that, in the average such classroom situation today, the teacher can possibly be an effective manager of every *individual* child's instruction.

As American critic Van Cleve Morris perplexedly put it years ago: "The teaching procedure we are looking for...must be a pedagogy which can rise above the physical sociality of the classroom to affirm the psychic identity of each of the several human beings located there."[1] Yet the fixed-in-place classroom group remains the basis of all administrative thinking, every innovation, including nearly everything which is sold to a baffled public as "comprehensive individualization" or "experimental management of instruction."

Where effective *individual* instruction is concerned, then, we remain at the stage of what in philosophy of science would be termed "revealed science." Thus however much the individual learner may be our real target, we are unable to "reach" him except through a group method. With our absolute presuppositions about this "fixed" system, as philosophers of the Popper school would describe them, we are prevented from any thought of experiment in instructional management which might depart from the basis of the "revealed" mode. Yet while we continue for now as prisoners of what ought to be seen as a self-evident limitation of method (the group as the only available vehicle by which individual instruction is to be managed), evolutionary pressures force us in new directions, on to a confrontation with the educational needs and challenges of a new century.

Time Lag and System Limits Within the Reform Context

In education we give lip service to the "sacred needs of the individual learner." At the same time we implicitly (and paradoxically) connive in the maintenance of a system which allows him to become submerged in the group process, even to a point at which we fail in our own pedagogical intentions. But what we also find it difficult to accept in our efforts to conceptualize any genuinely new system of instruction is the significance of *information interpretation* (including the desired functions of both information purveyor and information receiver) in the process. The philosopher Martin Buber wrote something much to the point on this matter:

> That man alone is qualified to teach who knows how to distinguish between appearance and reality, between seeming realization and genuine realization, who rejects appearance and chooses and grasps reality, no matter what world-view he chooses.[2]

But reality remains a difficult concept for the true reformer to confront in education. His cannot be the simple view of the world taken by the army drill sergeant. The sergeant's concern is training only, an inculcation of primarily passive response capabilities in the individual recruit. Intelligence has a clear but restricted role to play. This is true of both trainer and trainee. When we involve ourselves in education (as opposed to mere training), however, different conditions obtain. The logic of that situation requires a teacher and not a drillmaster, an interacting intelligence which aims to lead another intelligence toward the goal of self-realization; which, being itself intelligent and desirous of its own genuine realization, qualifies to teach—in Buber's sense of the word.

Nay-sayers belabor the point that modern society has a collective obsession with training (as opposed to education for character development). Though more simplistic reformers may identify this tendency as their principal *bête noire*, at the same time they ignore the further evolutionary aspects of the phenomenon—at some peril. A society focused on industrial efficiency necessarily has problems when too many of its members lack basic skills and remain ignorant even of the cooperative communal process itself. Truly all education must begin somewhere, and in a mass society a lack of the most rudimentary communication response skills (e.g., basic knowledge of language and maths) spells trouble for both individual and collective.

Yet it is also true that in the course of his growth and development every individual must achieve a given level of self-realization as a prerequisite to mastery of specific worldly skills or know-how. The two facets of development, that is, as Piaget's work so well shows, must move forward together, over time, in some optimum fashion, if a socialized, informed adult is to be the goal. As a standard outcome of general instruction, this goal continues to prove highly elusive. Such an outcome is dependent on numerous variables. The goal may not be realized in a generation, or even in several. It has an evolutionary, long-term aspect which demands patience and in fact may hide its face behind the "spinning wheels" of high-profile reform phenomena for decades. In brief, a blockage fundamental to the whole issue of instructional method—our inability to create change within the system, for lack of any social mandate by which really to "get at" the substantive problems inhibiting the process on an individual level—remains.

Over two decades ago perceptive American critic of education Harry Broudy wrote presciently of this issue: "The real dialectical joke being played on man is that the technological revolution is laying the groundwork for a new moral order—if individual men will exert the intelligence and effort to use the resources that technology is liberating."[3] Today's worldwide crisis of educational opportunity and instructional gridlock show how far behind the curve all societies remain in the struggle to comprehend the real possibilities.

Advocates of "core learning," such as University of Virginia professor E. D. Hirsch, make a cogent argument for delineation of "specific content" to be mastered by every child in every culture, at each step of a progressive learning sequence. This emphasis on a common "what" for all learners (a core curriculum) seems a move in the right direction after decades of an open-option, "learn-whatever-you-want" viewpoint on content (at least in the ultra-decentralized US system of education). Yet we continue to face, and in every national society, the even more comprehensive question of "how" such a more focused content might be taught, an issue which even the core knowledge group finds too big a problem to be tackled head-on.

Instructional Method and the Social Basis of Future Education

Soon, in the sense of evolutionary time, though not soon enough in terms of human expectations within one or two generations, advances in technology will force upon industrial-age man a comprehensive and public re-definition of the philosophical foundations of school instruction. Communications technology will in another half-century allow for direct contact between any one mind and any other, across the entire globe; all intelligences, in a word, will interconnect, and those left out of the loop will find existence meaningless. The local common school will, though, remain as physical center of instruction; an individual child can direct his mind to other locales through miracles of telecommunications technology, but he cannot escape (nor should we want him to escape) the social and intellectual nexus of here-and-now learning which the local school has traditionally provided. With this new and far more influential role possible for technology, nonetheless, society as a whole will have to attain a consensus—itself of evolutionary dimensions—as to both the *why* and *how* of individual instruction.

What is not yet well recognized, and probably cannot be recognized for some decades more, is the essentially blocking nature of administratively based reforms, when unaccompanied by philosophical consideration of the future application of high technology in instruction. It cannot be argued that any of these reform proposals actually does more than use technology as an adjunct of an already ineffective group management in instruction. True, the child-learner today often "learns" by playing with a computer. Too, administratively useful data on individuals and groups are routinely gathered and stored through technological means in educational systems. Thanks to administrative reforms, even mixed age and ability groups of learners are, fortunately, becoming more common. But not a single administrative reform program permits experiment with technology as a pedagogical tool for development of a philosophically defensible means for advancing abilities of the *individual* learner in comprehending the "what" of instruction.

This is a factor significant in social evolutionary terms. Of course average man cannot comprehend the subtleties of epistemology and theory of classroom method as these are discussed by educational psychologists and philosophers. He can comprehend results. Thus he stands amazed at the swiftness of general technological progress, even while he fails to grasp its meaning for school instruction—and how the appearance of individual learning within today's fixed orbit of standard technomanagement will eventually differ by orders of magnitude from the reality of individual learning in a future shaped by dramatic intervening change. For future instructional management—by technological means in conjunction with more comprehensive social-political decision-making—will be management *of* and *for* the individual.

The relationship of doctor and patient is not unlike that of today's teacher and average or below-average school learner. But important differences exist. A doctor has critical information on hand and a power of interpreting it immediately on his patient's behalf. School instruction is a far more hit-or-miss affair: whereas by common consent doctor and patient always function in a one-to-one interface, teacher and learner meet one another as information interpreters in primarily group settings. Individualization beyond a given limit not only cannot be applied in the classroom setting of group management; its possibilities are in fact overborne by the excessive and often anti-learning atmosphere of a collective external environment. Any adult with sufficient experience of today's world will concede that for the child of today who must live with the realities of a twenty-first-century tomorrow, hit-or-miss instruction is not good enough. Society should see to it that the child's learning is managed as a doctor would manage a patient's health. And because of technological advance, this will be possible.

A half-century further on in time will see the availability to one and all of artificial intelligences whose information-interpreting power will exceed that of even today's expensive supercomputers. Every such instrumentality will in addition enjoy a right of instantaneous contact with every other AI in the world. Psychologists may still be arguing over precisely "what intelligence is," but the results of advanced technology of this kind will already by, say, 2050, have proven to society at large that, for practical purposes, a machine devoted to management of a single child's learning program can "track, plan and reinforce" for that individual far more efficiently than a much more labor- and cost-intensive human system of guidance counselors and administrators.

Old-guard professionals, inured to traditional technocratic management beliefs, will cavil and complain, for to them the fixed class group remains the only possible basis for management of individual learning. How, they will ask, can the child have proper social experiences if not continuously in a class setting? Must he then interact with a mere computer day after day to the detriment of his growth as a primarily social being? The answer to these quite reasonable caveats lies in a new understanding of the term *management* itself.

The Basis for Instruction in a Future of Convergent Forces

Such an AI manager will not serve primarily as a delivery agent for instruction; rather it will function mostly in the background, analyzing its client's progress and needs, setting up meetings and group sessions—between human and non-human intelligences, within the single school itself, locally, regionally, nationally, even globally—and coordinating all these interactions in such a way as to prepare the individual learner *qua* individual for the reality of life in the new century's intellectually competitive global environment. Such management will encompass training and education in an optimally individualized program; it will lead to self-realization as well as social realization—provided society has become mature enough to accept this inevitable denouement. But none of this, however necessary in the evolutionary context of that time, however important in the struggle of the race to survive, will have come without costs or struggle.

I do not assert that a technology of artificial intelligence used in this manner is either desirable or not desirable from the standpoint of human evolution; it most surely will involve initially false steps and uncertainty, perhaps even some outcomes in the category of near-disasters. There are no sure roads to follow on the journey ahead. Experiment provides our one basic key to action—experiment informed by a sense not just of the limits of the technically possible but also of the morally desirable. And experiment in such a context carries a certain baggage of threat.

What I do assert, instead, is that both technological and socioeconomic trends have clearly begun to drive in the direction of this denouement to the effective elimination of other possibilities. If past history is any guide at all, there will be little purpose served in carping about lack of choice. We cannot evade the force or direction in which technological development leads; we can only attempt to bend it to our own rational purposes. All we can say for now with certainty is that, given time, such a relative "super-technology" will emerge, with self-driven computational and communications resources surpassing anything human manpower can economically provide for purposes of enhancing the aims of individually managed instruction. But what will we do with it? This question is already troubling that small minority of the better-informed who recognize the magnitude of difficulties lying in wait.

There are already clear hints of this within the community of scientists themselves, as between those who see a prominent role for AI in shaping human thought and behavior and those who reject such a possibility altogether. What the vitalist traditionalists dwell upon is the extent of differences between workings of a human intelligence and those of its artificial counterpart. They refuse to discuss the much more threatening issue of an already foreordained technological progress which will in a matter of mere decades have brought to birth better-then-human "thinking machines," devices which, while lacking still most components of typical human cognition "beyond the realm of reason," will nonetheless possess the capability for pursuing trains of logic, in simulation of human thought processes, surpassing anything the human working alone can achieve. This means we can expect to see mechanical tutors which will have a more intelligent and comprehensive approach—at least in the sense of professed societal expectations—in selecting a train of learning experiences for the human neophyte than will any adult teacher (or teachers) however gifted.

The vitalists, indeed, are evasive as to educational applications of AI altogether, sharing a view still common to a majority of educational administrators. They are unwilling to face up to the dilemma that science in the fullness of time will come to pose for education, with the development of a functional AI suited to the needs of instructional management for the individual learner. But scientists, in any case, like educators, have limited influence in any society. Eventually, since the problem cannot go away and will only increase in scope, it will have to be decided as other universal problems are decided in an era of mass democracy—through some sociopolitical means, be it referendum, parliamentary vote, or other form of expression of the general will. But without reference to the moral dimension in education, on what properly universal basis can the problem be resolved?

As French scientist Lucien Gerardin has put it, "Once we have found a general method, we will be able to leave it to the machines to do the rest. This is the proper role for artificial intelligence."[4] Such a "solution" leaves to one side, alas, the omnipresent question of political conditions and preferences.

Another Gallic scientist, Arnold Kauffman, more reasonably, awaiting a workable Science of Action (a "praxeology"), raises the underlying concern which this bland general statement leaves unanswered: "We must (first) decide whether science will be able to play its (legitimate) part or be a mere tool of ambitious men or groups."[5] In any case, it appears, society as a whole will have to be fully involved in deciding what the "general method" will be.

Inevitably we humans will surrender some powers of decision-making over the learner's program to the machine. We can hope to define its general principles of operation for a long time to come. Yet in matters of detail it will have from the first its own "rights" of decision-making, and as the number of these "detail decisions" swiftly increases, our power over its general operations could recede to nil. This is the old story of a Sorcerer's Apprentice, a machine which carried out its master's commands only too perfectly and whose mad pace of operation only a deus ex machina could finally restrain—except that very possibly in a future world of the kind we know will depend on intellectual mastery of information, no benign deus will exist and a demonic machine may well have its own way entirely. That outcome can occur, I believe, only if the machine, like that apprentice of legend, has no sense of the moral dimension of intelligent life.

Humankind's one advantage in this situation is the amount of lead time it has. What educators routinely identify as incremental (as opposed to fundamental) change is the only phenomenon we can expect to see much of for several decades more. Thus administrative "fixes" will occupy all public attention for a long time to come. Today's average man has no appetite for arcane questions of value or ethical practice, whether in education or—to revert to my earlier analogy—in medicine. Average man will continue to mull in his mind only the relative virtues of what Ben Franklin termed "useful" and "ornamental" knowledge. But it is possible that over several generations, as the information "explosion" does its work in the world, enough adults might come to comprehend the significance of even this moral dimension in education—for a time will surely come when a mass decision on the use of AI in individual instruction becomes a public responsibility entirely, when a consensus on fundamental change can no longer be resisted, when the connection between AI management and moral learning itself will finally be established as an educational necessity.

If there were no problem of improving the effectiveness of instruction and if technology could have no role to play in bringing change to the most critical human processes (e.g., those of genetics, say, and learning), school instruction could go on in its present mode forever. But technology inexorably advances, and with it the ever more insoluble problem of management of individual instruction within the group setting. We can claim we know why we educate. We can go on assuming that by training the child in this or that technique in the present fashion we do all that is possible, that our technocratic, anti-individualist method brings out all that is humanly necessary in the way of character development. We can insist that this age-old method suffices for both optimum development of intelligence and building of moral resources within the individual—simply because as a practical matter no alternate ways of viewing instructional method are available to us. Yet though convenient, this is hardly a rational way of approaching the future of school instruction.

Thus the value of lead time. Today consensus in any of our faction-ridden national societies on such a matter would be quite impossible. Even the best-informed futurists in discussion would find consideration of such an issue still highly premature. Management of instruction tends to be viewed by even the most knowledgeable observers as an all-human process pure and simple, not to be changed in its essentials for another thousand generations. But evolutionary pressures for fundamental change have a way of building not only in an unseen way but also at times in swifter ways than we anticipate. In the grand scheme of evolution, our human species too must eventually react to contain and adapt to inevitable challenges of the kind that scheme imposes. Where school instruction is concerned, our day of reckoning in this matter could arrive sooner than we now think possible.

Chapter 3

Socratic Approaches and the Problem of Communication in School Instruction

The conditions of human variability are correctly spoken of as infinite. In even a strictly statistical sense, we are highly limited in our ability to quantify this variability. Measures of central tendency, such as standard deviation, among other means at hand, tell us something about an individual case, true, but only in relation to the sum total of all other cases in a population. Thus who or what "is" the individual, and how society might best "reach" him without denying him his uniqueness of individuality—and specifically in such a critical process as education—remains a considerable mystery. What the socioeconomic rationalization of modern Western societies has not yet come to grips with in any but a superficial way is the function of the individual in the system. It is not by accident that the most effective critics of this failure have been Eastern philosophers like Aurobindo and Krishnamurti, men who think and write from a non-systems oriented perspective.

Educators as servants of society know to some extent what they expect education to do *with* the individual. What they might also do *for* him is another matter. Modern adult societies are competitive beehives, in which each system niche must be filled and each niche-occupier must function efficiently to meet economic and social expectations laid down for him. The neophyte must then learn, as his primary task, what society expects him to know to fulfill the obligations of an adult role gradually to be acquired. But while this may explain what must be done *by* a system of education, it provides no obvious explanation regarding method; it fails to enlighten the educator as to *how* his task might best be carried out.

Can a child be prepared for adult life by some pre-planned scheme of education, one appropriate to his family background and personal interests and aspirations? The search for such a "solution" has been never more prominent than in the present age of automated response to problems associated with the embarrassing facts of human individuality and constant socioeconomic change. As an example, so-called "career education," a fad of the 1960s and 1970s, sought to meet the need (as one devotee at the time expressed it) by "helping every student find and prepare for a rewarding occupation, whether he leaves high school without a diploma or graduates from college."[1]

Today, with the twentieth century already past history, such simplistic formulations seem fantastically naive. Competition grows apace. Even the college graduate, as studies have shown, will have fewer job opportunities in the new century than did his earlier counterpart. The average worker can anticipate changing occupations seven or eight times during a career, with corresponding demands upon him to readjust to new work conditions and to learn new routines —to transcend routine altogether, in many cases, if he is to keep up with the requirements of employment placed upon him at all. The old assumption of a mere K-12 education as sufficient for a lifetime of guaranteed employment has long since disappeared in the fast-growing global rush to constantly new and higher levels of workplace efficiency.

In the recent past the obviously outdated "career education" concept has been updated by American educators and business leaders who see in the traditional (though extremely costly) German apprentice training system a "way out" of the dead end of academic education for that two-thirds of US schoolchildren who are unable to continue into college and prepare there for higher-level jobs in the twenty-first-century economy. This may be an improvement on the career education concept of the 1960s, but it moves further into the realm of social engineering and raises ever more difficult questions of both moral judgment and curriculum almost impossible to resolve—at least in an American environment.

It seems inconceivable that as early as the middle grades American children could already find themselves shunted into a blue-collar career track, as is so commonly done elsewhere, though this is the most likely outcome of a system of "early manpower allocation" which increasingly forces career choices on a basis of bureaucratic necessity. Yet even more baffling will be the pedagogic fallout of such a scheme. In theory, any child pushed into a career apprenticeship at some point between, say, grade 5 and grade 12, with the help of brief academic studies (along with appropriate standards still imposed on such work through the grades), can indeed acquire a self-discipline and adequate work skills for succeeding in the work world—at his appointed level. But if his main energies are being used up in an apprentice learning program from so early a stage, will he benefit in any meaningful way from no more than a casual or occasional concurrent exposure to the more general content of academic learning in his most critically formative years?

Even adherents of this early apprenticeship training admit the futility of simply "upgrading" the lower-level work force through such a scheme if the individuals involved cannot also develop their powers of abstract thought and build their adult personalities at the same time. The age-old elements of a formal academic education thus assume an even larger place in the Information Age scheme of things. Instructional method has not yet caught up with the realities of such an age, needless to say. And perhaps understandably, given the systemic negatives with which it must approach the individual learner.

Politicians may lure the public with vast plans for apprentice and journeyman programs of education for the millions. Educational philosophy and theory seem remote from immediate political practicality. Yet the gap here is more apparent than real. In the offing lies an inescapable confrontation—with the issue of mind-to-mind communication as a central element in the instructional process and at the same time with that process in its moral effects.

The passion for practical results is not just an American mania. It is universal. Efficiency matters, and it comes down, increasingly, to a question of whether or not statistical data show "improvement"—and not much else. It is difficult, if not impossible, in any country of our contemporary technocratically driven world, to demonstrate that education can have a value which transcends immediate wants or priorities and, despite a lack of demonstrable practical outcomes as of a given moment, does something for both the person *and* his society which nothing else can do.

The standard college education, clearly, has become a glut on the market wherever one looks in the contemporary world commercial environment. India and other overpopulated Third World nations are not the only examples of countries with too many college graduates for the number of jobs to be filled. In a reversal of the rising expectations which generations of Americans were accustomed to think of as theirs simply by right of birth, we have seen that in the 1990s one in five US college graduates was obliged to work at a job not requiring a degree, while many more were unable to find work at all. As one stops to ponder this phenomenon, it becomes apparent that each new generation faces not simply an ever-shrinking job market overall. It also faces an inadequacy of the education available, in that the entire contemporary system for formal education, from kindergarten through graduate school, can neither fully prepare the learner for a settled work niche in later life nor provide him with the tools of personal adaptation in adulthood. In both respects it fails to connect the neophyte with what the philosopher Krishnamurti correctly labels the ultimate "realities (as opposed to illusions) of this world."

As Gilbert Highet has expressed it with respect to books alone, one may logically expand a simple principle to the whole of pedagogy: "All books communicate a selection of judgments about life. All books try to teach. The differences are between those which teach well and those which teach badly, and between those which teach valuable things and those which teach bad or trivial things."[2] It is impossible, in short, to speak of any education without considering its communications and ethical effects, along with its more readily quantifiable "delivery" and administrative aspects.

Two fundamental questions need to be asked: First, is the learner as an individual (not solely as a statistical element) "reachable" in a psychological sense? More precisely, does his instruction succeed in creating a complete communications loop which begins with a message from a competent source of instruction and ends in his having provably taken thought as to that which was intended as communication? Second, is there in this communication process some learning which demonstrably leaves an ethical residue? Has the learner "grown" in a moral sense, so that—to be specific—the negative effects upon him of an imperfect social environment are less likely to lead to motivational breakdown as he continues in development?

Among the commonest personal questions a reasonably educated adult of today tends to ask about this or that young learner is, "Why is he so unreachable as a student?" or, "Why is his moral life already so stunted?" The classic but not wholly satisfactory answer to either of these common and readily observed dilemmas lies in Plato's basic tenet of education: that education is for personal virtue and wisdom. A sane and whole society can be built on the basis of virtuous and wise citizens, but hardly on anything else. The individual's self-development and self-realization come first.

Today's education, from creche to graduate school, has evolved as a gradual response to universal needs for social order and restraint in a mass collective. It has little to do with individual self-development. Yet the collective itself can only suffer when the process of education becomes "over-massified"—as the decline of Leninist Communism in the world seems clearly to indicate. Is it possible, then, that in the next stage of human evolution a method of school instruction which builds on each individual's uniqueness and variability can be brought into being—to replace an increasingly irrelevant mass production system which worldwide, regardless of the level of culturally and technocratically imposed discipline, fails both individual and society? To answer this question in any adequate fashion, we must look both forwards and backwards in time, ahead in time to a new century of certain technological innovation and progress, behind us over time to the thinkers and doers of the past whose work lays both the foundations of our present impasse and the inspiration for a different future.

Socrates and the Dilemma of School Instruction

Socratic instruction is defined by some adherents as "maieutic teaching," or "teaching by asking or questioning (not telling or lecturing, and certainly not coaching)."[3] Even Mortimer Adler concedes that such a mode of instruction cannot by itself constitute the sole method. Two other, less sophisticated methods, that of didacticism (telling) and that of coaching (supervision of actual performance in some skill area) must also be employed. "The three modes of learning and teaching must be related—more than that, integrated—at every stage of the educational process."[4] But for Adler and his fellow proponents of Paideia, clearly the apex of all education rests with the rise or fall of Socratic dialectic in the individual's learning program.

In truth, the proponents of Paideia tend to be more circumspect in their claims for the uses or values of Socratic discourse than other enthusiasts for "new wine in old bottles" as the foundation of method in classroom instruction. Writers like Adler tend to stress the value of Socratic discourse for enlargement of understanding per se, not necessarily for direct inculcation of virtue. By contrast, in his 1991 book *Education For Character*, an enthusiast like US psychologist-educator Thomas Lickona claims that while in upper grade situations an adult teacher may well find himself a "lonely ethical voice, arguing with little apparent effect against a low-level peer-group culture," nevertheless moral discussions based on a properly chosen curriculum offer a "concrete" answer to the problem of basic understanding—and that of moral learning as well.[5]

Students, Lickona argues, "grow up" as they confront, however much in the abstract and at a distance, issues of moral content as these emerge in specific realms of knowledge. "The curriculum," he states, "creates a planned context for moral discussion, requiring students to gather and absorb information about a value issue. It poses the moral questions students should consider, and it structures their learning to bring out the desirability of the moral value (honesty, kindness, respect for the environment) under consideration."[6]

Yet all these claims for Socratic method overlook (or perhaps deliberately evade) the central point that must be made with regard to that method in our contemporary world: They may correctly identify the "Socratic approach" as a method with possibilities for use in our time and future times, but they make little or no effort to take into account essential differences in the underlying assumptions about mind-to-mind communication, in social conditions, and above all in philosophical basis for operation, as between today's collective mass systems of education and the system Socrates employed in his time. Nor, significantly, does the contemporary modus operandi in comparison with that of Socrates arouse the kind of fundamental questions those who develop and market modern computer and communication technologies need to be asking themselves as they look forward to a future world in which the buildup of information will tend to outstrip by far the capabilities of ordinary, unassisted humans to make sense of that world and act rationally within it.

Not only was the actual volume of units of information far more limited in Socrates' situation. He could also claim other and rather uniquely favorable conditions not often found in today's places of scholarship: His was a clientele of noblemen, leisured young adults for the most part, with minds already motivated and relatively prepared to think independently about serious issues; the Socratic circle consisted of lucky men living in a brief period of history when pursuit of knowledge and virtue—at least for a fortunate few—was not only considered possible but (by a significant part of the populace of Athens, if evidence coming down to us of the public role in religion, theater, and political life is accurate) quite desirable.

But there are also social and psychological, as well as philosophical aspects of a pedagogical method to be considered. The historical success of Socrates as a teacher only too readily leads us to lose sight of other facets of his activity which would have been required for that success, even given a fortunate historical set of circumstances. Socrates engaged in a process of communication, as we would today speak of it, with the conditions governing that communication, relatively, well under his control. As a result, the dialogues, insofar as we can tell, not only provided one especially bright pupil (Plato) all the necessary grist for a published philosophy later, but they also in every likelihood influenced all participants through their content in a way that directly affected their later behavior. In modern terminology, we might say that the issues discussed and the conclusions reached—because, admittedly, in large part, there would have been little information strongly enough of a contradicting or interfering nature, given that in a small community Socrates was by universal consent acknowledged to be "wise beyond all others"—had a lasting effect on the learners.

Throughout the dialogues Socrates is always a step beyond his interlocutor, often several steps. The conditions already mentioned and Plato's hero-worship may give us an unfairly positive picture of Socrates as well as of his reasoning methods. No less an authority than Bertrand Russell in fact even sees him as less than a wholly competent philosopher. But it also seems clear that if Plato and Xenophon, along with other Greek writers of the time of Socrates and later are correct, as a *teacher* he controlled the interactive situation with an aim of leading the learner (through endless questions, in his case) towards the truth of an issue. As a teacher, that is, Socrates (to use Gilbert Highet's phrase) "had a positive end in view, although that end was concealed from the pupil...to make (him) realize that truth was in the pupil's own power to find, if he searched long enough and hard enough.... In the combination of...the critical method and the positive purpose, lies the essence of (his) system."[7]

From this one can see that Socrates' intentions in his teaching were at once practical and philosophically grounded. The dialogue was simply a means to an end. If some other, more effective method had existed, Socrates' goal as a teacher would doubtless have driven him to make use of it. Maieutics, in short, should never be seen as the entire sum of Socratic method. Those who seek to utilize this method in a classroom situation today betray mixed motives. They say they employ Socratic dialogue in the "interest of the individual learner." Yet they also ignore the existing facts of classroom instruction as that setting affects individual management of instruction. A teacher's solitary, "lonely ethical voice" arguing the correctness of one or another moral point of view in a hypothetical situation may affect one or two students momentarily. It is unlikely to "get at" in the least the learning problems and needs of the vast majority; it involves, to put the matter as bluntly as possible, no provision for *management*—systematically over time—of each individual learner's instruction, in either a practical or a philosophical sense.

Group settings for activity are not the essential issue, in fact. They possess undeniable value in the development of instruction along many lines. But they are not suited as exclusive vehicles for either Socratic teaching as "maieutics" or for Socratic management of instruction in the larger sense. What has gone unrecognized for centuries, indeed, is the essential difference between mass process and individual process in educational method.

Since a mass system must necessarily work to maximize "mass-useful" results, it has somehow been assumed, at least on the administrative level, that only a mass system of management must also be applied—to the exclusion of other modes of instructional management. Certain predictable results tend to follow. Standardization of instruction obliterates individualizing tendencies in many ways, and the social benefits of group interaction are often not of a value sufficient to justify what is done by way of homogenization of the process. Yet standardization in the management of all instruction characterizes the greater part of classroom activity in our time just as much as in all past epochs.

Nor can teachers primarily be held accountable, in their supposed inadequacy to individualize within the class setting, for the failure of such large numbers of learners to comprehend the matter of instruction. Alone, they are unable to convey adequately to the majority of individual learners a view of the world which gives a proper value to quality in individual thought. As Thomas Molnar, a bygone critic of US education, put it in 1970, "(our education) permits its traditional concern, the cultivation of the mind, to be fragmented and dislocated until mass culture is mistaken for learning."[8]

The classroom teacher thus becomes a frustrated "lonely ethical voice" not only where discussion of specific moral issues or even instruction for rote content are concerned, but also in his or her larger role as guide to life-adaptation for the individual child. Society in its political and social judgments often seems to contribute all too readily to this denigration of the variability of the individual learner. One comes across such phenomena, for instance, as the fact that hundreds of thousands of US schoolchildren who happen to be of the same age and grade-status and who also happen to live in the same particular state must all learn from a single state-mandated text in such required content areas as social science or math—simply because the state finances text purchases and prefers to have its committees of textbook experts pressure large publishing firms to produce texts which can then, after an appropriate bidding war and emergence of a winning competitor, be bought in very large quantities. It is an ostensibly cost-effective but probably pound-foolish move in purely educational terms.

This example shows how far huge technocratic systems have come away from the ancient humane Socratic approach. Still, a locus of management, a primary source for decision-making for the learner, is always definable. That locus invariably gives power over the process to someone in adult society—ranging from a single tutor performing in an apparently Socratic fashion through various levels of technocratic decision-making (in which committees of experts and/or political appointees make determination of such important questions as what texts or curriculum patterns are to prevail) to the national society as a whole declaring its will on a given issue via referendum. Presumably of course the tutor has the ability to do what can be done by no other combination of powers in instruction: He has freedom to suit instruction directly to the individual learner's needs—the child's *variability* (to employ the term with which we began)—in a manner not otherwise attainable.

The problem with this way of looking at the instructional situation has to do with limits under which the Socratic tutor operates. Is he, in effect, a bearer of adult culture in a critical sense, or is he merely its slavish conveyor, ignoring cultivation of the individual mind and enforcing mass culture as the sum and substance of all learning? Taken in the popular understanding of Socratic discourse, he would be limited to merely asking questions dealing with highly abstract topics. In a mass system this seems unrealistic. Even if it is in a student's interest to become a competent discussant on a variety of topics, he must find other means for getting at information in the first place. There is no purpose served in providing the learner with a sequence of experiences which prepares him only to discuss. He must be enabled to go on by himself finding new information and making his own private judgments about it.

"The dialectic method," Bertrand Russell points out, "is suitable for some questions, and unsuitable for others.... The matters that are suitable for treatment by the Socratic method are those as to which we have already enough knowledge to come to a right conclusion, but have failed through confusion of thought or lack of analysis, to make the best logical use of what we know."[9] This the Paideia group acknowledges, advocating a variety of teaching techniques. But "moral educators," following the lead of late activist Lawrence Kohlberg, find it more useful to belabor the lack of sufficient "building of character" in both the area of content and that of instructional practice. What both approaches fail to take into account is the more general problem of managing the instructional environment of the individual learner in a context which includes him as the forever unique variant he—for better or worse—remains.

The progressive movement represented the most forceful effort in the twentieth century to develop theories for dealing with the contradiction of individual and group in education. Jacques Barzun in his critique of progressivism expressed what was achieved with grim honesty: "With respect to pedagogy...progressivism has made us face the fact that children are individuals in body and mind, and that they cannot be educated by mass methods."[10] This may yet prove the most lasting legacy of progressive education. But it is a legacy that has not yet led to any positive realization in practice. If the regime of exclusively mass methods no longer serves, then what must still be done to move us on into that evolutionary shift in instructional method which a new and far more information-dominated century will demand?

At this juncture we might pause to reflect on the failures of progressivism, in light of the claims and counter-claims for Socratic method. Progressive education in its various main themes still dominates US education and maintains an influence abroad out of proportion to its historical significance. Not only did the movement come later to distort Dewey's concepts of learning by overemphasizing the inherent sociality of the process. It demanded more in the way of adult resources, physical and psychological, than is consistent with economic reality. As *Fortune* magazine editor Peter Brimelow explained its American context, the result was trade unionization of the teaching profession, with all the economic waste such a development must entail. To quote Brimelow, "the prevailing orthodoxy in American pedagogy is umbilically connected with that section of the country's political culture that naturally thinks in terms of equity and social reform rather than economic efficiency."[11]

Putting the matter in even more global context, success of the process has for a long time now been of less significance than preservation of the system. If the learner has been communicated with, fine. If not, no matter; more important, the institution lives on, even though ossifying rather than adapting. No power existed which could have altered this elemental fact of life in the century just closed; nor, probably, will matters be different for some decades on into the next. This is a fact of life, in every nation, on every continent.

Yet there is no alternative to the common school, in America or elsewhere, for it alone offers opportunity to all in the struggle to learn and survive. But school remains a place of crowding and confusion, a socialized Babel in which communication between mind and mind is an infrequent happenstance. It is a mass system par excellence, an adult imposition of "reason" as it has been developed by intellectual elites out of the revolutionary ferment of the Age of Enlightenment. As John Ralston Saul argues in his book *Voltaire's Bastards*, the regime of experts and technocrats we endure today in every organized aspect of mass life has become just as oppressive and resistant to demands of the evolutionary cycle as the kings and aristocrats of Europe before 1789.[12]

Thus the cry from so many informed quarters in education for an application of "Socratic method"—a cleansing, in effect, of some degree of the miscommunication which the conflict between popular culture and functioning individual intellect in so confined a setting makes inevitable. The central question to be faced then has to do with the extent to which technocratic management of the process of individual instruction actually impedes, rather than enhances, communication. There is also a question of the advance in moral understanding which—as opposed to mere acquisition of rote knowledge—gives meaning to education. And these are both questions the inner gist of which few of those most loudly heard from in defense of Socratic approaches are thus far willing to deal with.

Socratic Teaching: Communication Versus Confusion

Our way of looking at the process of instruction easily leads us to a condemnation of the teacher. He or she "is a tiresome, socially misplaced person who among other faults fails to communicate." This is an ever-repeated story. French scholar of early education Henri Marrou characterizes the Roman-era teacher: "Like the Victorian schoolmistress or governess, the teacher of old was essentially a man of good family who had gone down in the world—a political exile, a wanderer without a land of his own."[13] Contemporary teaching in its demands for classroom efficiency without sacrifice of one's own personality already asks more than the average pedagogue can psychologically bear, and the child-mind she faces is truly a human riddle.

Consciousness in human context confers burdens on the individual unique in the universe. The ancients saw the problem clearly. Aristotle held that habit-formation precedes reason in the sequence of education and character formation. A born taskmaster, Aristotle dwelt, perhaps inordinately, on "right training" to bring appetites under control and make way for the true exercise of adult reason. But he saw the dangers of inexperience for every young mind, believing them to outweigh those of imposed discipline. Implicit in his scheme of education is the idea of a progression in individual mind from what today we would speak of as a lower to a higher consciousness, an effort to create habits more nearly in line with mature reason.[14]

In our own post-Freudian age, discussion of what constitutes consciousness and its supposed effects has become more convoluted. Theorists of instruction have no choice other than to confront the fact

Chapter 4

Experiment and Instruction:
Finding a Starting Point

To dispirited adults today there seems to be nothing further to hope for from the formal education system. With a cynicism born of despair they agree with Jacques Ellul's caustic analysis of the modern education process: "children are expected to become precisely what society expects of them. They must have social consciences that allow them to strive for the same ends as society sets for itself."[1] This is not a conclusion one accepts happily. Yet it expresses what in some degree we feel is inevitable. We reason that since the young will in any case be objects of someone's attention, why should their most crucial influence not come from society itself? Better this than that the dominant influence be only that of the street or underworld. Alas, such commonplace wisdom ignores deeper-lying realities of life in the modern mass society.

But is a better, or at least more formal, education really so necessary? And for so many people? In the cost-conscious 1990s some lawmakers, reflecting established public sentiment, often viewed education as a private, rather than a public, good. Private choice is what should determine how far the process will extend. If one values education, then he must expect to consider his own children exceptions to the rule and pay for an improved version of the product himself. The common school can do only so much for any single child, and schools already cost more than the public wants to pay.

Indeed, decades of high spending on not only K-12 but also college education from the public purse have disenchanted taxpayers, and often with good reason. Revolt against the school tax is always a likely political development. But in dramatically reducing financial burdens of property owners, as was done with California's Proposition 13, the "tax revolt" referendum, we may be ignoring the increasingly interdependent nature of an Information Society and the role of a better-educated populace in the operation of that society. To be sure, the wasteful use of public money at all levels of the education enterprise is shameful; but too few accept that substantive alteration in the internal methods of school operation—rather than abandonment of the school itself—will eventually provide the only sensible solution to the problem of society's educational needs.

The most overriding realities are often the most difficult of acceptance. As population growth and technological development together determine the shape of future collective existence, a better formal education for the average man, and indeed more of it in most cases, will be necessary as never before. Advances in information distribution and communications technology daily increase the processing load on every individual mind. Human beings who know too little—even in what appear to us now as wholly innocent contexts—endanger the working of the whole out of all proportion to their numbers. The child cannot wait for adulthood to gain a foothold in tomorrow's world of information overkill. School learning offers the only possible systematic "way out."

But what can the school do? Its reputation was never lower. A poorly informed public views convenient administrative alterations (e.g., the choice plan or voucher programs) as substantive experiment in instruction. It is easy to see why political interests with an ax to grind would come to make use of such schemes as political footballs. The public somehow fails to grasp that nothing about these so-called innovative programs attacks the central difficulty of contemporary school instruction: the lack of experiment which centers on what can be done differently *in the instruction of individuals*—irrespective of management preferences. While better informed people know that educational psychology has over the decades provided tantalizing suggestions of possible improvements in personalized, non-administered individual instruction, this has done little to influence actual instructional practice, either in elementary and high schools or in colleges.

Uniformity in curriculum and purposes of instruction for all learners remains important. Yet to focus on this issue alone can prevent emergence of a more balanced view of possibilities. If my assumptions are correct, a time is approaching when school education will be forced to abandon today's short-sighted overemphasis on the *what* of group instruction and begin to pay more attention to the *how* of individual instruction. Given our present settled assumptions about process limitations, we are literally unable to face up to a full range of alternatives in instruction. But tomorrow is, as always, another day.

Pitfalls of Innovation and Experiment

To provide a rationale for individual instruction is never easy; with time the task becomes even more difficult. Not only is the very concept of "individual instruction" itself suspect in an egalitarian society. There are also the profound psychological and ethical issues of all instruction to be confronted: How does instruction at one and the same time impose discipline yet grant freedom? How do we encourage self-fulfilling activity yet also secure the quiet concentration demanded in learning? How can any authority order the learning environment to allow maximum opportunity for a learner to prepare for the challenge of an unknown future—when that authority also bears the burden of a present of which the learner, however young, may already know too much?

America's way has been to seek a merger of opposites, to co-opt ideas, interests, and groups from outside the mainstream whenever a particular initiative threatens some traditional process. When progressive education arrived early in the twentieth century, for example, its emphasis on individual activity, learning by doing, and the primacy of each child's immediate interests was gradually (also in some respects successfully) merged into the pattern of existing organizational modes and managerial methods. Such tendencies to absorb what has earlier been anathema, then, may encourage flexibility and innovation in instruction up to a certain point—the point at which structural impediments of the system itself impose barriers.

Contemporary school instruction has reached a state of impasse because we are coming up against the residual element of the learner as an individual in the process, yet we cannot so far see how he is to be accommodated as an individual without threatening the overall scheme of traditional technomanagement. The system itself today prevents in-depth experimentation by its very most fundamental orientation—to the individual learner not as an individual in and for himself but as a strictly standard, replaceable unit. This has proven to be the point of built-in opposition beyond which instruction, or, rather, substantive experiment in instruction, cannot move.

Public awareness that we have reached a stage of educational stagnation has been growing. The knowledge of instruction's extremely subtle nature has likewise increased. We face widespread frustration with school instruction. Our tendency is to blame management for everything. This may be a mistake. Administration of school instruction does not fail simply because of some divine but unknown law which renders all management ineffective in face of individual learning variability. Rather, management as now constituted may fail mainly for the reason that, given the individual character of learning as a process, it cannot *by its present nature* extend itself to make adequate allowance for such variability.

Conventional wisdom holds that only a treatment which can advance the progress of group instruction provides a suitable criterion for experiment. Thus, we have no business proposing alternate modes of instruction which depart seriously from the exclusive classroom format. There exists, to be blunt, a persistent bias against the psychological fact of learner individuality—created by the very nature of the classroom as a management environment. Emphasis is accordingly directed solely to achieving permutations on the format of group instruction, rather than to creating more individually suitable modes and circumstances of learning. Indeed, only the former may be defined as acceptably "innovative" in any practical sense, at least for the time being.

Yet typical current administrative overhauls, say, magnet school programs or shifts to school-based management, are far from being experimental in any psychological context. They alter administrative arrangements by changing the criteria for makeup of classes, no more. Even efforts to vary the standard instructional format itself (e.g., among older concepts, team teaching; or as a newer concept, mixed-age group instruction) are experimental only in the sense that they involve treatments designed to provide, and altogether randomly, more direct and continuous contact between certain teachers and certain students.

Affected by a cultural blind spot, many educators view anything designed as an instructional treatment which, by altering the established hit-or-miss group instructional format in order to cultivate a single individual's learning, ceases to constitute education and enters a forbidden domain. Favoritism and elitism, perhaps even in some ideological contexts brainwashing, are automatically suspected. The public is forever suspicious, often readily convinced of the presence of evil forces secretly at work. Nor is public disapprobation hard to explain. Modern democracy is highly egalitarian. Since social "fixit" schemes are politically taboo, any shadow of possible "psychological engineering" in institutional settings is also always frightening, always taken seriously. In terms of mass consciousness, barriers to mainstream change in education, however obviously change may be needed, are many and high.

How easy then to confuse the fundamental difference in goal concept between classic behaviorist management à la *Walden Two* and management of an *individual's* learning in his own broader interest. But even while nurturing such popular fears and misconceptions and the public's preference for ultra-traditional ways, contemporary instructional managers can no longer obscure the underlying longer-term drift. The standard education system is headed downhill at a dangerous pace for too many learners. But why? What is wrong with the school as it now administers and delivers instruction?

For decades the profession has dwelt on the *what* of instruction. It patently assumes that by reworking and refining curriculum contents and patterns of use it does all that is needed to create the conditions for real change. Regrettably professionals still take it for granted that the *how* element in instruction has been by and large settled, cast in the concrete of "process elements susceptible of no further change." Yet an unavoidable core question remains: What has been done, or is being done, to improve the *individual* learner's progress? How this question can ever be answered positively without experiment which focuses on individual learner variability (though still within the instructional environment of the school) is a continuing mystery.

Critics may agree that individuality should not be sacrificed to collective principles. And we regularly hear from the same sources that "experiment" of some kind is a "good idea." But, these same critics then insist, since we must educate all children, how can instruction which *does* allow for recognition of the individual child's uniqueness ever, in any practical sense, be possible? This self-contradictory point of view is typical, revealing an excessive reverence not just for the past but also for the present with its ubiquitous political compulsions. Yet worse than this, such critics seek to control the future in this same context as well, seeing tomorrow only as a prolongation of today and its restrictive tensions. The real question about experiment has to be: Does it lead to a *different* future? Given the realities of a classroom method still unexamined in light of possible emerging alternatives, "experiment" which merely works a few variations on the surface of today's standard practice quite misses the point.

Decades may have to pass before today's method can be replaced on any broad scale. The modest present need, then, is for thinking which actually considers a theory of radical individualization within the common school. This has been for too long evaded. We cannot ignore forever needs for change. Indeed, the philosophic roots of innovation are implicit in the principles of democratic education. School has the socially approved mission of aiding self-development on an individual—as opposed to an exclusive group—basis. And this means—at some point—allowing genuine experiment with individualization. Otherwise we linger helplessly in the familiar rut of established habit, clinging to old routines even with the knowledge that this path only drives us around in circles of increasing frustration.

Aldous Huxley expressed some of the real despair of all adults who sense at one point or another in life the extent of unrealized possibilities within education. Decades ago he wrote:

> It is perfectly possible to combine a schooling in the local cultural tradition, with a training half vocational, half psychological, in adaptation to the current conventions of social life, and then to combine this combination with training in the sciences, in other words with the inculcation of correct knowledge. But is this enough? Can such an education result in the self-realization which is its aim?[2]

Now and again this problem of "self-realization" through education actually surfaces out of the psychic debris of our contemporary information whirlwind. In a bizarre footnote to a year of intense political bickering over the state budget for 1991, and with a looming deficit of more than $14 billion, California legislators nonetheless granted $40,000 to a school commission for "further study of ways to improve student self-esteem." To critics this seemed an absurd sum for an absurd cause. But the issue involves a point worth consideration. The very phenomenon of such an occasional grant itself demonstrates the extent to which society sees the standardized instructional enterprise as yielding less than it should in terms of bottom-line human benefits. Adults realize that something more could be done for the individual by the school than is being done, and when possible they would act on that understanding.

Whether we speak of self-realization, self-esteem, or any other state of personal improvement of an individual facing the world and its challenges, we refer to an achieved process of learning in which the individual has changed, and not always solely through his own efforts. Society invests in every person, through means both formal and informal. Through the school it aims formally to build that investment—helping him advance, so far as institutional structures permit, in knowledge and acumen. But there is a subtle element in this process, a factor hard to pinpoint. How easy it is to blame *only* the individual: "Johnny never learned to read; he couldn't hold up his end of the bargain and became another dropout." Yet perhaps the institution too failed in its part of the bargain. Many are the possible reasons for failure, and at present we can do little either to uncover or remedy them.

Given the rigidities of our present modus operandi, indeed, it asks too much to prescribe drastic forced experiment on any scale. Nor is large-scale experiment really desirable at this stage. If we are concerned primarily with individuals, it is sufficient merely to study the changes which an alteration of substance in structural method makes in a few individual cases. Common sense in fact tells us that small-scale experiment, in which differences between, say, group and individualized treatments in instruction are studied in detail, offers its own range of worthwhile possibilities. And—of great importance for the time being, in the sense of practical politics—it poses a smaller threat to powers that be.

One further point, a more global one, is worth making. The world is rapidly changing and an education for the twenty-first century cannot continue to be what was an already unsatisfactory version of nineteenth-century education. Experiment which "gets at" the real differences between effective and ineffective *individual* instruction thus becomes a critical matter in improvement of the process. Experiment for its own sake alone, with no other end in view, leads down a blind alley. This is the likely fate of every touted administrative "experiment," in which bodies are shifted here and there and into newer and more diverse group settings but minds are left untouched. In a word, the wholly administrative experiment lacks a philosophical basis. It fails to recognize human individuality and self-realization as integral elements of the educational scheme of things.

Education, as Huxley rightly states, must go beyond merely providing an individual with vocational and psychological resources useful in the struggle for existence. It must also open a way to his self-realization. This it has done only too infrequently through history to this point—for it has never truly recognized him *as an individual*. And the barriers to that recognition remain.

Can Instruction Reach Beyond the Stereotypes of Experiment?

Since instruction affects individuals first and groups made up of those individuals only secondarily, why should nothing ever be specified as to what an experimental treatment is to accomplish other than in relation to standard norms? If there can be norm-referenced results, then why can there not also be criterion-referenced outcomes in which an individual learner's performance is measured solely in relation to his own progress from a point of beginning to one of closure following an experimental treatment? The answer is that this kind of measurement will have no real value in the current climate of understanding; only the group matters, either in the actual environment of instruction or in judging the effects of experimental treatments.

Though norm-referencing of student performance and the nearly complete dependence on group modes of instruction are in many ways unavoidable in institutional settings, their limitations are seldom considered as major blocks to instructional evolution. This is hardly a matter of professional opposition to change alone. The "group approach, and nothing else" mirrors a deep-seated social ethos. Modern democracies are permeated by a widespread adult belief that society benefits most when equality in the status of individuals is particularly obvious and pronounced. It is not acceptable to think of "freeing" the individual if in so doing the collective fails somehow to profit economically or in a psychological sense from his "freedom."

In educational practice this short-sightedness leads to predictable outcomes. Far too often exclusively group-based instruction does best only what citizens of the most reactionary ilk prefer: It penalizes all parties to the process, holding back every brighter, quicker mind, while driving duller ones forward mechanically but unprofitably.[3] Yet resistance to change in education is never limited only to conservative reactionaries; the utopian liberal also, and out of similar fears, rejects the evidence of individual human differences and their effects. University of Michigan psychology professor Joseph Adelson has commented on the mind-set of many who cling to outdated 1960s views of the instructional enterprise:

> Differences in ability are a fiction....The gifted can take care of themselves, or are in any case not worthy of admiration or special attention. There is no special reason to stress cognitive skills over all others, since to do so is a bourgeois prejudice; it takes as much intelligence to survive on the street as to solve quadratic equations.[4]

Yet development of individual cognitive knowledge remains the principal business of school instruction. Few adults, if challenged seriously, will plead that school, after all, should for twelve long years be nothing more than a mix of meaningless fun and games. The case for change in modes of instruction grows consequently stronger. Is not the extreme move of a parent furnishing his child an education at home more than simply a rejection of group method? Is it not also a desperate bid for serious experiment in *individual instruction*—at a time when the very callous disregard of cognitive development in school classroom instruction itself invites parents' desperate measures to fill the gap?

But experiment cannot really be *just* a matter of "doing it for oneself." Home schooling may "work" for some few learners. It is no solution for the many; nor is it experimental in a scientific sense. Science and scientific theorizing are involved in any true experiment. If these can be called into play, then, yes, a study of instruction will be meaningful even when the experimental treatment involves only a single individual. But will anyone care, or even pay attention when measures are criterion- rather than norm-referenced? Oddly enough, they may. Society continues to be interested in the intellectual welfare of the individual child; evidence of this comes to us at times in surprising ways, most obviously in the school itself.

Teacher-student ratio is still the most fundamental aspect of instructional interaction where individual learners are concerned. What then is actually happening in this aspect of school instruction? We are in fact bringing education closer to the learner by bringing him nearer his teacher, at least if numerical data mean anything. As a portent of things to come, in 1991 all school districts in the state of California, for example, shared a public grant of $31 million to support lower teacher-pupil ratios. The legislators' basic concern was to make instruction available to every child on a measurably more personal basis. This trend to smaller class sizes is now universally favored in North America, as the new century begins; and it is implemented where and whenever possible, even in the predictable periods of severe fiscal retrenchment in the public sector.

The trend is significant. Yet it raises disturbing questions: Where does the principle lead? Who among so many millions of learners (there are at least 40 million school attendees below college level in the US alone, it is estimated) gets picked out to attend a smaller class and to have a more personal relation with his teacher? Do we choose only the "problem learners" for such specially favored treatment? The top-achieving students? What about average types, the great majority? Who among all these is most deserving? In an egalitarian democracy no one should claim preference simply because he is a "problem child," a genius, or "just average." As we move towards ever more individualization, what are the proper guidelines? Where does the process stop? In the present milieu of adult thinking, these are hard questions to deal with.

Withal, over and above these pressing thoughts we already face an in-place challenge of universal demand: Every parent expects his child to have the "best" instruction available. In the popular utopian view of communal life no one expects to settle for second-best. However we answer all the difficult theoretical questions, we have already as a practical matter accepted the obligation to provide every learner with the "best" education possible—meaning, in essence, the benefits of more *individualized* instruction, and sooner rather than later.

Future Needs and the Experimental Rationale

It is human nature to shrug off the irritating contradiction between individual and collective in the educational arena. We know there is little we can do for the present about the problems it presents. Besides, critics maintain, the problem of individualization of instruction cannot in any case be dealt with adequately unless and until technology (meaning a technology of artificial intelligence) becomes sufficiently advanced. For the foreseeable future, then, school instruction must remain a matter of stretching limited human resources over ever broader areas of demand. This is indeed a matter of recognizing limits—human limits. We cannot for now or for the near-future move beyond the limitations of organization in the "human systems" sense, cannot build motivation in the learner over and above what those systems permit. We certainly cannot yet automate individual instruction, somehow miraculously make it efficient over and beyond our given powers. Not *yet!*

Still, the nagging issue of future directions already intrudes on our thoughts. Future instruction not only should be "different." It will be different. What can be done now to prepare for a coming era of "higher tech" individualized instruction? Educational history provides some clues. But as with all human problems with a fundamentally moral core, we find no solution translatable directly into terms of instructional practice. At least not so far. But when we look carefully at man's educational past we find certain broad hints as to the choices that lie ahead. Again recall Socrates.

Socrates' method of teaching (for he *was* a teacher) made use of a single distinct means for providing educational experience. In that method one individual, an experienced human being, undertakes to guide another, less experienced person toward knowledge. Modern theories of pedagogy have not paid much attention to implications of this approach. This is so not only because, on first examination, the method seems too primitive and even simple-minded. A point of view on conscious intelligence is also involved, one with significant implications for instructional method.

Socrates did not assume that *collective intelligence* was unable to comprehend aspects of knowledge; this could in the best of circumstances always be possible. But significantly, both Plato and modern interpreters of the Socratic phenomenon (classical scholars like

Jaeger and Marrou) fail to concede anything further on this point. To put it in unequivocal terms, the nub of Socrates' teaching method was his unqualified acceptance of *individual mind* as agent of instructional direction or control.

It is difficult then to evade a disturbing assumption: that Socrates regarded as a physical and indeed psychological impossibility any attempt to convey knowledge from some "consensual intelligence." How could the one possibly think as do the many? Should we expect that he must, or ever will? In terms of modern communications theory, we find ourselves then confronting a problem of validity in information content. Is the real knowledge lost in the "cultural noise" of the transmission process? How can one assume that any teacher, however well-informed and mature, whether paid or not, can somehow represent collective intelligence and at the same time convey knowledge or truth effectively? Just as important: Why *should* education rest on management by and in the interest of collective intelligence?

Socrates did accept that knowledge was possible, that individual minds could acquire it by effort. Nor was knowledge of necessity a solely private possession, not shared by other minds. Some things the many can know. But Socrates denied that any knowledge was wholly self-evident. To attain knowledge inquiry is needed. A mind has to move beyond appearances, rules, illusions, to ask what symbols and phenomena mean, whether or not they are right, or true. Man must become familiar with the "stuff" of which knowledge consists. He cannot live through animal senses alone. But he must then risk hubris, the insolence of his own knowledge search. The whole undertaking, thus, has a certain dark side for society. The knowledge-seeker can only submit to "consensus intelligence" in a limited degree; to go beyond a certain point in the direction of "what others know" endangers the validity of his own efforts at knowing.

We are left with a disquieting conclusion: In a pedagogical sense the individual mind controlling instruction remains fully as important as the "message" of the culture. Recognition of this ambivalence as to the source of "objective knowledge" in education may once have been significant only on the philosophical level. But in the maelstrom of a post-modern, information-rich twenty-first-century world society, its relevance in psychological and pedagogical terms for all formal education becomes more pronounced as well.

This question of "what" or "whom" an individual mind represents cannot lightly be passed over in any serious consideration of future school instruction. It is too easy just to say that management of instruction will be under control of a "mind." That mind will have to stand for something, will have to be accepted for not only its stored knowledge but also for the "personality" which guides its actions in managing instruction. (One notes in passing that the context of mind—its origins, componentry, and tendencies—has already in the 1990s become firmly established as a top priority in computer software research; advances in artificial intelligence and virtual reality are indeed impossible without theories of mind in its major functions—knowledge acquisition, the drive to communicate, the manifestations of personality and intelligence.) And this leads us to ask: What is there in the concept of Socratic mind which cannot be done without in any future scheme of individual instructional management? In a more specifically historical context the query becomes: What *was* Socrates' characteristic advantage as a teacher?

Certainly, as Allan Bloom explains, the political lesson of Plato's *Apology* cannot be bypassed. A collision between Socrates and Athenian society at a certain point was inevitable. Politically Socrates was an intransigent: "Any careful reading of the *Apology* makes clear that Socrates never says he believes in the gods of the city. But he does try to make himself appear to be a sign sent from the gods, commanded to do what he does by the Delphic god."[5] His trial and punishment seem outrageous and cruel to us today. Yet "whatever scholars may say about the injustice of Aristophanes' or Athens' charges, the evidence supports those charges."[6]

But to interpret Socrates' case as exclusively political is to fail in grasping its pedagogical aspect. This in turn shunts aside a major question for any future education based on high technology. Few contemporary educators fail to cite technology, and specifically artificial intelligence, as tomorrow's major tool of innovation in the instructional arena. But most educators as yet have no vision of a future in which AI might be seen as something more than just a clever lookup aid for the individual student. The student's learning program continues to be managed exclusively by "wise" human adults. The contradiction in this way of thinking cannot forever be shrugged aside as not relevant. And the Socratic approach to pedagogy is involved in any effort to deal with the contradiction.

No purpose is served by using technology unless it brings men closer to possession of what they must have as adapting creatures. Only when we set humane goals and then use appropriate technology to aid in the achievement of those goals do we approach efficiency of process. Technology, then, will indeed remain a mere toy in the realm of formal instruction, until its use in achieving proper educational goals is made clear in a consensus view. But there would be small point in ignoring what this means for the shorter term, in which we have neither an advanced technology for individual instruction, nor a consensus on what such a technology (or education itself, for that matter) should accomplish. We have before us for the time being only a continuing and worsening stagnation in our mass education "processing system," a condition of things left over from Roman times in its administrative layout, and in its philosophical aspect a heritage of unduly utopian assumptions about human adaptability bequeathed to us by Enlightenment thinking.

The very word *education* connotes discipline. Broadly, we define education as the process of developing general and specific abilities of mind. If technology is ever to develop as a genuine contributor to *every* learner's education, it must function in an actively intelligent manner, not simply as an advanced, though passive, lookup toy which the learner can use or not as he sees fit. Its logical role then will be to create and manage the conditions of discipline for an individual mind, just as Socrates did for the young men of Athens. Human evolution brings new challenges, but also new opportunities. What Socrates did for yesterday's few, AI pedagogues will evidently have to do for tomorrow's many.

Employing technology as we do in education today makes use of it neither as a tool of systematic discipline nor as a psychological "individualizer" in a Socratic sense. Yet development of a technology of intelligence goes inexorably on. As robotics specialist Hans Moravec points out, management of some human activities by intelligent machines may prove an unavoidable denouement within the not-so-distant future.

There is no reason to believe that human equivalence represents any sort of upper bound. When pocket calculators can out-think humans, what will a big computer be like?.... So why rush headlong into an era of intelligent machines? The answer... is that we have very little choice, if our culture is to remain viable.[7]

One hundred percent human control of the instructional process is desirable so long as that process brings about reasonably adequate results. But today we see that *our* exclusive control of individual instruction, based on a method designed to reach the individual learner only as a member of some randomly defined group, has at best a doubtful future. Then what alternate path does tomorrow—if we are to have any human role to play in it—really allow? Can we go on forever ignoring the obvious lesson of developing technology?

Moravec expresses the overall problem concisely: "By design, machines are our obedient and able slaves. But intelligent machines, however benevolent, threaten our existence because they are alternative inhabitants of our ecological niche."[8] Still, humanity survives by virtue not only of its own intelligence but also through its willingness to *develop* that intelligence. We can keep ahead of the machines so long as our own minds maintain their innate—and individual—learning initiative. Nothing guarantees retention of this initiative so much as giving individual minds en masse the earliest possible opportunity to develop intelligently. A fundamental question about school instruction then is left to be answered: Can any real change in instruction occur without practical experiment which takes seriously the "mind-to-mind" nature of "artificial intelligence pedagogy"?

PART TWO

THE STATUS QUO: BARRIER POINTS AND POINTS OF DEPARTURE

Chapter 5

The Technological Enigma: Some Thoughts on Future School Instruction

For mass education the real promise of technology lies in its eventual combination of maximum versatility, efficiency, and cheapness. The maxim "more from less" will never be better applied than in the technology of the twenty-first-century school. But the long road to that outcome has as yet scarcely been charted.

Trial and error is the order of today—and tomorrow. For the short-term future schools will be deluged with machines most of which are not observably more effective than their predecessors, since they involve no conceptual breakthroughs which would incorporate in a machine system a capability for guiding the learning of any student on an exclusively individual basis. This will change, though surely not soon. Billions long since invested, plus more to be invested, in R & D as well as manufacture, by giant corporations in all the main industrial countries, are earmarked to take advantage of already built-in biases and limitations of the mass education market. Likely two or more decades will have to pass before the cycle of production, utilization, and obsolescence of this generation of technology can be fully run through—and the way cleared for a twenty-first-century educational technology.

Regrettable or not, the time factor here is a given of our late-industrial age; we cannot wish it away and overleap the current cycle except in the projections of science fiction. When some apparent breakthrough does occur, professional educators are reluctant to accept its implications for school instruction; delay and obstruction in designing and implementing specific instructional uses can be anticipated as much two decades hence as now. Nonetheless, since the school remains such a visibly resource-wasteful undertaking, cost-containment pressures continue of necessity to affect it. Current use of human inputs (excessive for remedial teaching, to say nothing of the areas of counseling, administration, and general teaching) is already inordinately costly in relation to results obtained. The only answer to the host of emerging problems in instruction is a substitution of advanced technology for expensive and too often ineffective human input.

Yet such a technology, in an era of public demands without cease for more measurably adequate instruction, will have to prove itself worthy on an Information Age scale of values. No small attainment, the barriers to which are still less than well understood even by experts. Even the briefest of reflections on the relatively slow development of technological potential in education through the later decades of the past century of otherwise runaway technological growth underscores the magnitude of the challenge.

All educational technology provides initial sensory stimulus or extends the grasp of external phenomena for some human user. There are two general classes of such technology. Both fulfill the broad task of expanding experience (and hence, presumably, knowledge, if human processing equipment allows) by mechanizing the experience of externality, directing it into logically organized event-streams. The first is the class of "mediative" communication technologies, including newspaper, TV, and radio. These as a group are termed "the media" because they bring phenomena of the external world graphically to our human input sensors (at the same time establishing a web of meanings within their presentations—increasingly through use of various editorial practices, e.g., emphasis, timing, sequence, pattern, shock tactics).

The second is the class of "simulative" processing technologies, machine systems capable of duplicating many (and potentially, in the view of a few scientists, all) of our human functions as we explore and manipulate the external environment. The major exemplar of such systems is the computer, in particular as it extends our reach into the external environment, via artificial intelligence in general and robotics specifically. The history of such "extension machines" as used in mass education reveals a record of consistent inconsistency in the pattern of application. This is not surprising, in view of the persisting void of constructive thinking about the ends of educational technology—both among product designers and equipment producers and those responsible for school instructional policy.

In the realm of mediative technologies, current and projected applications evoke a picture of only limited awareness by developers of how (or why) technical breakthroughs might be exploited to the advantage of the individual learner. The static condition of development of interactive TV systems provides perhaps the most obvious case in point. The potential is known, yet without greater interest and support—mainly from marketing firms and the public; school people, naturally, are of mixed mind, wanting improvements in instruction yet also fearful of what improved technologies of instruction will do to jobs—interactive TV as an instructional tool lingers on the vine, a hint of the future but not much more.

This is not too surprising. Ours has been the century for just a single category of media communication, what is termed "one-way" by specialists. Use of long-distance communications has developed along primarily two lines: the innocuous conversation-carrying telephone (two-way in principle, yet forever limited in practice by the perceptions and intellectual capabilities of individual users); and the one-way mass transmission media, visual print media only in the Gutenberg stage but later, in our time, audio, and finally audio-visual media. The information-using eighty percent of society now demands ever more forcefully the "entertainment power" of one-way mass media: radio, films, and above all TV—the real instruments of mass communication, providing an ever-expanding audience with ever-more-rationalized product content. It is impossible to make sense of the contemporary world without acknowledging the dominant role of one-way media communications in shaping human activities.

The triumph of one-way media is unquestioned, either from a commercial or a propaganda point of view. From those feeble beginnings, from Edison's demonstration of his kinetoscope at the 1893 Chicago World's Fair and Marconi's 1898 wireless reports to London of the summer yacht races off Ireland to today's blockbuster TV specials (in which millions around the world tune via satellite to a single drama, sports event, rocket launch, or political "happening"), all emphasis remains on the senders and their messages. Such one-way emphasis is also, unfortunately, nearly always present when media is made use of in education as well.

True, teachers often try to employ mass media products for valid instructional purposes, by encouraging classroom discussion of films, TV programs, and the like. Yet the range of choice among products continues to be narrow; the market sees little point in going beyond standard subjects and formats. School people are in no position to ask for more—or better. From the administrative side, given their current mode of operation, school leaders in fact see no need to make greater or more original use of media, or for media which are in and of themselves unusually original and different. Teachers create as well as carry out instructional policy; and in self-defense they will resist creative technology when it impinges on their territorial domains. Desperate teachers may also overuse films or recordings at times, but they have no wish to allow media to usurp their basic authority in any substantial fashion. Nor would any principal in his right mind permit his teachers to become over-dependent on instructional media.

All in all, with their education market essentially static, media producers have no cause to be innovative. As in the larger commercial market itself, each advance in technology is automatically accompanied by a corresponding simplification or degradation of product content. School children lack the subtleties of mental functioning which experience has given adults, so the information provided in any case hardly ever passes beyond the level of sophistication of an average adult TV or radio program. The educational value of media products in instruction thus remains low by any definition.

Schools with their culturally oriented approach to information content are at any rate not in an advantageous position to exert influence over commercial producers equally entangled with cultural forces. Nor do those few educators in a position to suggest change care to rock the boat by demanding drastic departures from a pattern of universally stereotyped media output. So the schools at each step of the way yield an ever-larger captive audience for so-called "educational" products of media technology, from recordings and radio through films, filmstrips, and TV, and now videotape. Each advance in technology ties end-users (teachers and children) to a steadily tightened leash-line, enjoining conformity to the single concept of "audio-visual resources" as exclusively one-way communication tools. This is taken, though not altogether accurately, as inevitable, something determined by the nature of communication itself. Yet it also genuinely reflects the limited educational possibilities in one-way mass media themselves.

A more complex picture obtains in the case of computers in education. For decades computers have been touted as *the* answer to manifold problems of instruction (notably those having to do with structure of the disciplines and with individualization of learning). In some respects, indeed, schools today would be even more backward than they are without these aids to instruction. Computer-assisted instruction, as a prime example, deservingly finds many boosters, not least among learning psychologists and programmers of instructional packages for computers. And in truth, with certain subjects studied at certain levels, the good effects of CAI unquestionably outweigh the bad. But the more significant issue is: Where are computers headed in education overall?

The late British psychologist and writer on computer history Christopher Evans pointed out three major reasons why the computer has been slow to fulfill any of the grand expectations laid down for it in the early decades of the computer revolution. First, no one knows if it incorporates in its processes the best methods of teaching, since those methods themselves continue to be undefinable in concrete terms.[1] Second, there are, unfortunately, persons of some influence who claim, with little evidence or support, that at base learning processes are no more than sequences of prearrangeable tasks which, with proper formulation, can already be entrusted to machines.[2]

Third, there are very large risks involved in bringing to the mass education market genuinely experimental products, and it is in the nature of all modern societies, capitalist or other, dominated by large organizations fixated on maximizing status quo operations, to avoid questioning either short- or long-term motives of the leading players. Experiment then is in the main left to small firms and the venture capital providers who underwrite them; hence momentum in meeting many real market needs can be difficult to develop.[3]

Some of the fundamental difficulty here, it would seem, has to do with a broad social outlook favoring one-way (as against two-way) communication in all societal processes, including formal education.

Perhaps partly for this reason machines for use in the educational sphere have been almost exclusively of a less interactive character than required, for they function on the basis of "right or wrong answers" only. In effect they present themselves to the user in a take-it-or-leave-it format, saying: "I question or present; you watch and answer on terms I lay down—and *only* on those terms, for I am incapable of communicating otherwise." Machines of this kind are, sadly, still the norm and they will dominate the educational market for some time into the future.

While we see occasional improvements in the "communication process" within such a restricted mode, there are also undesirable side effects. Every new "success" in the sequence of technological developments within the classroom (most recently videotape and VCR) thus far unfailingly clings to the one-way mode and probably reinforces it. The trend from a pedagogical standpoint likely adds to, rather than relieves, the troubles of already dependent learner minds and so demonstrates all the more the need for some kind of effective "reasoning dialogue machine" in instruction. (This last, an "umbrella" designation, and a necessary item of concern if one is to consider the full range of theoretical possibilities in instruction, would include any equipment geared to evoke not merely active but also *systematic* thought—in a given individual learner's mind.)

Both mediative and simulative devices as presently used are then obsessively one-way in nature. If we ignore for the moment the still slow-to-develop possibilities of interactive TV, all mediative "instruction" remains in fact one-way by definition. CAI and allied computer presentations are themselves typical examples. In such one-way didactic exercises, canned programs deliver precisely stated sequences of stimuli to the learner. Only a severely limited range of responses is permitted. Any reasoning other than of the linear and repetitive type has no place. Fact-learning for its own sake and memory drill routines, valid though they may be at certain times in instruction, tend to be far too often the sole pedagogic principles at work here.

Even so, one should not lose sight of the importance to education of the computer as an "alternative mind." It seems likely that if software improvements continue at their present rate and a genuine long-distance communications capability can be provided for school computer systems within the next several decades, computers, rather than mediative devices, will be the front-line technology for a more effective, individualized twenty-first Century school instruction. They are machines which, at least theoretically, will some day genuinely reason and, perhaps more significant, will also (though as yet, again, only in theory) create instructional situations free of the burden of inefficiency in direct mind-to-mind communication that, thanks to so many built-in distractions, infuses the typical school classroom.

The Lessons of PLATO

Following the fortunes of the computer as an aid to learning in North American schools gives some clues (even if only subtle ones) to the directions technology will follow in mass education.   Progress is anything but automatic; stop and go is the only pattern so far discernable. Still, improved access to information stored in data banks and better management of instruction—both key elements in any improved teaching-learning process—are being realized in slow increments as the technology of CAI matures. At the leading edge, considerable achievements have been recorded by way of "evening-out" and rendering more credible the elements of instruction.

Control Data Corporation's PLATO learning system provides a good case in point. PLATO is a comprehensive CBE (Computer-Based Education) environment, consisting of several subsystems incorporating four interrelated instructional components: instruction proper; testing; record keeping; and information/learning resources. The interactive CAI instructional subsystem is linked to a Computer-Managed Instruction (CMI) sub-subsystem, which handles the tasks of student diagnosis, resource selection, testing, record maintenance, and decision-making as to which among several directions the learner shall next pursue. Another linked sub-subsystem is the resource data bank itself, called CSLA (for Computer-Supported Learning Aids). From this the user is able to retrieve data of many types for solving problems and to answer questions.   As examples, CSLA provides routine calculation, accepts and stores student-originated formulas for later use, summarizes statistical data (such as Census Department figures), and so on. The system as a whole allows for interaction between user and "machine instructor" in a variety of classic teaching-learning modes: drill and practice; tutorial; dialogue; inquiry; simulations and games; direct problem solving.[4]

As a model for other advanced interactive "learning systems" in the last few decades, PLATO has shown, indeed, a fair instructional potential. With flexibility of design, capability for individualization, provision for network access and long-distance interaction, and relative comprehensiveness as a pedagogic processing agent, the system performs as an often admirable aid to learning in a variety of situations. As its authors state:

> The PLATO system is a delivery system. It is not based on any one set of training or instructional principles. It can present instructional materials according to any instructional theory, philosophy, or methodology, or according to any training method or plan.[5]

One of PLATO's segments, as an example, involves a math curriculum for Grades 4 to 6. This courseware, typical of the system's breadth, actually provides sufficient lesson material to engage the interest of a student at that grade level for half an hour daily during the entire school year. The scheme of instruction was designed to "accommodate a wide range of student abilities, prompting and tutoring the slower students while challenging the curiosity of the most able."[6] Provision is made for a balance in each lesson between review and new information, with games, graphics, and other elements of variety to modify the pace and extend concentration. This flexibility is characteristic of all PLATO software. The degree of interaction possible with this whole system, in addition, adds to its sophistication. Contemporary PLATO represents, indeed, a remarkable advance on the original teaching machines in respect to such basic system components as memory capability, variation of response, and choice of learning materials and approaches. It is, at least in concept, the very prototype of a high tech learning system.[7]

With such laboriously and carefully developed technological enhancements of instruction, it is then no longer suitable to speak, with that hint of condescension, of the continuing inadequacy of "technological solutions." Yet even with PLATO no signal peak of accomplishment has been reached. Serious questions of both rationale and practical effectiveness remain. A large-scale study in which PLATO users were compared to non-users revealed no significant differences in either student achievement or attrition levels. The use of PLATO materials in addition to traditional instruction was readily accepted by students as helpful and interesting but had no apparent effect on performance in standard tests.[8] One is left searching for explanations. Why has no more catalytic outcome for mass education resulted from the increasing availability to learners of such a relatively advanced instructional technology? Aside from the fact that some costs to the user (such as telephone hookup) are built into the program, it seems impossible to identify—at least in the present context of mass education—any primary reason for the inability of PLATO to "click" with a larger market of academic consumers.[9]

A response that says "such a system will replace teachers and even administrators, hence it is being successfully resisted by the profession" seems patently simplistic and insufficient. Nor can one explain the phenomenon very well with the comment that "no learner, young or old, wants to sit still and converse with just a machine, even if for only a half hour every day, for a whole school year." In the case of PLATO, we cannot even fall back on the most often-voiced explanation heard in computer circles: Educational software involves too many instructional "errors" and is too often hastily conceived and marketed by authors and publishers more interested in a fast buck than in a quality product.[10]

The fact is that users at all levels, not the system, create the real instructional problem. To gain a tangible advantage from the system, a user cannot approach it with a mental slate that is blank. He will have to have been involved from an earlier time, pursuing his subject continuously, with motivation, and he must have developed a general understanding of the field and its relation to other aspects of knowledge. In his interface with the system, he will then be doing not simply "some work which the teacher or the course outline prescribes." The learner will instead be pursuing a self-imposed developmental regimen, in which he is psychologically too involved to allow his "backing away" at any stage of the process.

Only at this psychological point, then, will one encounter a person who is adding to his already well-developed dimensions as a learner, something finally possible for two reasons: (1) he has already "learned how to learn," so he can profit from such instruction; and, (2) the system, given its developed capabilities, can open up new, attractive, and otherwise unavailable intellectual opportunities for him. The sad fact is that not many children do reach this stage at any time through the spectrum of K-12 instruction. Lower schools today cannot routinely build up in average children this kind of "set" in favor of further, more concentrated learning as a vital part of experience. Only the minority which reaches college, indeed no more than a fraction of that minority, develops such a "set." The gap at lower levels, moreover, was not being addressed in any comprehensive way, even in the 1990s.

As a US National Academy of Science briefing panel statement on the uses of information technology as an adjunct to pre-college instruction summed up a few years ago:

> In addition to traditional competencies, students increasingly should learn the thinking skills to manage information, formulate effective probing questions, test hypotheses, make judgments, express themselves logically and lucidly, and solve problems. Unfortunately, our present educational resources are inadequate to meet these objective...as a result many students fail to correct even minor misunderstandings that nevertheless prevent continued advancement, and to develop skills for assessing their own learning problems... (yet) information technologies can provide the means to deliver some aspects of instruction not only cost-effectively but also in a deeply individualized and integrated way.[11]

Technology for the Individual Learner

Information technologies, nonetheless, remain a puzzle to educators as well as to the public. The degree of confusion where instructional applications of technology are concerned is generally profound. Many educators, as well as a majority of members of the public, I believe, would actually be inclined to agree with the following view of mass elementary and secondary instruction as it ought to be carried out some time after the turn of the new century:

> In the new Information Age, teachers train and programs teach. That is, the role of the human in the education system is to facilitate use of computerized modules and to foster social relations. The federal government supports production of thousands of multi-media modules at all levels. So instead of thousands of teachers redundantly teaching algebra or physics, we have one (or two or three) Hollywood-scale efforts involving video action, computer feedback, etc. Teachers coordinate the use of these programs and assist special students. The educators who

remain (down 30% from 1980) find the new system rewarding and challenging.[12]

This futuristic estimate, from Alan Porter, a professor of industrial engineering, should not seem unexpected, in our day of swiftly whipped-out technocratic "solutions" to problems large and small. Yet what really would be resolved in education by this approach? The individual will have been relegated to a yet further level of insignificance, while the new "learning" such a system was supposed to have promoted will have been conveniently forgotten. Soon enough, as with all systems that ignore the primary fact of human individuality, society will be reduced to nothing more than its usual after-the-fact search for "what went wrong this time." Every step in such a negative direction will reap a larger whirlwind in destruction of the values on which a rational society can function.

It is sufficient here to record that, long before the twentieth century, with its scarcely believable disregard for the individual, inspired such satires as *Brave New World*, J. S. Mill pronounced an eloquent verdict upon all such propositions, which were, if not as common then as now, at least as cocksure:

> All that has been said of the importance of individuality of character, and diversity in opinions and modes of conduct, involves...diversity of education. A general State education is a mere contrivance for molding people to be exactly like one another...as it is efficient and successful, it establishes a despotism over the mind, leading by natural tendency to one over the body.[13]

Yet simplistic, mechanistic formulas for the collective use of educational technology are still the norm, alas. More fundamental philosophic and psychological issues continue to be pushed aside. Moral and ethical concerns are still too embarrassing to bear widespread public scrutiny. Projections of vast schemes for one-way teaching modules and a reduced role for (and diminishing numbers of) human teachers provide little more than a temporary smokescreen hiding the fact that such formulas are devoid of any defensible basis, either in human values or in what is known of the psychology of learning.

Certainly there will have to be an increased use of technology, and in a diversity of forms, in the school of tomorrow; this would be necessary just to keep up with increased needs. And certainly the number of teachers, overall, must diminish as well: Today's over-swollen staffs exist to attend in part to various baby-sitting and make-work functions far too often, and without doubt the teacher-student ratio could over a lengthy period be reduced by, say, 30%, if greater attention could be placed on focused instruction using educational technology.[14] But those who think mass-management, Porter-type plans can somehow evade the basic facts of individuality and resistance to regimentation in instruction have another think coming.

Even so, the need to face up to preposterous technocratic schemes of this kind may also provide an impetus for our reexamination of the real fundamentals in education. This will be necessary in any case, if educational technology is ever to assume a rightful place in school instruction. But discussion and argument are not the same as consensus. A viable technology will not emerge until those who design and those who formalize and sanction use are both agreed on *who* that technology will serve and why (the social-philosophic issue); and *how* it can be made to serve (the psychological issue). In this, we can expect at best over the coming decades only a slow and uneven progress. PLATO represents no more than the earliest example of a somewhat sophisticated system—the crudity of those first teaching machines has been fairly well left behind—which finally presents these philosophic and psychological issues to us in a more realistic light.

It is of interest that the PLATO project already boasts a lengthy history, having been begun as long ago as 1960. Relatively speaking, it has been one of the best-funded and -manned projects in education over the years. Yet as early as 1974 the presence of factors inhibiting further development was noted. These factors have clear social-philosophical and psychological dimensions. In the words of Professor Ernest R. House of the University of Illinois, Urbana (where the PLATO project had been developed):

> The most critical question now facing PLATO is precisely (the) problem of universal application. For some time it has been promoted as a twenty-first-century blackboard, that is, every teacher is his own author and puts his own materials on the machine. The alternative is a twenty-first-

century textbook in which materials are centrally developed and 'piped' out to the classes, like Sesame Street.[15]

In either case, however, application never quite succeeds. Some psychological factor, some primary instructional element, is still missing. An individual "author and his materials" can evidently never be all things to all learners. Neither can one "centralized text." And what about the learner himself as a "receptor" of knowledge? Has he the needed capabilities for what he is expected to do in the first place? Data show reading skills declining in US and other school-age populations. The whole age-group from grade-schoolers to the thirty-somethings, in fact, lacks the benefits of that more concentrated school reading experience which was once a matter of course. But if the average learner cannot read well enough, should instruction depend to a greater extent on alternative approaches—more audio-visuals, more listen-and-learn and similar experiences which stress passivity in the learner in the same way as does TV? Clearly there are limits inherent in instruction encouraging passivity beyond a certain point, and it makes no sense to bypass those limits.

Then what alternatives are there? Media such as the mass-produced textbook or one-way TV, however enhanced, cannot by themselves "get the job done" with any expectation of cognitive closure. The child who cannot read has no reason to pursue by himself what books have to offer. TV, the mass medium par excellence, yields only momentary benefits of an intellectual character, even under the best of classroom conditions. By contrast, the human teacher who can actually "reach" the individual learner becomes, with passing time, a constantly more expensive and harder-to-find resource, and this source of instructional input, though the most desirable in a pedagogic sense, may prove ever less available for the deeper future.

Some additional, more genuine teaching element must then be present if instruction is to succeed in developing learning capacities and habits among the mass of children. It is this which all artificial systems for instruction still profoundly lack. All the expenditure of effort needed to create and develop PLATO and similar teaching programs has failed to confront this underlying psychological barrier to "universal application." At today's level of development, machine instruction lacks the power and flexibility of even a less sophisticated human mind in stimulating another mind comprehensively—and thus directing it toward the independent search for knowledge. As "agent" of individualization, the human mind still, as of this writing, has no peer whatever.

Yet the past offers no ready basis for prejudging the future. While machine intelligence has been over-ballyhooed as the solution to any number of problems in education, we are still unsure as to which specific tasks are best suited for machine handling and which, in the nature of things, must be reserved to humans. What we do know is that machines are developing far faster than humans in the ability to deal with problems of information input, processing, and output. In the jargon of science, the machine develops according to the rules of Lamarckian evolution, while man continues to move forward at the slower Darwinian pace. This raises a painful question, of great relevance to education: How much processing power needs to exist in an entity other than man for it to be capable of improving on human management of what are essentially human mental processes?

As scientist Robert Jastrow explains it, the astounding development of computer intelligence in only a brief four or five decades is "the kind of evolution that Lamarck...envisioned...wrong for flesh-and-blood creatures, but right for computers...(it) can proceed at a dizzying pace...the designer can tack on a piece here, and lop off a piece there, and make major improvements in one computer generation."[16] This pattern of development brings with it unavoidable implications for school instruction of the future.

Then on what basis, on what fundamental theoretical postulate, can technology contribute, as it must, in the development of future school instruction? Can we limit the role of technology forever to no more than that of a special toy with which to amuse the learner during brief periods of respite from a primarily social nexus for "collective learning"? The computer is evolving into something more than what it originally was; while a machine does not yet exist which scientists agree possesses powers of intuition, insight, or other characteristics of human consciousness, machines have already come into being which display what most scientists accept are "reasoning capabilities"—of the kind we associate with human intelligence. The simple machine, in brief, appears without question to be evolving in Lamarckian fashion into an ever more complex one, with inevitable consequences for human processes of adaptation.

All computers, of course, compute. But that can hardly be the end of their story. Their potential applications defy our imaginations. Thus, when they also teach, and effectively teach in the most basic sense of that term—meaning that they can manage in some significant way the instructional program of an individual, rather than simply feeding him somebody's canned lecture—then the world of learning will no longer, in any sense, be what it was.

Society and Its Machines—Where Consensus Still Fails

To this point, even with an advanced system like PLATO, we are using technology primarily as an end in itself, rather than as a means to some genuinely human end. The scientists who design such systems are an easy target and take an inordinate share of blame. We ignore that the scientists are not solely responsible for failing to see the road ahead. They too are mere travelers along a road that still remains to be defined through popular consensus. Lack of such a consensus is a problem just as much as is the scientific challenge of creating an advanced instructional technology itself. Science can hardly make progress in this sphere on a technical level alone. The issue is one which also demands social imagination for its resolution. As Norbert Wiener once expressed it,

> Operationally, we must consider an invention not only with regard to what we can invent but also as to how the invention can be used and will be used in a human context. The second part of the problem is often more difficult than the first...we are confronted with a problem of development which is essentially a learning problem, not purely in the mechanical system but in the mechanical system conjoined with society...definitely a case requiring a consideration of the problem of the best joint use of machine and man.[17]

Science is not standing still. Over a decade ago a leading developer of basic research in instructional technology could speak with some justification of "sitting on the edge of a revolution in the way in which instruction is delivered to students of all ages and varieties."[18] Yet really useful applications of instructional technology even today still seem to lie decades on in the future. For one thing, basic research in this field is singularly unappealing to those who control R & D funding. There are few government programs to support "general intellectual investigations of a fundamental kind," which (to use the precise language of Patrick Suppes of the Stanford University Computer Learning Laboratory) "will not, in the course of ordinary affairs, be undertaken by industry.... "[19]

But this is something we should be used to. Of more immediate interest to observers of the current educational scene is the nature of the conceptual barriers confronting those scientists who actually aim at breakthroughs in educational technology. Yes, technical obstacles themselves are formidable, and will continue to be. But there are also remarkably hard-to-pin-down issues of epistemological and cultural content, which a priori inhibit agreement on a direction for development. The era of "thinking machines" may already be upon us, yet we are still decades away from a universal picture of what those machines should actually do, and why.

If computers can be made to communicate, that is one thing. But another is their ability to know what knowledge is worthy of being stored and used. Even beyond this, there remains the question of how to combine various elements in a useful psychological context so as to provide an individual program of instruction. As Professor Suppes put it: "...the least-developed feature of this technology...is the theory of learning and instruction. Even if you can make the computer talk, listen, and adequately handle a large knowledge base, we still need to develop an explicit theory of learning and instruction."[20]

One has the uncomfortable feeling that science is working in this area with its hands tied, and not merely by the lack of interest from sources of funding. The public still looks on instruction as a simple and not very important process of force-feeding a mass of neophytes certain bits and pieces of fixed data of experience—and nothing more. Until this attitude itself begins to shift in favor of a more experimental approach, yet one with a socially acceptable philosophic basis, little change can be expected either on the scientific front, with the development of an artificial tutor/manager of instruction for the individual learner, or in the nature of day-to-day school instruction itself.

Chapter 6

Power over the Instructional Process: The American Experience

It might be asked what the education profession is doing in response to the crisis in school learning, since clearly that leadership has its own vital interest in reversing educational decline. The US situation foreshadows what the rest of the developed world can expect in decades to come, if no new options are developed in administrative outlook and technological applications—based in both cases on defensible philosophical foundations. Without question, the pressure to "do something" is evident, and not surprisingly most forcefully in North America. As never in the past, the education profession faces growing demands to "deliver the goods," and from many quarters. Society as a whole is responding to crisis, and in its accustomed way—with cries for action.

Contemporary educational leaders benefit, fortunately, from ample historical hindsight. They know the mistakes of the past; they also are preoccupied absorbing the lessons of contemporary management theory from industry and commerce. And they recognize their increasingly decayed popular image. They accept that the public mood is one of threat—threat to stand-pat assumptions and business as usual. At the same time, however, they realize the value of a continued breathing-space unavoidably granted by that same public, as with baffled hesitation it seeks to evade confrontation with the hallowed (even if patently under-productive) ways of the traditional system. Today's

technocrats of mass education are nothing if not pragmatic; as leaders
of a profession they are not out to shake that system to its foundations.
But they must somehow build better schools, and they say so.

Ex-California School Superintendent Bill Honig has spoken for these
new and pragmatic managers. "If the last quarter of a century of failed
revolutions in the educational arena have proved anything...it is that
"top-down" reform doesn't work. On the other hand, anarchy isn't a
very inviting alternative either."[1]

The answer? Like many of the currently dominant pragmatic school
of thinking, Honig demands all-around cooperation to push "down-up"
reform. Communities and parents must therefore be more involved.
The intention here is admirable, surely. Yet in the last analysis can a
reform which fails to motivate teachers and students themselves, the
front-line players, bring the results people at large keep demanding? It
is well known that the fine line between toughness and conciliation in
the demeanor of management of any undertaking readily has its way of
getting lost in the rough and tumble of managerial practice. And what
real internal changes does this new style of leadership actually bring
about? Why should nothing more than a greater level of activity on the
part of community members—or managers themselves, for that
matter—somehow automatically translate into a higher level of student
achievement across the board? Brave words are the perpetual coin of
every higher manager, but when does life on the front lines truly begin
to change?

Not, of course, that the reform-minded pragmatics of today lack a
perspective on what should have priority. They do not. They know, as
well as any liberal of the 1960s or classical humanist (say, a supporter
of the Paideia Program), or even any reasonably alert classroom
teacher, that anything to be called either "reform" or "progress" must
magnify the basic academic core. They are only too aware of the
extent to which academic work—if one is to speak of formal education
as a meaningful experience at all—is what school has to be about.

It is hard then to disagree with the ground-level principle on which
the US pragmatists operate: that the level of academic work in all
schools has fallen far too low, and that it must and will be improved on.
It hardly makes sense, either, to quibble over which general areas of
school activity can be, in the shorter term, pinpointed as targets for
reform. Honig revealed a ready grasp of the problem in describing his
own four "main leverage points" for reform, the pressure points to
which "people in the trenches" as well as members of the community

can all apply their enthusiasm and powers of persuasion: There will have to be: 1) tougher textbooks; 2) more effective discipline; 3) a return to meaningful homework assignments; and 4) continuous testing using standardized instruments—to show not just what students have learned but also how teaching and course structure/content relate to measured achievement.[2]

These are certainly four areas in which improvement can and should be striven for. These and like goals, if attainable, might reverse the trends with which we are so familiar—to always lower levels of achievement which, indeed, as establishment critics now point out, the laissez faire open-education excesses of previous decades did so much to promote. The public mood, up to a point, suggests broad support for whatever can be done on these lines, provided costs are not visibly increased. Yet there remains that aura of militant, almost fanatic determinism about such a program which smacks of the same self-certainty that marked the mind-set of Washington bureaucrats fashioning America's Great Society programs with public money in the 1960s.

The question of whether or not, in the midst of all this "toughening up," we are improving the education of the individual seems forgotten. It appears, indeed, that even with the best of intentions this approach is merely one more mobilization of mass resources, no different in its process aspects from the arrangements used by totalitarian societies, this time aimed at reshaping American youth to make them better able to compete as a mass system in the difficult global century ahead. It is not experimental in any pragmatic sense; nor is it an effort at breakthrough in resolving the underlying problems of instruction for the *individual*.

In short, the new pragmatics depend on all the old assumptions and all the old machinery to resolve a problem defined not pedagogically but politically, in terms of public discontents. They have but a single theme, which is a repetitious playing on popular fears that the economy will go bust if US schools fail to graduate masses of people who can become (in the sense, unfortunately, of automata) more efficient and motivated workers. But can such a form of what really still amounts to top-down management succeed, even when (by admission of those very interests most concerned) the only means for attaining the desired kinds of change will be "from-the-bottom-up" initiatives? Something is missing in all this, and that something is vision—a vision of genuine system change. So the chances are good that, if reform depends on what the new pragmatic managers have to offer, school instruction will be no different from and produce no better results a decade hence than what we see before us today.

But why such a negative outlook for what appears, on the surface, to be a hopeful renaissance in school management? Because (and one can only interpret the "down-up" pragmatic approach to management by its public stance at this stage) what the new pragmatics offer takes too little account of the underlying nature of life in an Information Society. Since an Information Society depends for success on not just the dispersion of information as a commodity but also on the ability of individuals to deal with information knowledgeably, cultivation of individuals as knowledge-users is of the essence.

On this critical variable adherents of the new management offer us as evidence only possible minute improvements on test score averages within a given segment of the school population; they still take for granted (in fact leave wholly unstated their views of) social and personal change as direct outcomes of the educational process. They are looking forward to a future which is unreal—unreal because intended to be without risk, only the past warmed over, a "mass method" which differs in degree but not in kind from what has gone before, which still targets only a collective audience and leaves the individual learner unaffected.

Despite its absurdities and trivialities, the uptopianism of the 1960s was not without its spokesmen for a recognition of the future as it is more likely to evolve. This the new pragmatists, with their bias against substantive change, seem to lack. One doubts that any "new pragmatic" in management, or today's education-reform-minded politicians for that matter, would even deign to comment on the implications for future school management of such a statement as that made several decades ago by George Leonard: "the age of man as a component—whether of a pyramid-building gang or a space system—is just about over.... A world in which everyone will be in touch needs people in touch with themselves."[3]

To be sure, such pronouncements were (and continue to be) premature—if our view of man's life is wholly circumscribed by only an appreciation of where we are now. It seems a miracle that even the current semblance of order obtains in the world education enterprise. So how can one look forward to less, rather than more, group regimentation tomorrow, or to real achievement instead of further decline, when nothing essential in the process has been altered? The question is more than rhetorical, for tomorrow's realities inevitably catch up with today's omnipresent security preoccupations.

The new pragmatics speculate on the future by blotting out possibilities that do not jibe with their preferred expectations. The facts of life in an Information Age do not, unfortunately, solely concern management strategies for "universal cooperation" and "getting the job done." They also concern the reality of the individual, conflict between individual and collective, and realistic definition of the risks that will have to be taken in every society, rich or poor, developed or underdeveloped, in order for that society to coexist with the individual. When this reality cannot be recognized in an effective manner by professional management, it soon becomes more than ever the burden of society and political authority—as we see, an increasingly common development nowadays.

Related Fallacies of the New Pragmatism

The impossibility of doing without a certain amount of unavoidable change, of course, is already reflected in the pointedly conciliatory rhetoric of new, "down-up" managers. In this they respond to a current popular wave of vague resentment against the school as an expensive but disorderly environment, a place in which liberal theory has run amok. Failures of Dewey-inspired laissez faire principles, in fact, have soured a whole generation of parents and this backlash could make life rather more difficult for obviously unreconstructed Deweyist administrators. Thus, though themselves heirs of much of the free-wheeling and spending tradition of the 1960s, today's pragmatic technocrats take care to distance themselves publicly from the excesses this liberal tradition symbolizes. The result is a curious, politically treacherous middle-of-the-road management line.

Honig represented this approach with a typical combination of modesty and well-tuned public rhetoric. Adroitly bypassing deeper issues of conflict, he visualized success arising from a neat balance of old and new styles of management. This effort at synthesis is in fact no more than the latest chapter in America's troubled recent educational history. Till the radical sixties, a tighter hierarchical control, a more exclusively top-down form of administration, largely prevailed. This led, naturally, to reaction. During the 1960s and 1970s, as open-education and laissez faire liberalism played out their cards, the pendulum swung to the opposite extreme. School people were caught between two stools. A conviction grew that a measure of chaos is impossible to avoid; one does what can be done to "get by," and forgets the might-have-beens. This became management's guiding principle.

Today's new management has had no choice but to disclaim recent over-acceptance of chaos, admitting it as a surrender to expedience. Yet at the same time it becomes politically unwise to ignore entirely the "feel good" residues of sixties liberalism, with its deep popular roots. These inspire a nearly complete tolerance for childish confusions of mind—which of course reflect only too accurately the confusions of adult popular consciousness itself. In this way school administration of our day is led, by its own wisdom, to a new Hegelian blending, a somewhat neater combination of carrot and stick suited, if to nothing else, at least to its own short-term survival.[4]

The pendulum, in any case, cannot swing back towards any absolute insistence on old-style discipline. The new managers are well aware of the limits of any theory of overt instructional discipline in popular consciousness. Still, the mere appearance of "better results" on academic measures (if obtainable) does equate to "improvement in discipline" in the eyes of a confused public. Hence the appeal of modern theories of organizational compromise—"with a new role and new expectations for both management and line workers"—of the kind current industrial management theory preaches. (One can regularly discover the varied facets of this wisdom by a steady perusal of the financial pages of his daily newspaper.) In the educationese of Bill Honig, such theories hold that "a successful corporate enterprise creates a guiding spirit or vision that informs local effort, legitimizes standards of excellence, maximizes the autonomy of units to operate under that vision, and holds everyone accountable for measurable results."[5]

In short, one cranks up the old machinery and actively seeks to make it function better—but (be it well noted) with no effort to alter the substance of methods used. That would lead down the forbidden road of theory for its own sake. The impetus to "do better" will come simply from a change in attitudes elicited by management, a phenomenon analogous to what is thought to be Japanese experience in industrial organizations. (In Japanese industry, as we are so often told, great effort is expended to improve interpersonal relations among management personnel and between management and individuals lower in the hierarchy. Once achieved by sufficient efficacious jawboning, these improved relations supposedly also bring about the desired end-result of higher industrial output.)

Educators also fall back on popular theorists of management Tom Peters and Robert Watterman, citing their theory of "bias toward action" to rebut the savants of education who have "become paralyzed by the complexities they see in things."[6] The "excellence" concept of business management makes clear that decision-makers have no alternative but to go forward on the basis of prudent hunches. Companies with a bias toward action (as Peters and Watterman presumably show) are demonstrably more successful.[7] So, the theory holds, must it be also with local schools, once the concept of excellence takes firm hold in management thinking.

This outlook conveniently overlooks one important and indeed overwhelming truth where education is concerned: Even when privately supported and even though they too must provide balance sheets and operate on standard accounting principles, schools are *not* business organizations. We are thus comparing apples and oranges. In business the organization always functions, ultimately, for profit. The product must measure up directly to a market standard, or the organization will be pushed aside by competitors. Would that this were so for the school, but it is not.

Schools can by their very nature have no such precise bottom line. True, the school by common understanding functions to "prepare" for adult life. As adults we are concerned about its "output" in relation to the real world we already inhabit. And one form of valid end-result in education is typically held to be test scores and school grades. But education can never be managed, literally, to insure a "better-prepared" life-product; we know only what the current record shows of any given learner, and that is little enough. Anything we predict about a graduate's future life course will be sheer guesswork (though in bothering to make such predictions we may be acting unconsciously to salve our consciences over what—in our private belief—we acknowledge as society's failure in giving that learner a better life-preparation under school auspices).

Test scores, in any case, are dubious measures of either present attainment or future promise. Even if average performance on standardized tests improves somewhat, how can one know that this has not come about by simply "teaching for the tests" and that our students are not as fundamentally deficient in bona fide intellectual habits and skills as before? Whatever our standard of measurement, whether our concern over results is short- or long-term, one remains at a loss to see how a mere cosmetic alteration of the managerial regime of instruction

as dictated by a new pragmatic code of industrial management will
make a difference in the quality of our educational end-product—even
under a regime of increasing "toughness," whose results *may* show up a
decade or two down the line.

It is difficult, in short, to envision how the imposition from above, as
at similar stages through the past, of tougher texts, greater external
discipline, more homework, and the other recommended vehicles of
pragmatic school reform adds up to a recognizable "bottom-up
initiative." Nor does an engineered management scheme of this kind
seem likely to produce results any more enduring than those produced
by earlier across-the-board "crackdowns." Such a regime may well, for
a while, create an improved educational atmosphere, both in the school
and among the supporting adult communities, simply by virtue of the
energy put forth by its supporters. However effective for however
long, though, it should not be mistaken for a *substantive* change in the
nature of instruction. The old basic method, treating the individual
only as a legatee of the collective, focusing on group processes and
group norms, continues as before. Bluntly put, the "how" of school
instruction, along with the "what," remains in the same old rut.

Contradictions of Instruction Lacking a Component for Individualization

How deep that rut may be we now know fairly well. Few words are
minced any longer. The observer wandering in from outside soon feels
the underlying cynicism of all who have experienced the system.
Standard subject matter and age-old methods of pedagogy provide the
normal bill of fare, often regardless of their inappropriateness. This
troubles responsible minds, even among establishment regulars. Yet
correctives are almost universally seen as limited to the usual narrow
range of administrative shifts; change in the actual substance of method
is still unsuited to present management wisdom. As time passes a tone
of incredulity over the persistence of such absolute stasis in
management thinking pervades the criticism of even the most even-
tempered of observers. UCLA education professor John Goodlad's
sarcastic resume of "what" and "how" in school instruction, in his 1984
report on US elementary and secondary education, is typical:

> It is charged that schools neglect the basics and have abandoned
> traditional ways of teaching, but the data...suggest quite the opposite.

Mathematics and the language arts dominate in the elementary schools we studied and are well represented in the curricula of the secondary schools. And the traditional procedures of telling, questioning, reading textbooks, performing workbook exercises, and taking quizzes were infrequently interrupted by so-called progressive methods of teaching and learning. If a predominance of rote learning, memorization, and paper-and-pencil activity is what people have in mind in getting the schools back to the basics, they probably should rest assured that this is where most classrooms are and have always been.[8]

Do school administrators have an appreciation of the stagnant situation this picture of the learning process conveys? Certainly they do. But they can claim, and with considerable justification, that they are not by any means solely to blame. The lockstep arrangements for instruction forced on them by state and district requirements, as well as by fixed expectations of the general public, permit little or no leeway to do anything substantively different. This is in general true for almost every foreign system as well.

No analogies so far permit us to construct some convenient Theory Y2 (or even a more modestly ambitious set of management principles such as those devised by the industrial psychologist McGregor in his original "Theory Y")[9] for optimizing classroom operations as one could do on a factory floor or in a business office in the adult world of fiscally rationalized organizations. In the school—as even the most casual observer recognizes quickly—one is not dealing with adult, already developed workers but rather with young learners who lack both the experience of personal decision-making and the already established habits governing time and energy use common to adult minds. And the tasks to be performed are abstract, foreign to childish natures to begin with. Can a theory of method for instruction in such a situation then be simply a re-hash of whatever is current in industrial management?

Every question about "new ways of doing" in school administration leads back to the issue of instructional method. This in turn drives us back to the psychology of childhood and the limits of pedagogical entree. Learning tasks can be handed out to all children indiscriminately, but the point of any valid down-up philosophy of instructional management would logically be to insure that, through the spectrum of passing time from infancy to late adolescence, tasks will be imposed on learners in accord with their individual capabilities. This is an implicit message of every major learning theorist of our times, from Dewey to Ausubel, from Montessori to Piaget—that each learner's available instructional time can be used effectively, yet without destroying his sense of play, *if* management works from a basis of that learner's own interests and perceptions of the situation before him.

Thus readiness for learning and for the explicitly formal instructional experience on the child's part remains a critical concern. But lack of individual progress in reading, math, or motor skills is in some degree no more than an effect which traces to developmental or environmental causes. Certain prior or parallel experiences in both cognitive and affective domains, it appears, are critical as prerequisite to success in formal learning, even with the very youngest child.

Learning researchers and child development specialists have begun to insist, indeed, with an almost monotonous regularity, that the age span from three to six years is the really critical period. It is in this phase of life that a normal child comes to attain not just a grasp of symbols in their relatively full complexity but also the basic sense of initiative and self-direction that is the foundation of adult personality.[10] During this age span the child enters school and begins adapting to its social norms and its modus operandi of formal instruction. If the school organized along present lines does not fail in its socialization function, it may still fall woefully short in another critical function—as source of motivation for the normal individual child as an information processor.

Perhaps the most telling indication that pre-schools and elementary schools face problems of instruction almost beyond their present power of resolution has been the activity of watchdog groups like the National Association for the Education of Young Children. The complaint of such organizations, based in part on Piaget's findings in genetic epistemology, today raises to a new level of public consciousness caveats voiced in the past by only an isolated few early childhood education specialists such as Berkeley professor Milly Almy. These caveats boil down to a simple message: The very young child cannot endure successfully, or profit from, a diet of too much cognitively oriented instruction.

Led by David Elkind, a well-known theorist with a background of research in both Montessori and Piaget practices, the NAEYC insists that too many children are already being "pushed" at too early an age into "force-feed" learning situations. There they must focus on an excessive load of academic lessons, instead of being allowed to move through learning stages at their own, more natural rates. This argument carries, understandably, a certain weight, given the evident problems of learner stress and resistance now regularly uncovered in the various pre-school and early grade programs dedicated to speedup of academic learning.[11]

Thus an increasing ambiguity attaches to the role of pre- and elementary-school experience in the child's development. It seems possible that what the child experiences, and how he reacts, during these critical years may do more than we have before been willing to concede in the way of shaping him for the later, adolescent phase of school, when the tendency to psychological rejection becomes so evident. This can be said in full knowledge of a great diversity of opinion among experts on the usefulness of early academic exposure[12] and of the contrast between American and foreign practice in early childhood instruction. (Abroad, typically, children undertake a heavy program of academic work from the kindergarten year on, and for the most part all children are obliged to learn a common subject matter. Also, little allowance is made for differences in individual background and native abilities, i.e., ability grouping is not practiced.)

Too, American children, as is regularly pointed out, are rather coddled intellectually from the outset, and not only in their home environments. The difficulty of enforcing any single standard school curriculum arises early and continues to the end. Habits of avoidance of intellectual discipline are endemic through the whole K-12 spectrum. So the exact significance of findings that suggest an early arrival at some kind of "rejection-limit" among the youngest learners remains hard to determine.

It is difficult, however, not to ascribe some of the tendency towards rejection of academic endeavor to specific habits developed progressively *in school*—as opposed to more general, outside cultural forces. Why would one otherwise find a drift in this direction already so apparent among four- and five-year-olds attending pre-school or kindergarten? Is this due only to the influence of "bad apples"? Could the problem be mitigated by forms of instruction which dealt with the child's program as an individual matter more than as an issue primarily of conformity to expectations for the class group?

What is beyond speculation, in any case, is the clear inability, well-established by the high school years, of a high proportion of learners to engage as individuals in genuine and sustained intellectual activity. Even establishment-oriented critics like Goodlad lay much of the blame for this problem directly at the door of school instruction. As the Goodlad study found, for example:

> What the schools in our sample did not appear to be doing...was developing all those qualities commonly listed under 'intellectual development': the ability to think rationally, the ability to use, evaluate, and accumulate knowledge, a desire for further learning.... A current misunderstanding about the improvement of pedagogy is that teachers simply need to learn to do better what they are doing now. It is important, of course, for teachers to be superb at lecturing and skilful in questioning students. But providing inducements for improving only in these limited aspects of teaching is to reinforce what already is grossly in excess.[13]

Yes, exceptions exist. Here and there Goodlad and his colleagues did find remarkable and effective cases of teaching and learning, just as did critic Charles Silberman in his major study, *Crisis in the Classroom*, a decade and a half earlier—just as other scholars would find if they carried out similar investigations now.[14] But the point is that these *are* exceptions; what is normal, standard, and in the final analysis unacceptable is the average situation so succinctly described in the above Goodlad quote. Inevitably one must probe further.

The classroom, in and of itself, as a sole nexus for the daily routine of instruction, may not so much have exhausted its overall possibilities as it has now revealed its inadequacy as a single universal environment for management of individual instruction.[15] It places ever more formidable obstacles in the way of individual confrontation with the more subtle and developmental avenues of thought. And if these aspects are not a major goal of education by anyone's definition, then we are paying for nothing more than a system of random social interactions in maintaining our schools.

Sometimes it becomes necessary to accept that a point of absolute stoppage has been reached in human processes. There may be by now no way of avoiding a predicament which is summed up in the single phrase—the failure of group-managed instruction as the "only possible" format for learning. There may then be, likewise, no remaining avenue of progress left open save that of experiment and risk-taking. For given present cultural and institutional circumstances, inevitably the inflexible group method of management, used to the exclusion of all other possible approaches, may do nothing more than produce ever more unsatisfactory results. If this indeed does prove the case, we shall have to acknowledge that we have reached such a pass by having ignored for too long the most elementary fact of all education: that it can have no lasting beneficial effects unless it reaches the individual as an *individual*.

The pro-status quo claim that such studies as that of Goodlad, with its dour conclusions about the value of instruction as presently carried on, lack credibility or validity seems out of touch with essential reality. Goodlad's study involved inspection of more than a thousand American classrooms, at all grade levels. The implication is strong that other unbiased investigations would lead to highly similar judgments regarding teacher and student achievement and morale. It is also very likely that other investigations on a comparable scale would lead to the same general conclusions as those of Goodlad *about instructional methods* currently in use and their educational effects—or lack thereof.

Social Lag and the Directive Function in Instruction

A pattern of relative failure thus persists and is likely to become yet more pronounced with time, regardless of administrative nostrums. But what prevents movement in some alternate direction, some kind of trial and error effort with more fundamental aspects of the instructional process? It is often argued that this can easily be prevented by the school management professionals, and will be, since the administrators (and many teachers, as well) see no gain to themselves in drastic changes in the realm of instruction. This is not a realistic interpretation; professionals in large numbers are only too well aware of the present system's inadequacies and, while perhaps fearful of change, are only too cognizant of the depth of the present system's crisis, as well as of the contribution to that crisis of a persistently hit-or-miss method of instruction.

Professionals in large numbers in fact concede the inevitability of large-scale alterations in modes of instruction, later if not sooner. With intimate experience of the education system as it is, they are only too aware of the dangers of systems of instruction built on an intellectual house of cards. It is, rather, the larger public itself, caught up in a profound and growing lag of social consciousness, which in many respects remains the principal barrier to substantive experiment and change.

Too many non-professional people, in short, have yet to recognize the need for evolutionary shifts in the *how* of school instruction. This is a hard social truth to face. Yet the mass public is still content, for the most part, to view learning as exclusively a group or even a mass activity, in which sergeants (teachers) put recruits (the learners) through a series of exercises, the sole effect of which is that all recruits become, quite automatically, adults of sufficient standing, capable of negotiating wisely and successfully, a world of settled standards and norms, unchanged from one generation to the next. The error of this way of viewing the process of education, its failure to identify tomorrow's responsible adult as one who today learns to be not just a "team player" but an independent thought-taker as well, has not yet sunk into popular consciousness.

But the demands of evolution can be suppressed only so far, and only for a time. Slowly a crisis-stage of public decision-making is being approached, one in which this issue will be critical and central. A generation ago futurists like Alvin Toffler began demanding a reordering of education away from industrial-era norms, away from a standardized classroom format, away from technocratic management as an end in itself, toward decentralization, community involvement, and experiment in organization and instruction. The reader can judge for himself how much real progress has so far been made in this direction. Yet to a certain extent, the static condition of our educational practice can be misleading.

If it seems evident that little has in fact been accomplished by way of movement away from dead center, whether toward such vaguely expressed mainstream shifts as those envisioned by utopian futurism or toward more tangible, precise changes (such as those in which human teachers are superseded by computer programs for one-on-one drill and practice sessions in elementary schools), the twin specters of human need and advancing technology are gradually making their effects felt, even in a lagging mass consciousness. But the professional in education really has as yet small leeway for innovation. Caught in a straitjacket of tradition, line educators struggle to find a way to negotiate the labyrinth of social limitations and prohibitions they inherit. They have no firm authority, in fact, to create anything radically different in the sphere of instructional method.

Nor do upper-tier leaders either, once the limits of their mandate are admitted. What today's "new" managers recommend brings no change to instructional method but merely overlays the existing system with a new set of verbally delivered "enforcement" techniques, of dubious promise over the long haul. Then does this mean politicians alone must decide "if and when" any change is to be permitted? Hardly. Neither a federal Congress nor state legislatures can dictate successful outcomes in instruction simply by passing their own "tightening up" legislation to endow the technomanagers with more authority to "get things done." If the issue were that simple, the situation would already be far different than it is. History appears to suggest that before anything significant in the way of innovation comes about, the mass public itself must first comprehend the absolute demand for change, and then submit to a consensual program for such change. But the time for such a development in school instruction is clearly not yet.

How, indeed, could such a consensual program come about? It goes without saying that it will not appear so long as only a "business as usual" approach is the sole principle on which school management operates. The needed elements, I believe, are two in number, the first being of greater importance: 1) There must be substantive experiment in the field of individualized management of instruction, using whatever technological aids are currently available; and, 2) a "from below upwards" flow of information, as opposed to the usual "top-down" directed flow, should provide the governing modus operandi of instruction.

It could be added, as well, that this approach will really require an "end-run" around establishment obstacles by its very nature. An experiment in instruction, correctly interpreted, will proceed from a theoretical base. It cannot have its basis in the "ordinary" ways of doing, and this very fact delays its arrival by additional years or decades. Standard practice constitutes a formidable barrier in any mass social process, but nowhere so much as in school instruction. The traditional role of management in prescribing both the "what" and "how" of individual instruction cannot be underestimated where issues of experiment and genuine process change are being considered—for the "business as usual" approach has many dedicated supporters, both within and without professional ranks. This may not be all to the bad, of course.

But beset by their own blind spots, such "business as usual" advocates are more difficult to appreciate when on occasion their policies overstep rational bounds. In early 1991, for example, a milestone of political invasiveness in US education was achieved: The National Assessment Governing Board, a body created by Congress to insure maintenance of performance standards in US schools, set the first-ever government-decreed national achievement standards for math tests. These apply to all students in grades 4, 8, and 12. The testing scheme is designed to gauge (also, presumably, to promote) learner proficiency—at least for those gifted as test takers. Norms are available; the tests specify a passing level at each of the three grade levels. But how such a Stakhanovite set of goals is to be fulfilled without any change of substance in instructional method remains the mystery of educational mysteries, at least where the objective critic of the system is concerned.

What, though, can such an unusual government initiative suggest other than a spate of future "toughening up" legislative items which, though foreign to US education tradition, is aimed at *forcing* improvement in school achievement?[16] One recalls King Canute commanding the tides. The implication for professional management seems clear: The authority of school personnel has now become insufficient, and political authority must more purposefully be added to the technocratic structure. Politicians and bureaucrats alike will go on in all this assuming they are obeying a popular mandate in at last "really getting tough." And to a degree they are right.

Yet how much progress can reasonably be anticipated through such command maneuvers, in an era when by admission of the education profession itself (and many outside the profession) "down-up reform" alone will succeed? Is this not simply another attempt to force the educational technocracy, even in some measure against its own wishes, to do no more than tighten yet again the same old screws when the chances of success via such a course are recognizably dim from the very outset? One must ask: How does the welfare of the individual learner fit into all this picture of management pressures from ever more directionless sources of authority and power?

For the profession a fundamental distinction is involved here, one analogous to that cited in the 1930s debates over technocracy. A technocratic management does not by definition have to operate in a top-down fashion exclusively. Yet in practice, for lack of countervailing powers, this tends normally to be the case. Leaving to one side the newer problem (for education) of political interference, there is a residual issue of management in any large organizational system still to be faced: At what point does the enforcement power of management come to be applied in such ways that the organization's primary goals are no longer capable of being met, and when the responsibilities of management to the organization and those beneath its hierarchical umbrella are replaced by nothing more than the will of management solely to preserve itself?

Sociologist Daniel Bell accurately echoed the substance of this distinction in his discussion of the original technocracy movement: "Interestingly, when the word (technocracy) became nationally popular through (Howard) Scott, it was repudiated by (William Henry) Smyth (originator of the concept), who claimed that Scott's use of the word fused *technology* and *autocrat*, 'rule by technicians responsible to no one,' whereas his original word implied 'the rule of the people made effective through the agency of their servants, the scientists and technicians.'"[17]

A body of technocrats may be a necessary evil no organization can do without, regardless of the social outlook of individual managers. In any case some form of management must exist in every mass enterprise. But who do the technocratic managers in the collective school enterprise represent? In the last analysis they have to serve as conduits for the thinking not solely of those classes in society whose conceptions of "how things are to be done" have always governed, have automatically applied in every realm of organized public endeavor. Beyond this, by the very nature of modern democracy, they inevitably have to interpret and faithfully execute the essential wishes of the majority, whose servants they are.

Today this majority public is characterized not so much by indifference to fundamental issues of education as by puzzled incomprehension of them. Yet need and the inalterable advance of technology must in time push instructional practice into new channels, often antagonistic to earlier reflections of traditional popular culture. When enough evidence has accumulated and been made available to the public that mass technocratic management on the old lines alone cannot do the job—and that methods of instruction must change drastically as well, away from a single group format and toward a technologically based *management of individual instruction*—then, but only then, the always latent power of the masses over the education of their offspring may at last come to bear a better fruit.

Chapter 7

Individualized Instruction: Historical Issues and Practical Efforts

Perhaps no evidence so well illustrates the extent of cross-purposes bedeviling contemporary mass-administered universal K-12 education as that which comes from the one field of social science most intimately related to pedagogy, namely psychology. Specifically, various long-term studies in the psychology of pedagogy, along with the implications of their results, must leave any disinterested observer wondering what counter-proofs those defending a wholly non-interventionist, solely technocratic, non-individualized management of all school learning will in, say, the next two or three decades be able to put forward.

Hidden from any broad public knowledge, in a long-term scientific quest, a small band of psychologists and educationalists has been at work for several generations developing a schema for maximizing the effects of individualized instruction. As might have been expected, the American effort in this direction has maintained the greatest level of energy and persistence. It is illustrative of what has been achieved to date in a still largely unknown realm. And enlightening as the history of experiment along this line may be, it also reveals, as could no other aspect of modern educational history, how vast is the gulf between theory and practice, between supposed cause and actual effect, between public perceptions of how the instructional process is supposed to function and the depressing reality of results in terms of human adaptation to an Age of Information.

One fact of instruction no one can evade: Every learner is an individual. He has his variability. What follows from this? Does our interest in a student's learning style, his unique background, his immediate personal concerns—in a word, his individuality (as opposed to his identification as a unit in some social mechanism)—mean something for instructional method that we have so far not perceived? More specifically, can theories which aim to maximize instructional effects through individualization actually be translated into institutional reality with meaningful results? Beyond even this, and putting the case yet more precisely, since human resources are both costly and so often inadequate to need, on what basis in philosophy and social consensus can we expect to employ intelligent electronic systems in the management of future individual instruction?

These questions are not yet answerable in terms of any such philosophy or consensus. Indeed, the issues are so rife with elements of conflict that few adults even care to consider them. But escape them we cannot, or the challenge they present for future generations. Instruction continues to be a tradition-shrouded, seemingly unalterably pro forma undertaking, both as actually practiced and in the public's vision of it. Yet thoughtful people know that it must in time yield to an evolutionary mandate of change, if the process of knowledge transmission is to continue. It too must bow to the onrush of new human needs, must embrace what Margaret Mead asked for—a "new kind of teaching altogether."

Little in psychological research over a long period contradicts the basic tenet that effective learning requires an adequate level of individualization, often the more the better. The seemingly continuous demand from education professionals across the developed world for a reduction in average class size to a ratio in the 15-to-1 or even 10-to-1 category, with all the extra spending this would entail, speaks for itself as an indicator of longer-term trends in instruction. But this trend carries in its wake disquieting questions: Once started on such a course, can there be any turning back? What happens when we run out, as we inevitably will, of suitable human teaching talent?

It may be unnecessary to pay attention to such matters when we look at "school reform" solely from an administrative point of view, but these questions are already nascent in the more successful recent programs involving drastic management reorientation to instructional practice (e. g., in America, the individualization scheme begun in the Hammond, Indiana, schools during the 1980s).[1] These "new" methods require typically higher levels of individualization; there are few programs of this nature underway which are not formed on such a basis. The supposition is already current, nonetheless, that until individualization as a root principle can be tried out in some genuinely broader fashion and its application made to some extent universal, individualized instruction cannot really be judged fairly for its potential, whether applied in traditional settings or under more genuinely experimental circumstances.

Many people indulge in a kind of utopian dream, that of a future individualized instruction guided by some magically endowed mechanical intelligence, able on its own to create instruction exactly suited to the needs of any single learner. But this happy set of assumptions ignores underlying questions which humans themselves must first answer. What, it must be asked, does individualization expect to achieve in human terms? What are its possibilities and its limits as a practical tool? What are its effects intended to be in society's eyes? Can greater rationalization of the individual's instruction be evaded, as a distinct trend to more individualized teaching replaces the routinely hit-or-miss method of today's classroom management?

We are then still, as the adults who make society "work," faced with unresolved technical and moral issues of control in the instructional process. Classroom management is really all we have. Today's typical textbook is no control medium in the sense of a long-term resource of mind-development. Ditto for a computer. We cannot just hand a child a fancy hardcover book or snappy piece of machinery and in effect tell him, "Play with it as you see fit." Yet this is substantially what we are doing when we use such tools with no one other than a single overburdened classroom teacher expected to guide the learning program of every individual student.

If it is actually his formal instruction we are concerned with, the child's program must have a goal and a plan; his progress must be monitored, evaluated, and guided comprehensively. His learning, in a word, will have to be managed, in the most modern, complete sense of that term. The ever-more competitive nature of national societies as linked units of a single global economy forces events in this direction—in fact only in this direction—whether liberal sentiment in richer countries cares to admit it or not.

Management of individual learning, potentially, could in any case be something other than the haphazard affair we put up with now. Indeed, rationalization of the learning process has been an acknowledged subject for psychological research for a long time. I am not thinking here only of work with chimpanzees and other human-related primates under ultra-controlled laboratory conditions. The specific concept of mastery of knowledge by an individual human learner after completion of a series of predetermined steps towards a "mastery criterion" already has a considerable history of development, as well.

Naturally, definition of "mastery" has always proven something of a difficulty. Still, the concept of "teaching the individual learner"—as opposed to the autocratic assumption that all learners must function in like manner and always be exposed to a single standard curriculum—is central. Individualization of instruction emerges early in man's educational experience—before Socrates—and reappears in every epoch and every culture from which records survive. But it is also the case that only in the century past has steady effort been applied to describing what it is and how it functions in an instructional setting.

In fairly recent times we have seen a distinct trend toward innovative trials of quite carefully tailored individualized instruction. This has not been limited to formal psychological studies alone. It has been part and parcel of various movements and experimental programs carried out in the schools themselves. Given a persisting climate of public dissatisfaction over the effects of traditional instruction, initiatives in this direction have continued. In all these twentieth-century efforts aimed at development of individualized "instruction for mastery" there is also a tendency for a number of schemes and conceptual breakthroughs to overlap and reinforce one another in a fairly steady chronological progress. Something new, some fructifying syncretic element, to make the concept of "complete learning" that much more valid, has come along every decade or so.

It seems important, both for professionals and for today's layman concerned with problems of future instruction, to gain some knowledge of the all too little-known history of this line of development in education. The aim of actually "causing learning to occur," rather than simply assuming that it should, and for the most part under relatively uncontrolled conditions, raises to a higher plane of discourse such questions as "How is school instruction organized?" and "Can there be such a thing as effective learning?" This train of historical development deserves brief further exploration.

The Evolution of Mastery Learning

Can a learner and his subject matter be placed together in an optimum instructional milieu? This is the primary concern of individualization. The earliest significant scheme for individualization in English-speaking countries accorded a substantial trial status during the last century was the Dalton Plan. Now largely forgotten, the Dalton Plan somewhat paralleled the Montessori approach, but was more clearly focused on individual guidance and its effects. It had, in the pre-World War II era, rather more success in England than in the US. Its characteristic features already suggest developments to come, especially those of Britain's "free schools" and "open education" of a later day. Yet its emphasis on individualization of the learner's program in fact influenced research developments more profoundly across the Atlantic.

The scheme calls for a school with separate laboratories for every subject taught; a learner can move from one to another or carry on successive units of work in any particular lab according to his own initiative or prevailing interests. A "program of work" is laid out for the individual; this is a series of progressive units in each laboratory (English, arithmetic, etc.), with a teacher on hand to advise, interpret, and give general guidance, also to administer tests and quizzes at appropriate intervals. The plan allows each student to learn at his own pace.[2] The Dalton principles, quite innovative in their own time, seem more than familiar to us today.

The Winnetka Plan of Mastery Learning developed next, in the 1920s. It involved, prophetically, reducing subject matter to a group of learning units, complete mastery of which, in sequential order, was required of the student. Diagnostic testing on an individual basis dictated the amount of time a given learner might have to spend working on a particular unit. Along with a somewhat similar plan developed at the same time at the University of Chicago Laboratory School (and named the Morrison Plan for the professor who guided it), the Winnetka Plan emphasized an optimum learning sequence within each subject area. It broke down instructional units into smaller and prerequisite elements. These developments contributed to the eventual emergence of programmed learning per se, a phase commencing with the work of psychologist S. L. Pressey, intellectual father of teaching machines, also active as early as the 1920s.[3]

Out of the work done by Pressey, Morrison, and others the integrative concept we now call programmed learning gradually developed. Its basis was the mastery of subcomponent learning. Largely through the influence in general of behaviorist psychology, and in particular of B. F. Skinner, the Harvard experimenter whose pioneer studies of rat and pigeon behavior carried on the tradition of E. L. Thorndike's operant conditioning, the refinement of positive reinforcement was added. (The unique element Skinner's work provided, indeed, was the "enhancement" of feedback to a learner: Incorrect answers had to be "extinguished," while correct ones would be appropriately reinforced.)

As finally presented to the public in the 1950s through the device of the teaching machine, programmed instruction called for mechanized presentation of sequenced items to an individual learner, the usual pattern involving the reduction of a text to single "frames," to each of which the learner had to respond successfully before proceeding. As ordained by Skinner, there are three essential elements in all programmed instruction: a) sequentially ordered input (frames); b) a desired response by the learner; c) immediate feedback, which can correct a wrong answer or reinforce a right one.[4] While Skinner rationalized the externals of instruction thereby, he did not, indeed, could not, provide any element of control over individual psychological conditions or the specific locale in which learning took place; the teaching machine as an instructional tool, while an innovation at the time, like the later "new math" and similar novelties, was doomed to die on the vine of lagging public interest.

"Mastery Learning" was the next and last major development in this general direction. A modernized, highly integrative combination of all the earlier strategies for individualizing and rationalizing learning, Mastery Learning was developed by, among others, John B. Carroll and Benjamin S. Bloom in the 1960s, mainly at the University of Chicago. The scheme recognizes the gaps in instructional control which such a limited device as the teaching machine permits; it is therefore a more holistic, inclusive approach to problems of individualization of learning. It takes into account affective as well as cognitive factors. It also requires adequate diagnosis of each learner's levels of subject-matter interest and general interest, his attitudes toward the school and school tasks imposed upon him, his self-concept, and even his state of mental health.[5] In short, it assumes (at least in theory) a far greater control over the immediate conditions of individual instruction than has been historically possible outside the idealized world of Rousseau and Emile's divinely guided tutor.

This control is exercised in a variety of ways. In the operational plan of Mastery Learning, several quite non-traditional assumptions regarding individualized learning are implemented: Aptitude is measured not by a score on an aptitude test but as the amount of time required by the individual learner to master a given learning task. Quality of instruction is treated as a variable and defined as an "ordering" of elements of instruction in line with some reasonably optimum result expected of a particular learner. Beyond this, an assumption is made that a learner's ability to understand and profit from instruction depends on his experience and abilities; hence, modification of stereotypical patterns of group instruction and in materials, as well as the way they are used, becomes necessary—unavoidable, indeed, so long as mastery is expected as the outcome.

Finally, there is the treatment of time itself. Adequate time for mastery must be made available for each individual. Evaluation processes assume this availability of learning time. And evaluation itself is diagnostic in nature; that is, it aims specifically at providing feedback to both learner and teacher as an integral element in a continuous process. It continues instruction, rather than interrupts it. It cannot be limited simply to the standard function of a grading procedure and nothing more.[6]

Clearly, the theorists of Mastery Learning, along with their human subjects, learned as their work evolved. By this stage of development, one aspect of individualized learning had become clearer than ever before. This was the issue of control over the environment for instruction. Benjamin Bloom put the issue of group vs. individual instruction in blunt terms, in effect demanding an answer to the traditional assumption that individuals must always learn in groups. A particular subject matter outcome can be stated as an objective that should apply uniformly to a collective of learners; yet this does not obliterate the fact of individual uniqueness, in both style of learning and motivation.

In a rationalized learning environment every learner must in fact bear responsibility for using his energies in pursuit of his learning target. Yet the instructional manager must do his part by providing suitable conditions specific to that environment. Providing such conditions in classrooms as we now know them is the major problem of contemporary instruction. In a single, unchanging, forced-group milieu, real managerial flexibility becomes virtually impossible. As a result, resistance by the learner to coercive circumstances is to be expected; this is in the nature not just of the young but of groups themselves. Only when sufficient variety is permitted in the individual's learning environment, then do the possibilities for control over instruction logically increase as well.

Bloom explained in these terms: "We persist in asking, 'What is the best method of instruction for the group?' 'Who is the best teacher for the group?' and 'What is the best instructional material for the group?' One may start, however, with the very different assumption that individual students may need very different types and qualities of instruction to learn the same content and instructional objectives."[7]

This seems like nothing but the straightest of "straight talk." Obviously, we need to "get at" the individual in some more effective way in education. But how? What can be done, really, other than to arrange his environment so as to focus his mind temporarily for the purpose of making him respond to instruction which in another setting he would ignore?

A standard learning environment, the class group, nonetheless, is still accepted as a universal necessity by both society and the professional managers. Our only visible alternative, so far, has been the occasional tutoring or counseling session designed to move the individual learner into a momentary one-on-one relationship for "more concentrated work"—an experience ordinarily soon forgotten against the backdrop of the learner's always far more influential general environment.

Fundamental questions then arise, which our current absolute dependence on a largely social format for instruction otherwise has until now caused us largely to ignore: What form of management might contrast substantively with that of the class group? How can effectiveness in an individual learner's instruction be optimized unless, at certain times and under certain conditions, given the negatives of constant group interaction, the learner can be obliged to interact with or be managed by another individual intelligence? And will that intelligence then not be one dedicated both to his successful attainment of educational objectives and in possession of a surer rapport—at least during the period of interaction—with the learning mind itself?

Educational and Social Policy Aspects of Process Change in School Instruction

Earlier in the twentieth century proponents of "life-adjustment" theory openly conceded that in a mass education system there will be a "lower sixty percent" of the school population which cannot be given a serious academic education.[8] With this majority, it was thought, the school could not accomplish much. Today, as a new century begins, many professionals in education, if honest, admit to a belief in that same percentage, and that same dim outlook—but likely now with a proviso that "many of the so-called uneducables could be successful if a means existed for reaching them psychologically." Such a proviso is not attached by accident; it is more significant than we may care to admit. Even if sixty percent of today's learners are still unfitted for an academic education on lines of the past, the very conditions of present and future employment markets alone demand that the psychological substance of such an education is precisely what they—and the country—now and in the future most need.

European and Japanese critics of America's educational system correctly point out that, while in excess of sixty percent of American high school graduates do not go on to college (or at least do not attend with serious intent), no substantial public provision is made for the continuing education of this group. Europe and Japan tend to do far better than the US, in fact, in educating their non-college workers, both in the schools (where, relatively speaking, discipline, social and intellectual, remains firmer) and later at adult work sites. The huge expenditures borne by US business and industry in "re-training" this army of non-college educated workers simply underscore the magnitude of US problems in this realm. Yet neither foreign nor domestic critics have more than vague suggestions for remedying this situation—though all unfailingly criticize the waste and inefficiency of US K-12 school instruction itself in its abject failure to instill intellectual discipline in this segment of the student population.

The implications here for school instruction can be no secret. Every businessman and other outside critic who speaks publicly about US education today asserts categorically that "our schools must turn out people who can think." Then can America afford to shrug off the failure of more than half these school learners, with no effort at resolving such a treacherous problem? Clearly not. Public pressure to "do something" about the historical sixty percent is growing. More effective instruction provides the obvious answer. But instruction of what kind? Of what intrinsic communications mode? Do test scores alone really reveal "effectiveness" of instruction? How does one develop "people who think?" This is not solely an American problem.

Surely group learning modes have not yet been fully utilized in instruction. More, in fact, is being done with group work than ever before in schools, and certain rationales for grouping (e.g., cooperative groups) have promise for instruction.[9] But the key to interactive learning in groups is clearly adequate individual preparation for the new learning experience.[10] This presupposes either sufficient experience of "self-instruction" or some more fundamental interactive form for effective instruction than the classroom group. Either of these is hard to come by in even the best of cases.

The complexity of communicating even what was once taken for "simple knowledge" poses new burdens as well. No-nonsense critics like E. D. Hirsch reveal to us these days the difficulty of passing on even the most rudimentary data for centuries assumed to be self-evident fact, obvious to all. Unless the individual learner has established both motivation and prerequisite capabilities, of what use is any exercise in "advanced learning," especially such anticipated Hollywood-scale efforts as TV lectures (which for effectiveness will demand complete and in-depth advance preparation of every student participant)? It is no accident that remedial work has become so much more important than it once was. We are now routinely forced to reassess the whole sequence of a learner's experience of a subject, seeking out and trying to fill the lacunae in prior programs of learning too often in the past erroneously assumed to have provided satisfactory preparation.

It is pointless to pass over the role of the standard school learning environment as a major culprit here. Lack of suitably individualized instruction, along with an environment of built-in disincentives to personal initiative in pursuit of academic work—these are more than a recurrent aggravation to classroom teachers. They are also a constant drag on administrative flexibility in dealing with the real needs of individual learners. Administrators literally find their hands tied, whenever questions of real change in the individualization of methods of instruction arise. Thus educational reform resting solely on a basis of measures which "tighten up" the existing system can yield no real answer to the problem of instruction.

But can't something be done for at least a segment of these under-achievers by catering to their special needs in some way? If even no more than thirty percent of US K-12 school learners (rather than the historically assumed sixty percent) are problematic in the academic sense, we are still speaking of millions who could potentially, via more individually designed instruction, be aided in "making it" into the realm of higher achievers. Much needed knowledge is currently closed off to such students by the combination of their own anti-school backgrounds and the antagonistic environment of classroom instruction. It is nevertheless conceptually possible to bring some of this knowledge to these learners, if greater flexibility were made available in the instructional environment. This is especially important in certain typically disliked subjects (history, math, literature, etc.) which are of such long-term life value.

The truth is that under existing circumstances not much can be done along this line for the great majority of learners. Once again the problem is a lack of resources, plus the already built-in bias against on-site initiative so typical of vast hierarchical systems which tolerate only a minute element of local self-determination. In our age of mass-produced texts and mass media dominance in communication, any scheme to prepare and utilize "local resources" to greater effect in meeting local needs gives little promise of early realization.

Knowledge for the masses in effect has been pre-determined; it comes "from the center." A suffocating barrage of uniformly required studies and credits is laid down by state legislatures and education authorities. Worse yet, the unending wave of mass printed and screen media for the adult community devolves for the school into that of mass TV lectures, documentaries, and "learning entertainments." Even if real human mentors were available in greater number and in one-to-one settings to those who have need of them, this still would only haphazardly attack the nub of the problem: how to make knowledge in general appeal to an individual in such a way that he will in fact want to pursue it steadily over time.

So, if conditions are so retrograde for the present and near-future, what about the longer term? The existing system will doubtless have to disintegrate further before it can be truly reformed. Though the trend will be hotly resisted by stand-pat traditionalists in method, schools have no real long-term option other than to open their doors to full scope of "individual tuition." But what does this really mean? The question of how to achieve greater individualization of instruction is already of more significance than the original issue of whether or not to move in that direction at all. The march of individualization continues and grows inexorably, even if unnoticed and unpondered by the wider public. From this truth itself emerge certain global conclusions about what must happen over coming decades.

Already evident are political and social consequences of an increasing exercise of family rights of choice in the struggle to improve standards of learner performance. Consider these issues: Why do private schools prosper as never before? Why is "choice" so popular? (Some Americans, be it noted, with some logic ask if choice programs sponsored by Washington and the states will do anything other than decimate the vast majority of public schools as now operated. Indeed, the political aspect of education—the question of who gets what in the way of scarce instructional resources—is already, though perhaps not always obviously, taking center stage.) What criteria will determine who can best benefit from the use of scarce educational resources? Who decides all these critical matters? And how public can or should such a decision-making process be?

Social attitudes to education and its purposes indeed remain a source of grave uncertainty. It is easy to state that instruction must be made "more effective." But how will people react when confronted with a change in method which could actually bring about increased effectiveness? Would society accept a more individualized or "private" management of the learner's instruction, as opposed to the existing "open and collective" type if the former were proven, even on some universally accepted standard measure, more "effective"? This question is not altogether theoretical only; already today it looms larger than ever in the past in practical context, as angry parents opt for home instruction in preference to local school offerings, and as the proliferation of tutoring services and private schools continues. For the growing numbers of parents who give their children home instruction or afford special tutoring, the matter of a provably more effective method is long since settled. But this is not a suitable resolution of the problem for most families.

There is no choice long-term, other than to probe technological alternatives. So where do we stand with efforts to create effective instruction directed or aided by a non-human intelligence? Scientists struggling with theories of learning and instruction have in fact been unable to achieve a breakthrough—not only because "machines are still dumb," but because there is so much fundamental difficulty identifying what the source of instructional control or direction will be. The history of Mastery Learning and its predecessor efforts at rationalizing individual instruction to this point resolves neither the basic problem of how individualization is best carried out in the context of school as a social nexus nor the problem of maximizing technological applications. Yet in a general sense it does provide us with some directions we would otherwise lack.

Mastery Learning views the individual learner (not the group) as sole target for almost all instructional experiments. (He is a given, and—such must be the underlying assumption—once we discover how to deliver instruction to one, we could presumably simply modify machine programs to accommodate individual differences as they are found among all learners.) But the final source of instructional control itself, on the other hand, cannot be so readily pinpointed, and therein lies one more major difficulty. As AI technology matures, as we approach ever more closely to an optimum theory of instructional AI, it becomes necessary to deal with this critical issue.

(In the gradual development of Mastery Learning theories, the issue of what or who influences instruction and its data was never dealt with squarely. In large part experimenters saw no necessity for raising such a question. A behaviorist bias against "social concerns" in any psychological experimental context is understandable. Yet in a practical sense today, it is difficult to think of "effective instruction" without considering the influences which affect instruction from outside the immediate environment of learning.

Variation in any subject's reactions are to be expected, since individuals always vary from one another. But both the personae of control agents and subject matter were viewed by behaviorists as fixed elements, neither of them subject to influence from a wider external environment. The what of learning, defined as specific subject matter, for example in the simplicity of Skinner-type designs, would either be absorbed by the learner and his mastery of that matter demonstrated through testing, or it would not be absorbed, and with failure a repetition of some part of the learning sequence would be required. In the real world of mass education this treatment of curriculum as a "fixed" element—the same information to be learned by all—seems an oversimplification designed only to bring about trouble.)

But with these sharply behaviorist limitations of Mastery Learning we can become too concerned. The movement's real lessons may lie elsewhere. The underlying concept of a controlled milieu for the individual learner, necessary if effectiveness is our real goal, carries within it a clear expectation that how instruction is managed is an issue of equal importance with the what of instruction. Even so, what or who will actually make the critical decisions? It is no longer enough to specify some distant authority as source of curriculum material and then simply assume that a "standard method" applied by a "qualified" teacher suffices to convey that curriculum content to this or that child. Some entity with an arbitrary power to deal with both what and how of instruction must manage the process to the specific advantage of a given individual learner.

We should not, in brief, lose sight of the fundamental, indeed implicit acceptance—by Pressey, Skinner, Morrison, Carroll, Bloom, all those attempting to create a comprehensive learning environment prior to the advent of high-speed digital computers—of the basic element of the how, something perhaps best described as a "dual-entity" undertaking: There must be both an identifiable single source of control or management of instruction and a definable individual who is the learner; it is not sufficient to hope that "experts at the state capitol" or "society in its wisdom" can advise comprehensively on a process which demands not only knowledge of subject matter but knowledge of a particular individual as well.

There is, indeed, a philosophical link, however much we may wish to ignore it, between Socrates' approach and that of modern educational research. While each of the conceptual schemes already mentioned, from the Dalton Plan to Bloom's and Carroll's Mastery Learning, allows for broad interaction between teachers and learners, and among students in peer circumstances, primary emphasis remains on a sustained dialogue between the learner and whatever individual mind controls and guides his instruction. This is the major agency, invariably, for "fixing" cognitive knowledge in the learner's mind. The fact that Mastery Learning implicitly accepts the twin concepts of a Socratic "control agent" and an identifiable individual learner has not been accorded sufficient significance by educational critics. Progress in instructional development has, as a result, suffered.

This is demonstrated by the fact that more recent work in instructional research and development has not yet really broken any new ground in the realm of practical application. This is something that can be stated (allowing for some few exceptions) about most research and experimentation in learning—even (to consider, as an example, a line of development less bound by standard academic rules of operation) the work of R & D firms not connected formally with school systems or commercially exploiting existing school instructional practice.

Wherever one looks in the realm of new theoretical work he finds with no sense of surprise that developers seldom fail to continue with the concept of the individual (not a group) as primary target of instruction. Group management of learning poses problems beyond the scope of learning psychology, to put the matter bluntly. The gap between the focus of investigation in psychological studies (the individual) and the focus of school instruction (the group) remains a barrier stronger even than in the past: The separate establishments for psychological R & D on one hand and for school instruction on the other have such decidedly vested interests in maintenance of the status quo and keeping existing problems unresolved that their paths never meet; progress, if occurring, would be difficult to discern.

Although it is still too early to make lasting judgments, this has so far been true of newer variants of the older CAI currently in use as well, including the most sophisticated versions developed to date under the acronymic designation ICAI.[11] One can hardly fail to note, incidentally, the steady and increasing dependence on high-speed computers such advances in the technique of instructional management require. Contemporary machine-guided instruction, though, in a newer (and certainly not a final) manifestation of the concepts of the original teaching machine, thus clings to its already well-established roots in psychology. Nor should this be seen as a wrong turn in pedagogical development, any more than was the primitive version Skinner adapted from Pressey in the 1950s to deliver what he so modestly termed "programmed instruction." We have simply reached another stage in the long-term development of a technology of instruction by virtue of which the individual learner will, through managed experience, be given better opportunities to mature as an interpreter of information. But what this will mean for schools, who can yet say?

Fortunately no machine can manage a group's learning at this stage, nor is it likely to be used, even on a trial basis, for such a purpose in the future. (Some administrators, to be sure, for reasons of their own, might actually prefer increased standardization of instruction via machine management of group activity.) But neither is the intelligent machine as yet finding the rational opportunities that it could eventually inherit as an agent of instructional management for the individual. Any actual implementation of possibilities for primarily machine-driven management of individually tailored instruction, given the prevailing cultural outlook, remains for now far beyond the pale, both to public and profession.

The differences between R & D in advanced electronic instruction, on one hand, and standard school classroom instruction on the other, insofar as individual pedagogy is concerned, are then starkly obvious—and at the same time not very promising for the near-term future of individual instruction in actual school settings. Talk continues about "experiment" with school instruction. But insofar as the average individual learner is concerned, this remains largely talk. Experiment and common practice in instructional method, indeed, if we look critically at what is happening in ordinary schools, with their increasing dependence on texts tied to simplistic popular conceptions of science or literature and media-influenced classroom "entertainments," seem to be drawing farther apart instead of coming closer together. This is happening not for lack of public or professional interest in better instruction, but evidently to a high degree because of the impossibility of dealing in any practical way with the child as an individual in the socialized classroom.

One major factor in this situation is surely the lack of alternatives to an established regime designed primarily to promote egalitarian "collective learning." Yet puzzling as it may seem, generations of research workers in the psychology of learning have paid little direct heed to phenomena of group instruction. The strange assumption that "if something works for one, it should work for all" has led the community of educators down a veritable primrose path. But why have the experimental "methods for learning" discussed in this chapter all taken for granted a necessity to isolate the individual learner and engage with him in dialogue prior to assuming that he has in fact succeeded in learning? Why does current experiment in instruction and learning also take for granted the need to place a subject in a controlled dialogue setting, while on the other hand in instruction as carried out in schools we apply the quite different assumption that a group setting—where dialogue cannot possibly be controlled in the same sense—remains the uniformly accepted context for learning?

Means for Individualization and the Future of Instruction

No good explanations of this contradiction other than those of tradition and management preference are available. But perhaps a more modest historical view is needed: Classroom instruction was simply a necessity, given resources at hand; any more overtly tutorial approach has never seemed imaginable on a mass basis prior to our own era of microprocessor intelligence. Still, it cannot be accidental that so many different investigators have been independently led in the direction of the same pedagogical truth, one acknowledged by classicist Gilbert Highet in language of a rare clarity: "This (i.e., the tutorial) system is the most difficult (to use successfully), the least common, and the most thorough way to teach...(the method) is based on the principle that education is the art of drawing out what is already in the pupil's mind. It helps (him) to become what, potentially, he already is."[12]

Contemporary appearances are deceptive. My perception is that we are as yet only at the beginning of a drastically altered regime of mass education, and the signs of change are not all that obvious. But a shift of great moment has begun, nonetheless, and in a currently small-scale phenomenon like the IEP (Individualized Education Program) we glimpse a fleeting hint of the larger future. Mastery Learning schemes may well have fulfilled an unintended historical function: by their very adherence to the implicit concept of one-to-one managed instruction, they suggested a lack of confidence (that people in general, once properly informed, would share) in group methods as the only way to manage and direct instruction of the future efficiently.

The underlying implications of such a trend will seem frightening only to those who strongly feel that the value of any existing process inheres in the social and economic traditions of the process itself. Mastery Learning avoids this desperate dead end. It does not reject group learning activities out of hand; instead it regards the group as only one of several options for implementing instruction. Mastery Learning makes no claims beyond those of traditional practice for any one constantly maintained instructional situation. It never asks that the learner be limited solely to conversations with a tutor, either human or mechanical. What it does suggest, however, is that the key to efficient instruction is clearly management of the individual's learning program as an individual matter, something apart from, even while still connected to, management for the group.

But a troubling fundamental question remains to vex us: For what practical reasons of their own have investigators in educational psychology focused their work so largely on the individual subject in learning studies? It is possible to do more experimental work not only with groups which can be separated on the basis of global variables such as age, race, socioeconomic background, and the like, but also on a basis of achievement under a system of group management as contrasted to one based in the main on a tutorial approach. True, psychology is the study of how an individual interacts with his environment, and why. But surely one would expect that fundamental research in the psychology of learning could focus more than it has on group phenomena, or on the differences that occur when an individual's learning is managed in a group setting and when it is not.

Why this relative bias, then, and from so many innovators and experimenters—as the record extending from Dalton Plan days to contemporary work with ICAI so well reveals—against group learning environments as the more practical basis for instructional investigation? Why this pervasive line of division between what science holds significant and what goes on in the schools? Even if both today's researchers and school administrators are by now locked into bureaucratic systems ultra-resistant to the dynamism of real change, what explains the acceptance of this direction of things over generations of experimenters and innovators concerned with maximizing educational outcomes as—presumably—mandated by society?

Shortly before his untimely passing, Robert Hutchins issued a final manifesto called prophetically "The Learning Society." Typically, Hutchins stressed an issue the resolution of which should be obvious to all but too often is not: "The aim of education is not to fit people into a system but to help them develop their human powers."[13] That this is not possible given the existing arrangements for instruction was, to no one's surprise, the writer's theme. And by no means, to the author's credit, was that theme developed with escapist logic.

When he came to speak of method in education, even at that date (the late 1960s), this old-style liberal intellectual could nevertheless admit that educational method was already bound by absolute ties to modern technology. And he wondered then, even as we do now, if an educational technology could, in a mass age, be successfully wedded to the real needs of man, be so developed as to contribute in some bona fide way to his humanness and moral character. Hutchins went further, to ruminate over a possible "electronic midwife of the mind," a personal dialectical tool for every learner. Nor did his vision fail to accept the burden of intellectual effort which tomorrow's learner would have to bear. If anything in all this, the one-time boy-wonder of academia was a jump ahead of later futurists, an astute appreciator of long-term trends as they would in time affect education everywhere.

In a broad sense the inevitabilities of man's longer-range future as seen by Hutchins differ only in degree from those for which a practical scheme like Mastery Learning would prepare the learner. A twenty-first-century world must necessarily be a more competitive environment, Hutchins recognized, in terms of institutional demands on the person as well as in the effects of competition upon his private emotional life. While the desire for escape from intellectual struggle would never in human history be stronger, there could be no educational milieu of mindless fun and games for future learners. Through an "electronic midwife" (in Hutchins' vision), the method of maieutics, i.e., Socratic discourse, would be brought into play, tirelessly to hone the individual learner's mind, driving it on to Socratic "clarification and comprehension of basic ideas."[14]

Of course such a vision, seen in today's afterlight, may seem as premature, even as impossibly utopian, as some scenarios of futurist science fiction, and flawed on both scientific and cultural grounds. The problem does not have to do entirely with the slow pace of technological development. There is also the matter of lag in social consciousness. Learning is still widely understood as a mass enterprise without a significant individual component. In a mass system one pumps a standardized product—raw information—in a standardized way into a mass of learners and simply notes their output as the testing industry records and interprets it. If thought is applied to the issue at all, this seems to be how society, except for that minority of better-informed citizens which exists in all nations, thinks of the educational process.

Such a view was not consistent with the conditions of life even in a twentieth-century world, though, and it has for too long effectively impeded real innovation. The individual and his variability must be better recognized in the instructional process. As Hutchins trenchantly put it, education does not come about if method is entirely limited to mere training or transmission to individuals of inert information, to rote learning as opposed to reasoning and understanding. (Thus he could yearn for some means of "universal education" to replace an obviously failed "universal schooling."[15])

In any event, regardless of technological advances, individualization of school instruction has barely gotten off the ground today. In good measure this situation traces directly to a lack of social support for genuine experiment and innovation. Society cannot yet comprehend the extent of individual differences among learners, or the negative effects which ensue when these differences cannot be taken into account in the design and management of instruction. It also still assumes that an overworked and underprepared (also likely undermotivated) human teacher can manage individual learning among scores and even hundreds of students.

Parents and the public at large at this stage then as yet see neither an instructional nor a social basis for the kind of drastic change which must come from bold technological intervention. Yet already a long generation ago even an educational traditionalist (but also a confirmed humanist) like Hutchins, to give him full credit, could foresee the necessity to take into account technological possibilities as the "only final way" in a future universal mass society. Unfortunately for man at the millennium, he is still confronted by a still-unresolved issue of the kind of future technology—and its philosophic basis—which will provide the instructional management twenty-first-century learners require.

As for Mastery Learning and the schemes and primitive hardware devices that preceded it, where then do such efforts eventually lead if not in this same direction of technologically guided individual instruction? In the 1990s we saw daily dramatic advances in artificial intelligence, in virtual machine and storage techniques, and in multiprocessor and neural net technology. Science moves forward ever more briskly, approximating ever more closely "human equivalencies," embarrassing (though hardly convincing) those who still ridicule the concept of an electronic "midwife" of the mind.

Too, on the school instructional scene itself gathering evidence, both from the past and from our continuing practical failures in the management of the individual learner's instruction, suggests that we can ignore more focused mechanical intervention as an evolutionary "given" for at best only a few decades longer. All this leads to a hard-to-accept but unavoidable conclusion. We may still be sure, as through all the past, of one thing: that no technology can come into the stream of social life without its quota of new problems for human resolution. And in modern democracies this means achievement of basic social consensus for doing what must be done—insofar as possible in advance of accomplished fact.

It would be a less painful matter if we lived already in societies in which more people (again to quote Hutchins) had developed "the habit of thinking and the capacity to think about the most important matters."[16] But the prevalence of ignorance remains an unfortunate given. Everyone in the adult world complains about the impoverishment of school instruction, yet action to deal with the problem in its fundamentals lies still far over the horizon. For the next decade or two, the best one can hope for is a series of small moves in the direction of AI-managed individual instruction. This follows inevitably from the work of a long line of would-be change-agents, and in the course of these moves one can only hope that a socially as well as technologically defensible "line of experiment" can emerge.

PART THREE

INTO THE UNKNOWN:
WAYS, MEANS, PURPOSES

Chapter 8

Experiment in Instruction: Can it be Made Meaningful?

Public knowledge of such long-drawn-out professional efforts as the Mastery Learning program remains slight. For the great majority, such schemes arouse anyhow a natural reaction against the behaviorist view of the universe. Why? Because they necessarily shut off some possibilities in order to secure others. They abrogate the individual's "freedom" to do anything he chooses. But this majority ignores the fact that every existing environment in any event also places its own limits on that individual freedom.

Nevertheless, in North America, perhaps because the need is already so much more self-evident than elsewhere, there is broad public awareness that something will have to change in a very fundamental way if the process of school instruction is ever to bear useful fruit over the decades to come. But what avenues of approach to fundamental change are there? If not movement in the direction of a more successfully controlled management of individual instruction and increasingly through mechanical means, then what is the answer? What alternatives for the long haul are really available?

Experiment is, or should be, the basis of policy—experiment with fundamentals of the process. In time it will come, though it is surely too early to say on what consensual basis, philosophical and political, such experiment might take place. We know only that, as a matter of evolutionary necessity, its logical place of beginning is North America. Beyond this, one can also say that, since existing public tensions created by the issue can only heighten over time, speculation about it becomes not only more necessary for the man in the street but also more necessary as a goad to professionals in education and science, whose ongoing work provides the practical groundwork for new developments to come.

American education justly deserves credit for instructional innovation in several aspects: We create administrative "experiments" like magnet schools, choice programs, or school-based-management which at times go beyond mere arbitrary head-office-dictated "on-paper" reshuffles and involve genuine efforts to innovate. We have also a lengthy tradition of laboratory and private school tinkering with standard formats of instruction; some, like the now-forgotten Dalton Plan, have been as illuminating for instructional practice as they have proven too ideologically radical or administratively unsustainable for their times.

Also, educational psychologists for over a century have carried on both laboratory and in-school studies from which we have derived manifold insights for instruction (for, as Robert Gagné explains, "How people learn, and the conditions under which they learn, are questions that have been investigated by several generations of American psychologists, as well as by those in other parts of the world. But learning has always been a favorite problem for American writers and researchers, partly no doubt because of a philosophical tradition that tended to place great emphasis on experience as a determiner of knowledge."[1])

US school instruction has nonetheless been of declining effectiveness for decades. All efforts to provide an unassailable basis for controlled change prove inconsequential. As Rutgers University professor Milton Schwebel points out, even richer suburban school districts no longer provide (if they ever did) an education which creates an "autonomous learner," one with power of "self-control in the learning activity."[2] Though instructional challenge is missing everywhere, this affects college-bound suburbanites less than the numerous disadvantaged. For the large mass of non-college-bound children, their experience is that of a "second school system," providing only second-class instruction and directing them forward into a palpably second-class adult status.

Certain existing experimental programs, Schwebel notes, lead to the conclusion that "content of learning is less relevant than the conditions in which learning occurs."[3] Critical opportunities for "self-monitoring" and self-control are particularly missing in "second-school" formats of instruction. Nor are they likely to be provided by proposed changes of a predominantly administrative character demanded in political and some professional circles (tougher academic standards, longer school day and year, etc.).[4]

Administrative changes tend in the main to take form as new requirements, testable only in the course of practice, and these tests to be valid must measure what such changes do *to* and *for* the individual learner. When such changes fail, as they will do, perhaps more genuine experiments may then take place. But these too require a basis in theory. It is hard to see how any future program of experiment, to be honest, can further evade more positive assumptions about the individual learner and the conditions under which he works.

If past experience is to provide an indication of future directions, we are driven toward a recognition of these deeper fundamental points about anything to be called real instructional experiment: First, since average individuals make up the bulk of students and a large percentage of these learners must attend schools in which intellectual opportunities are highly limited, the major locus of instructional experiment ought in fact to be the "second school." Second, the individual learner's potentialities cannot be comprehended on a basis of "norm-referenced" measures alone; the "criterion-referenced" measure, a determination of the individual's degree of progress from a beginning point to a later stage of closure, also matters. Third, issues of method (as opposed to content) are still not being squarely faced, (this very obviously in so many of the current purely administrative innovations). Fourth, psychological aspects of the learning environment of individuals subjected to experimental treatment will have to be more completely controlled, otherwise results will still tend to lack meaning.

All these are points of reference for future action. They derive from a single fundamental premise for experiment: that the individual learner, rather than the group, constitutes the fundamental unit in instruction and learning. True, there is a revolutionary aspect to this premise. Yet it seems evident that only with such a drastically new approach will substantive experiment ever become possible. The thrust here, clearly, is away from experimental schemes making solely a vague "collective sense" and toward measures which could demonstrably change the individual learner's thinking as an information processor and consumer.

Educational Technology and Socratic Method: Can There be a More Effective Pedagogy?

What alternative scenario might then be sketched? Broadly speaking, short-run changes in instructional practice will, for political and cultural as well as economic reasons, remain limited. But within, say, three decades, underlying pressures reflecting evolutionary needs, should begin to drive innovation at last in substantively new directions. Yet without the guide of new experience drawn from the realm of experiment, random trial and error could well lead for decades more to "innovative" practices essentially meaningless.

What is important is that instructional experiment should move away from the limitations of a basis in cosmetic administrative change alone. This can only happen, I believe, if and when public opinion reaches beyond the mere fact that the method of school instruction as now carried on is inefficient in and of itself. Until experiment does take place with the *substance* of instruction (as opposed to its external forms solely), the educational system will indeed remain mired in perpetual crisis. And such experiment will only occur when adult society at large lends support to more innovative approaches at the theoretical level.

Possibilities for improvement through innovation derive from a combination of several main factors: 1) ever-increasing individual student needs; 2) swift-moving technological development; and 3) the eventual abandonment of certain cultural misconceptions about the process and purposes of education. Once a paradigm shift which acknowledges these elements has come about (that is, when the practical steps such a shift demands have received social sanction), real experiment in instruction is finally likely. Following that stage, for experiment to bring meaningful results system policy would seem to entail three critical points of entree:

First, there must be a turning away from management of instruction which makes the group the sole locus of management; second, learners in deprived environments should be given priority when technological means for individual instructional management have reached the stage when their use can be implemented with some chance for success—for political and social reasons primarily; and third, Socratic method as the basis of individually managed instruction (not as a direct "method" of teaching, however) should be given a decent opportunity to show what it can do in guiding learning uninterruptedly—that is, in directing the activity of the learner's mind over time. Some comment on each of these three unquestionably contentious recommendations is necessary, to forestall criticisms that may suggest they were designed to force a totalitarian regime of lockstep discipline upon the learner—when quite the opposite is intended.

Recognition of the inadequacy of an excessively socialized formal learning environment comes hard, but come it must. Traditional psychological inquiry itself, by isolating the individual as a unique unit for observation, has shown the way for future learning management systems. In time the individual as a school learner—thanks to meteoric advances in computer processing techniques, allowing for comprehensive psychological appreciation of the single individual—will himself finally become a completely legitimate focus of instructional experiment, and the public will have not much choice other than to support such efforts. Thus over time old-style episodic "observational studies" of the student will metamorphose into "continuous experimental observations," in which experimenters will be provided with a continuous "picture" of the individual learner, both for purposes of judgments about the person himself and his needs and (though quite secondarily and more traditionally) to provide data for standard group comparisons.

Where experiment should take place and how its progress is to be judged are other knotty problems which will by no means be easily resolved. No moves in this area are possible, in any event, until an artificial intelligence useful enough for experimental purposes is available. Then it will be up to society to decide. Any true artificial intelligence, since it also remains a machine, will by definition act in the interests of its user. So for the practical reason that society has a great deal to gain by so doing (and not as a matter of political expediency in implementing more egalitarian instruction by the first available means) technology and the experiment it supports ought to be put to use in those identifiable common schools where culturally induced ignorance is at its most pronounced and there is a large untouched potential for academic achievement.

But is this still not a matter of trying to brainwash society's more unfortunate children, and in this case by a new and potentially enslaving technology? The answer to this question must be an emphatic no, because Socratic management will be built into the system, and that kind of management tolerates both success and failure, both achievement and recidivism. The only thing it will not tolerate is total inattention to stimuli, and the range of stimuli it will have to draw upon will be so extensive that danger from this source should recede dramatically—in comparison with the predictably narrow range of stimuli present in the teacher-managed classroom setting of today.

Such technology can be used experimentally to locate and reduce blocks to any individual's learning progress in any school environment, but it makes better sense to give initial experimental emphasis to at-risk learners within the "second system." Later, in any case, experimental resources would be better distributed more evenly and broadly, shifted away to a greater number of schools and less problematic students. Universality of access (and hence of achievement) is the only rational goal, given the character of the future society into which these learners must ultimately emerge. For society will not benefit finally from any form of change which seeks *only* to "bolster the less able"—and stop at that stage.

Throughout, the starting-point for analysis and planning will have to be the individual learner, regardless of his socioeconomic niche. If individual progress is what matters most, then in the deeper future a criterion-referenced individualized experimental treatment (i.e., a treatment following a beginning measure of skill or knowledge, to be succeeded by a later stage of closure and testing) will become the primary tool of evaluation for instructional experiments. More sophisticated instructional software will certainly have to be developed as a result, and of a kind sensitized to a particular individual learner's psychological background yet also based on commonly accepted developmental principles.[5]

But beyond these immediately difficult practical concerns, it seems altogether likely that Socratic method as a pedagogic basis for experimental management of the individual's learning will itself constitute the greatest block of all to genuine experiment, because it provides the ground for a wholly tutorial form of management independent of collective technocratic rationalizations. To appreciate this point, one need only ponder the difference between mere "Socratic discussions"—piled onto the usual didactic and coaching functions performed by human classroom teachers—and a form of instruction in which an individual intelligence as tutor (be it either human or artificial) possesses from one stage of progress to the next that directional *control* needed to deal with optimization of the learner's mental development and, equally important, can act on that information appropriately, whether the learner himself is then pursuing work in a group or an individual context of instruction.

People have not yet come fully to understand or appreciate that individualization is not a goal in itself but a means. Thus the need for experiment. The word derives from the Latin *experimentum*, to try. Individualization may do nothing for the learner or a great deal. Its overriding purpose is to provide the individual with an environment suited to self-controlled thinking. Without this, too much time spent in schools is wasted, in terms of both society's and the learner's needs. Since we cannot yet provide such a milieu, trial (and probably in the early stages, much error) cannot be avoided.

Group methods alone can never exclusively provide this environment. Already today an "ideal tutor" à la Rousseau has been partly realized in a variety of undertakings ranging from various "adult mentor" schemes depending on human guides to wholly electronic programs on the lines of PLATO. Yet in general both human and machine tutors adequately informed about the individual learner and his needs are equally rare in formal instructional settings. Whoever seeks to understand the problem of instruction as it will be faced in tomorrow's world must therefore ponder this conundrum of the intelligent and informed tutor as "ideal agent of instruction."

Why though, some will ask, in an age when costs for professional manpower grow in clear disproportion to our ability to pay, give any further emphasis to one-on-one methods, whether in experiment or routine instruction itself? Why not, instead, concentrate on the opposite, a large-group method which, in the words of its enthusiasts, can be turned into "Hollywood-scale" media spectaculars—"big" lectures, interviews, colloquies, etc., "canned" by film production experts and, with the usual economies of scale, made available for pennies to every school district in the country?[6] Isn't this "wholesalers' approach" the only logical way to circumvent the professional manpower problem and the so far intractable problem of a lack of good instructional software? To this seemingly sensible but unfortunately simplistic question there can only be an emphatically negative answer, one which has its basis in inescapable conditions of modern life.

There is no escaping the inevitable fact of individual differences which has become ever more a source of primary difficulty as mass processing systems grow larger and more unwieldy in both the adult and juvenile worlds. "Big media" information schemes, indeed, as they seek to control always more extensive populations through manipulation of information at a mass level, in education exacerbate the very problem they seek to solve. The system-bound educator, like his counterparts in other information dispersal systems, cannot cope with individual variability beyond certain very finite limits, and when he hands responsibility to a mass medium he simply opens the way for yet greater media diversion of the learner's attention—a prime result of which will be an increase of the growing chaos of inattention we see in today's school classrooms.

What really is contemporary media instruction? It by definition is a mass product, useful to a certain point and no further. It offers the same opportunity for passivity of response as mass media in the adult sphere, and to view it as of anything but minimal use in the individualization of instruction would be a serious error. Pedagogically, it fails on the same psychological grounds as does its more general analog, mass non-interactive TV. Conceptually it both teaches and entertains, but mainly it entertains. A fundamental difference exists between instruction and entertainment. The latter aims at a multitude, expecting to reach the individual only incidentally. The lessons of educational history suggest strongly that not more than a small number of learners at any one time can be served equally well with a single instructional product, and mass media fails on this score just as have past mediums.

Mass media instruction, of course, should not be altogether overlooked for its occasional possible benefits to instruction. The problem is not with media in toto but with *mass* media. As efforts to commercialize school instruction by mass media methods (e.g., the Whittle Corporation's programs in US schools in the 1990s) are likely to reveal in due time, a smaller (not a greater) exposure to mass culture through the media in school instruction will serve the better educational purpose. Experience comes to the individual from many quarters, and Hollywood-type productions expected to bring about miracles, by merely repeating the already established stereotypes of mass social and economic life, interfere too blatantly with other and more pedagogically justifiable sources of information needed for balanced mental development.

At the opposite extreme from a mass media emphasis stands the Socratic dialogue in its original form—the discussion format intended to probe some question or issue of common interest. But pitfalls abound. It is easy, for example, to say that a film or tape program generates a need for follow-up discussion. Yet all too often in the easily mismanaged fifty-odd minutes of class time it is the film which gets shown and the discussion which is dispensed with. Any increased dependence on mass media instruction will in all likelihood come at the expense of discussion as a tool for learning, since workbook activity and test-taking are already so comprehensively built into the typical classroom schedule. (This could merely then prove another, though perhaps unintended, drawback of mass media intrusion into the instructional arena, and an unfortunate further loss of opportunity for genuine intellectual exchange.)

Small- and mixed-group approaches to instruction, discussion-builders par excellence, will surely continue to reveal their value in interactive aspects of pedagogy in any case. Yet not if they are routinely crowded out as a matter of convenience to the schedule. And much discussion, when it does occur, goes admittedly nowhere anyhow. From a psychological point of view, immaturity of the other-directed childish or juvenile mind itself in fact presents a possibility for anti-learning outcomes, whether a discussion is based on a just-viewed mass media presentation or on some more usual teacher- or text-initiated subject-matter issue. In the one case, a group has watched a film or videotape, in the other each student has presumably listened carefully or worked alone at his reading in the expectation that he would find some meaning in information presented. But in both instances, if the discussants—as is so commonly the case today—lack a background that allows them to comprehend critically the information initially presented, little is gained beyond that often all-too minuscule value which resides for the individual in the original data itself.

Yet discussion, whether termed Socratic or not, is important, indeed indispensable, in any developed scheme of individual instruction. Thus in time another and more fundamental issue than merely that of "exposing the learner to the information" as a preparation for discussion will have to be recognized: The individual performs best in a group when he has first attained a direct *personal* knowledge of the matter of instruction; he must have gained "a prerequisite knowledge of the subject," to put it in educational jargon. And the link between "prerequisite knowledge" and "Socratic understanding" is abundantly clear. But how is prerequisite knowledge obtained? Few educators would deny that this is best come by (assuming alternative modes of initial instruction are available) through an intensive, continuing, one-on-one formal encounter to which response must be given, a flow of stimuli which absolutely holds the learner's attention—in short, a Socratic encounter. No small accomplishment, since prolonged individual attention is something more and more difficult to secure among today's information-encumbered child minds.

It is difficult, in fact, to evade the evolutionary significance of such a more comprehensively guided, "before-learning" (and indeed "Socratic") form of management of individual instruction over decades still to come. Effective closure of individual knowledge is a uniquely Socratic concept, yet one wholly at war with the information chaos of our age. But Socrates, unfortunately, has been misunderstood for two millennia as one who "explained philosophy by conversation" and nothing more. This is an injustice from a pedagogic point of view. Gilbert Highet, among others, has attempted to correct the misunderstanding. A tutorial system like that invented by Socrates is "the most difficult, the least common, and the most thorough way to teach." The pupil, Highet writes, "when the work is over...feels that nothing has been given to him, merely that he himself has grown."[7]

This polite way of putting the matter actually understates the inherent usefulness of Socratic method in systematic pedagogy—once the learner has been matched with a suitable interlocutor/manager. Socratic instruction potentially enhances both cognitive and motivational aspects of learning in a fashion not theoretically possible under any other set of controlled circumstances we can formulate. What historically restrains this mode of instruction is, first, popular distrust, and second, the inability of any nation-state to afford a large corps of human teachers both talented and dedicated enough to put it to use.

Socrates' approach was quintessentially different, and not merely because he lived in an era of low technology and would probably not have wanted anything to do with a mass media production. Socrates accepted the learner's right to and need for direct feedback, an impossibility in the circumstances of mass media instruction (though, to be sure, a handful of call-in questions or comments from individual audience members of a radio talk show may erroneously be identified by the uncritical observer as genuine Socratic feedback.)

The question of how to provide individual learner feedback via a source which has come to "know" the learner remains indeed a core problem in formal instruction. So does an obviously negative trend in the economics of human instructional resources. There cannot be "one teacher for every one child." Experiment with individualized instruction can never lead in that direction, for there are not enough gifted human teachers to allow such an approach to be made in a meaningful way. But we *can* experiment with machine intelligence as our human control agent in the management of instruction.

Today most scientists are rightfully fearful of allowing any machine to control a human being's flow of experience in some comprehensive sense. Such a machine in any case does not exist—yet. But many scientists would already be forced to admit that a well-programmed artificial intelligence could "see" what was possible and profitable for a human learner within a limited time-span more adequately than any overworked and insufficiently "available" teacher or parent. The experience we already have of so-called expert systems in medicine and certain areas of industrial technology is instructive for instructional theory. Sooner or later an AI with its own significant learning capabilities will attain expert status in arranging instructional experiences for a human child with whose mental and affective characteristics it had become familiar.

A disturbing question is then worth posing: Assume that in the not-so-distant future there could in fact be an experiment contrasting the effects of instruction via mass TV (the canned lecture, say, with a minimum of direct learner feedback) and instruction managed for individual learners by an artificial intelligence. What happens then if the evidence—as gauged by quality of post-event student discussion, achievement test scores, and other variables of measurement—indicates that, as between AI on one hand and TV (or another media form for managing instruction) on the other, the former has become clearly and consistently superior?

Coming to Grips with the Problem of Experiment

At this point of time it is hard to see why the emerging and unavoidable issue of individually managed instruction requiring machine control of the learning sequence should be so difficult to countenance except on primarily cultural grounds. Hardware already exists which, at least for experimental purposes, could be adapted to such management. Inadequate instructional software cannot continue to be an excuse forever either. The crushing problem of resource-need must force expert thinking in this direction too, once the lack of any genuine alternative becomes more fully evident. There can be no real choice, long-term, other than to supplant in some degree over-costly (and too often under-performing) human intelligence with expert mechanical pedagogy.

This sounds threatening. Yet it may not prove as harsh a medicine as it at first appears. As subtle capabilities in AI thinking come more to be realized and applied to instructional problems, these systems will produce better results without destroying (as is happening under the now-in-place regime) the intellectual basis of school instruction. But the vital non-technical question still hangs fire: Will society accept and support the new basis for method in school instruction?

It would be better, one cannot help thinking, to stand up to reality than to go on courting present illusions, which maintain that standardizing technocratic measures constitute the only real answer. Science and technique advance with an inevitable dynamism, and explicitly toward that point of time when a machine will exist which could control management—though not delivery per se—of an individual's instruction in a manner superior in every practical respect, and on every criterion of achievement. When this stage is finally reached, economic and social pressures to use such mechanical systems will become almost impossible to circumvent. But what if the philosophical and social issues that underlie this phenomenon have by then still not been worked out?

The great problem, philosophical and political, will certainly be, "Who or what gives the AI system its underlying orders?" Experiment may have proven the usefulness of these systems beyond a peradventure, but that will not mean much until the issue of "who controls the machines" is opened to general debate. But science, to be blunt, has not yet even entered the stage when it permits itself the luxury of applying the already fantastic information processing capabilities of, say, a contemporary supercomputer to such a pervasive and socially troubling problem as that of school instruction.

The paradox here is that even science, though possessed of its own mantle of self-determination, still recognizes the need for society's mandate as it becomes entangled inescapably in politically dangerous universal issues. On this crucial matter science indeed awaits a show, however insignificant, of social approbation—as well, one believes, it might.   For a terrible open question which even the scientific community cannot answer with a single voice looms over the whole scope of possibilities: Can an artificial intelligence entrusted with this or any other assignment that involves serious human consequences be prevented over time from overriding essential human purposes, and from thereafter developing further its own intelligent existence—at our expense?

Machines can and do destroy legitimate human rights. Fear of their power is a reasonable fear. Men cannot monitor a complex machine's every move. As AI develops, our capabilities for ordering its decisions are slowly but surely reduced. And yet a machine able to guide human instruction will in some degree have to be able to make independent decisions, to have a "mind of its own," thus forcing the difficult question of who actually does control what is happening.

Sooner or later, this dangerous issue must be faced. Today's mushrooming failures in school instruction may be only temporary phenomena, to be succeeded by a new era of educational renaissance achieved with no fundamental change in method. On the other hand they may also prove to be only the initial signs of a much more prolonged future descent to ever new depths of non-achievement, which only can be reversed by the development of new technologies of individual instruction.   There are few signs, if any, that on a worldwide scale school instruction in its historically established forms can serve adequately the needs of a twenty-first-century global civilization immersed in information flows of an unprecedented magnitude.

Every past age of evolutionary advance in civilization has demanded the throwing off of some socioeconomic or cultural shackles, some long-preserved but ultimately excess baggage which no longer suits the circumstances, and replacing that which has served its usefulness with something new and, in fact, experimental. In this connection one might reflect not only on the fact that the school inherits an ancient and noble tradition of learning as the most important of human undertakings, but also that the classroom system—in essentially the same form of organization and operation—has existed almost as long as has man's own recorded history.

The key to adaptive change in instruction lies perhaps more than anywhere else in an understanding of what Socrates was really doing.

For over two millennia, men have tried to ignore the pedagogic implications of what Socrates, so long ago, was trying to accomplish. This was a man who spent his days not in obviously "productive" labor but in wandering about Athens, discoursing with young men about such seemingly self-evident subjects as truth and justice and the good life. Clearly, Socrates did not think of himself as an educational planner or "delivery agent" of knowledge in any popular sense. He had no ulterior motive, was keen on abstractions, scorned teaching that merely aimed (as with the sophists) to show pupils how to get along and live well in the present world.

Yet there was another, often overlooked side of Socrates. He was no believer in unfinished business. Commentators have for centuries pointed out how, after their sessions with Socrates, his Greek friends from slave youths to aristocrats "looked at things differently," or had "suddenly grown up." Socrates, it seems, "made their brains go to work." Implicit in his method was the concept of "process thoroughness." This dangerous fixation was, perhaps, one major aspect of the Mastery Learning approach which in its day doomed it for practical use on any scale—and similarly with PLATO as a tutorial agent later. But these early way-stations on the road to the future, though perhaps all too quickly forgotten by professionals and public alike, just as with the method of Socrates himself, reveal possibilities which, in however modest a fashion, open the way for eventual change of an evolutionary character.

Socratic method, if we translate it into present-day terms, not only allows but requires a complete cycle of analysis, planning, and delivery of instruction geared to an individual. Science can in time introduce an unlimited degree of such "process thoroughness" into an artificial intelligence (AI) system of individualized instruction. Once experiment with the real "stuff" of individual AI instruction can take place, science will know far more about its possibilities than can be guessed at in our present state of ignorance. But how much of this is as yet palatable to adult society?

Education can in theory produce a Shakespeare or a robot. In large measure it is up to society to decide how much of the one and how much of the other in the typical case it would want. Social awareness of this problem, again, is the great difficulty. Science cannot move forward unaided; society's will must be respected. Until society does achieve a better appreciation of Socratic method and its larger possibilities, and can give voice to that appreciation, science lacks the needed supporting consensus. We are thus caught in a vicious circle—at least for the present.[8]

Today's Individualized Education Programs and Chapter One (of the US Elementary and Secondary Education Act of 1965) programs in any event offer a first small hint of future directions. But such developments remain vague in both their philosophies and specifics. Too, the Socratic basis has never been seen by educators as particularly distinct in and of itself, different in substance from other approaches. Yet it also must be conceded that the inherent "differences" of this method seemingly are today becoming better appreciated. This is demonstrated by the very fact that, as a test of their support, adults outside the education profession (backed by many professionals themselves) are demanding in ever larger numbers greater individualization of instruction in schools at all levels.

The Burden of Choice—Conceding Failure or Striving to Adapt?

No convincing argument can be made in support of the use of any technique for its own sake in the management of so deeply human an activity as formal instruction of the individual. But the argument that technology properly used in this endeavor could function to safeguard (rather than enslave) the individual remains difficult to refute. The operational issue comes down in essence to one of where intelligence resides and how it can best be developed to suit the joint purposes of its possessor and the collective.

In the evolutionary sense, societies and civilizations, even whole species, live or die by use of intelligence. Nineteenth-century sociology, among its other credits, was the first science formally to develop the concept of a proportionate distribution of talents within a society, and the equally significant linkage between a society's success and staying power and its manner of employing that talent—its division of labor. Work, it was discovered, can be shared out among different intelligences in any number of ways, but it would be impossible on even the most commonplace pragmatic grounds to accept that all ways are equally justifiable morally or effective economically.

The division of labor, French sociologist Emile Durkheim wrote, optimally "presumes that the worker, far from being hemmed in by his task, does not lose sight of his collaborators, that he acts upon them, and reacts to them…is not a machine who repeats his movements without knowing their meaning, but he knows that they tend, in some way, towards an end that he conceives more or less distinctly."[9] That this ideal is not always attained, Durkheim also acknowledged, citing the "forced division of labor" found in all modern societies.[10]

With the coming of artificial intelligence as an alternate occupant of our human niche in the web of universal life, the division of labor picture is altered even more drastically. Artificial intelligence now invades an already wasted traditional human scheme for division of labor. Education cannot remain immune from the newly emerging framework which sets new and higher values for some forms of labor and dispenses altogether with others.

In this new era of labor productivity, dedicated individual intelligence is the single key element in collective use of energy. But this is an intelligence freer in its capability to pursue its own lines of inquiry than any known to Comte or Durkheim, for in their day developed intelligence was limited to only a relative few. (And certainly few could foresee a machine that would deserve by any standards to be called intelligent.) As sociologist Daniel Bell has stated the new social outlook:

> The most striking aspect of mass society is that, while it incorporates the broad mass into society, it creates greater diversity and variety and a sharpened hunger for experience as more and more aspects of the world—geographical, political, and cultural—come within the purview of ordinary men and women.[11]

What adults often fail to appreciate adequately is the significance of formal education in the development of the kinds of intelligence needed to make such a society function. Labor is not only more specialized; it can and should be more fulfilling to the individual. When it involves too much of one and too little of the other, trouble ensues. But intelligence, once developed to an optimum point by formal education, allows both individual and collective to adapt more comprehensively to the unremitting demands of a constantly changing environment. School learning is thus quite fundamental.

In all spheres of adult labor some form of machine intelligence, however limited, has already intervened to alter the balance of work functions. The trend continues and strengthens. From advanced scientific work at one extreme to repair of the simplest household equipment on the other, all endeavors of men now depend in increasing degree on testing and measurement devices which are in themselves extensions of—as well as sources of correction for—human intelligence, which can no longer cope unaided with the information processing demands required. (Yet strangely, in school instruction, that most basic of all modes for aiding the human intelligence as an adaptive tool, those who manage are typically still less than convinced of any bedrock future role for extra-human intelligence.)

Both teachers and students are, certainly, in the broader sense factors in the overall division of labor in society. They too are expected to "produce." But while use of intelligence is the "stuff" of instruction and learning, and development of intelligence is in fact the ultimate goal of the process, present organizational structures fail to optimize the use of either teacher or learner intelligence in furthering instructional purposes. Organization of work in the instructional setting, still designed to suit outmoded technocratic preferences, ignores issues of both motivation and fundamental subject-matter comprehension in the individual learner's behavior. Routine, and its accompanying symptom of individual reaction, that familiar absence of personal interest in all but the social aspects of the process on the student's part, effectively block those very outcomes which society expects of school instruction.[12]

Without doubt a great deal of purely animal energy does get expended by both students and staff in every school classroom setting. Yet the question of process optimization remains entirely unresolved. Does instruction confined so entirely within traditional norms of management fulfill a twenty-first century's demands for developed intelligence in the individual? One can only wonder. And looking at the process in light of future needs, does it at all represent any significant labor contribution to what Durkheim and the other early-day sociologists saw as the increasing "organic solidarity" of human society?

Today, speaking of school instruction, we maintain a system, but do we have anything that can be called an efficient method? Of course, experiment is necessary; on this, in principle, there is broad agreement. But on what real-world basis? The Socratic model for many goes against the grain, even if it is hard to visualize any valid theoretical alternative: It possesses too many anti-democratic biases. A similar criticism holds for technological control over instructional process: No scheme for advancing the possibilities of Socratic or any alternative method can ignore technology. But the very trend to "machine intelligence" itself leads finally, so it would seem, to an agent of instruction with *independent* tendencies of mind, rendering infinitely more complex the decision-making which must precede experiment.

Critics will contend, and rightly, that once an independent "thinking entity" is entrusted with the task of fully individualizing instruction, a new and more dangerous phase in the universal rationalization of human energies will have been reached. Arrival of machine management of individual instruction will without question usher in an era of wrenching breaks with the human past. But this need not be a form of management guided in its absolute essentials entirely by the machine. Indeed, how can man knowingly abandon *all* human control over this vital process?

Instruction and learning must still concern the development of an individual *human* mind primarily, and that of a machine only as a secondary issue. In the best of cases we will, assuming no mistakes from which recovery is impossible are made, simply find ourselves altering a basic process in such a way that it is no longer so completely dependent on those negative elements now predominant—propaganda and cultural moonshine from outside the school; social interactions within it; the profit motive among professional staff and media suppliers. Society as a whole will have to lay down and enforce the general rules; human teachers will guide individual learners according to the spirit of those rules; the machines, within limits human thought allows them, will simply handle management functions and details.

But again, what about politically or community-inspired reforms? Why assume that current efforts at reforming standardized instruction will fail, when such vast resources are directed towards their success? Can't the institution itself be successfully redirected without forcing such a drastic change in how we treat the individual learner? The answer to these questions, unfortunately, lies as much in the irreconcilable traditions and limitations of our institutions themselves as in society's inability to comprehend the scope and character of coming change. Mandatory attendance laws may enforce a learner's physical presence, but they cannot make him an active participant in a process whose significance he fails to acknowledge or understand.

As Montesquieu put it long ago, "In our days we receive three different or contrary educations, namely, of our parents, of our masters, and of the world. What we learn in the latter effaces all the ideas of the former."[13] More than ever, today's traditional formulas of instruction compound the felony, leaving the solitary mind helpless to defend itself against the rigid claims of human culture and the moral confusion of the world. We are doing too little to aid the child mind towards maturity as, unprepared, it must face the infoglut of today and the further information deluge of tomorrow. Until instructional experiment is taken into a more strategic realm, this situation—and the disappointments it brings—cannot but continue.

On what defensible basis in theory *can* we then experiment? The argument will be made that any AI medium of management will operate outside the direct control of society and its consensus structures (committees, commissions, superintendencies, councils, legislatures) and thus can never be "permitted" any substantive role in pedagogy. As I have pointed out, such a view will be tenable for only a limited time longer, for very practical reasons. Also, this view conveniently overlooks the fact that before AI management can be brought into effective practical use in instruction anywhere, generations of committees of scientists, politicians, religious functionaries, and all manner of similar interest groups will be involved in cumulative decision-making on the issue.

All these special interests would, at least to begin with, seek to insert their private biases into the development of any AI management schemes. But none of this will obviate the fundamental and sure-to-continue disparity between resource input and results obtained. Experiment with method will not be experiment while these culture-bound entities go on enforcing the gridlock of culturally justified technomanaged instruction. They are putting a cultural "spin" on the concept of AI management which is sure to fail. The sole alternative to committee-dictated instructional practice, it seems all too clear, can *only* be a form of instruction engineered by an individual intelligence making its *individually* crafted on-the-spot decisions in the service of another intelligence.

Chapter 9

Economic and Infotech Factors in Instruction: Twin Motors of Change

In developed nations some improvement in measured effects of school instruction may be expected over the short term, and for two reasons: First, public attention has been called to the "test score problem" as never before. If nothing else, "teaching to the tests" will become more common and test results will show a consequent slight upward trend. Where no alternative form of evaluation is seen as meaningful, either to laymen or professionals, test scores—and the need to improve them—will be taken seriously. Second, management structures are themselves being altered to promote better instruction. Some positive motivation, as the non-professional adult community comes to enjoy greater input to instructional policy (as, say, with school-based management), should filter down to the classroom level and give some teachers and many students a temporary sense of purpose in the pursuit of higher test scores.

Such gains, however, are likely to prove one-time or short-lived phenomena. What neither public support nor management reorientation can alter is the institutional-cultural framework of instruction itself, and this failure is certain to bring in its wake a continuation, longer-term, of declining school achievement, regardless of the measurement process applied. The impossibility of making more substantial headway under the circumstances does not go unrecognized. As American education analysts John Chubb and Terry Moe, in their 1990 Brookings Institution study, stated:

The schools' most fundamental problems are rooted in the institutions of democratic control by which they are governed; and, despite all the talk about 'restructuring,' the current wave of grab-bag reforms leaves those institutions intact and in charge. The basic causes of America's educational problems do not get addressed.[1]

As to which of the various proposed reform schemes making headlines merits further consideration, Chubb and Moe are hardly sanguine, except, oddly, in the typically American case of "choice," a concept which allows parents within a given district complete freedom to choose the school of that area their child would attend. "A true choice system," they conclude, "strikes at the foundations of democratic control." In their view, choice can be a "self-contained reform (which) has the capacity *all by itself* to bring about the kind of transformation that, for years, reformers have been seeking to engineer in myriad other ways."[2]

But is this claim supportable? Of course choice goes well beyond other currently considered reform concepts. It would turn "market rights" to instruction literally over to parents, the decision-makers closest to the ultimate consumer—the child-learner. And even if this initially provides no more than a few options as to *where* the child will learn, it moves far beyond past proposals for change. Wholesale implementation of this principle would unquestionably shake the old lockstep mode of administration to its foundations, even in the already decentralized US system. If choice makes the headway its many adherents seek over the next decade, it may well succeed where Progressivism itself failed—in obtaining that degree of continuing public support which could permit stirring up the old mindless routine with some genuine trial and error—not just on a broad scale but also, and of equal importance, over a lengthy time span.

Yet will this necessarily make for a real difference in individual instruction? What we are apt to overlook in choice is the lack of any plan for alterations in the psychological (not just the physical) locus of instruction. In 1989 I pointed out several nearly certain adverse effects of choice: too many people (parents and students) uselessly chasing after too scarce goods (more effective providers of instruction); potential breakdown of less favored schools in which millions are still "left behind"; enforced further de-individualization of instruction as "schools of choice" become not only dominant but much larger and their student bodies harder to control (and this at a time when, in fact, individualization will be needed as never before); increased competition for both teachers' time and grades, under conditions that give average and below-average learners actually *less* rather than more opportunity for that individual direction which can make the difference between mere attendance and actually progressive learning.[3] Taken altogether, the psychological effect of these outcomes as the individual learner himself would be impacted by them is, to say the least, likely to prove both discouraging and disturbing to adult society—even before a nationwide program gets underway.

Choice, in addition, if carried out on the proposed national scale, could also have negative effects in another area of administrative concern. It would allow, perhaps even encourage, yet further oversocialization of instruction, in a form, alas, often stereotypically represented to the public as a necessary adjunct to progress. This might well create additional barriers to effective individualization. More, not less administration would be needed, as a means of policing ever larger numbers of ever more undisciplined children and youth within a space too confined in both a physical and a psychological sense.

Social chaos under technomanagerial control could well, in fact, be the only lasting heritage of choice. For all its innovative character in the administrative realm, choice actually allows for less, not more, innovation in the instructional process itself. Unless the individual learner can be challenged psychologically—as himself, not always as a member of some collective and nothing more—even choice will bring about only the most ambiguous of results in the end, leaving its proponents and the broader public alike wondering what they were fussing about in the first place.

Learner Needs in the Instructional Sphere vs. Contradictions of Institutional Outlook

As it is, the system goes on short-changing the learner-consumer in the psychological domain, without so intending. To be sure, he will later, as an adult, be in any case "on his own" in making the many momentous decisions mature life requires. Yet whether we see the school years as "preparation" only, or as in the Dewey canon merely a "different" form of life itself, an unanswered question which our loose system of instruction governed only by "institutions of democratic control" cannot possibly address grows in significance: Can instruction, with the aid of technology, be altered in some substantive way for *every* learner's benefit? Can technology be made to take into account the unique psychological factors in his school experience and, in so doing, both give him a better preparation for what lies ahead and make his immediate learning efforts more fruitful?

Men are still amateurs in the domain of educational technology. This comes not so much from a lack of knowledge of computer and communications systems and their capabilities as from a kind of built-in resistance we all share, a dislike for challenges of any kind to traditional "ways of doing" in educational practice. Critics with expertise in the new technologies, indeed, often subtly suggest that momentum for change fails not so much on the scientific side as on the side of the education profession, and its silent ally, the unaware and uncritical public. For truly, so long as the administrative approach to instruction cannot be altered sufficiently to permit real experiment—through technological intervention in instruction—no one will know what possibilities exist for beneficial change.

What then is the proper role for technology, and what are its ultimate limits in the management of instruction? Because we choose not to grant it more extended authority, no computer as yet exercises totally unquestioned power over human events. Only in occasional scenarios of science fiction are machines (like HAL in *Space Odyssey 2001*) made to do some actual bossing of human underlings. The machines do, nonetheless, carry out an increasingly significant amount of the raw processing of data required to maintain even basic social and economic order. They can in fact (as with computer-generated billings and mailings) go much of the way in actually enforcing society's various compliance processes. What they are *not* doing yet is to set overall policy, to determine what should be done—and why—by humans in the first place. The appropriate division of labor, in short, needs to be spelled out, not for human society solely but also for man working in tandem with intelligent machines.

We have not even begun to face this question of the real and proper limits of machine use in education. Our inability to think about such matters seriously, and our habit of treating them, all too often, as beneath contempt, traces not solely to the obvious fact of current hardware and software inadequacy. It also has to do with our traditionally sentimental adult picture of the child. We prefer to see him as an already competent creature, a "little man" or "little woman" whose primary need is for "just a bit of time in which to grow up." We tend to downgrade the extent of the human neophyte's lack of experience in processing the ever more complex data of contemporary reality.

Where AI as an educational tool is concerned, then, we cannot yet bring ourselves to admit that we may soon have something to gain by handing over to the machine some powers of decision. We refuse to acknowledge that *in certain ways* the machine possesses greater knowledge and control over information than does the child, and that this situation could be turned to human advantage. As the authors of a recent text on use of computers in schools have noted,

A computer's strength lies in its capability of producing, storing, and manipulating information. In order to tap this power, schools will need to direct their curriculum toward teaching students to be users of information, rather than being recipients of information. Were this more of a real goal for the school, the computer's role would be clearer.[4]

This distinction between a learner who is a mere passive recipient of information and one who is an active user is vital to pedagogical science, obviously. Every reform program aims to turn the learner into a more active participant in the instruction-learning process. But just as with mainly administrative schemes which seek to achieve this goal, so too underlying the use of machines to encourage active learning lurk unanswered psychological and indeed ethical questions: Who is technology primarily intended to serve—those who make the machines, adults at the school site, parents, society at large, *or* the child-learner himself? If our scheme does not psychologically include the latter, then can we really expect his cooperation?

The history of school as a locus of instruction provides a negative lesson here: Instruction never loses a certain aspect of coercion, and students are aware of that coercion. Why should the learner, already held in a vise of legal-situational circumstance, follow the lead of a machine which manages his instruction, when his increasing opposition to a human being in that role is already evident? If he is passive before the human manager, why should he be other than passive when confronted with machine management? That necessary, indeed fundamental "something different" about instruction and learning which a mechanical mind must provide has yet to be seriously investigated.

False Economy: The Passion of Record-Keeping for its Own Sake

Today, school systems large and small and in many countries hover on the edge of bankruptcy in terms of sustaining morale. The school fails to meet either individual or societal needs, as even the less critical adult mind perceives them. But no one quite dares to suggest that a cause-effect relationship may exist between a process of education still almost wholly dependent on human inputs and the observed conditions of deterioration and breakdown. To a given degree, this universal unwillingness to engage the issue at a deeper level comes about understandably, for despite awareness no one yet knows what to offer as an alternative to traditional method.

Calling for an advanced technology of instruction to resolve these difficulties is, while premature, therefore no longer as surprising as it once may have been. The corresponding need for genuine *experiment* as instructional technology advances, though, is less well appreciated. Meanwhile, adults by and large also remain almost unaware of the fact that, though the school still depends altogether too heavily on human resources alone as the means of direct instructional control, administrative activities are already increasingly directed toward technologically oriented process management. This phenomenon, like it or not, also affects the learner's own performance over the long run.

In all school systems a more exclusively quantitative basis for management has been growing in importance for a century or more. In the US, use of standardized tests, of grade point averages, of average daily attendance data for funding, of Carnegie unit requirements for graduation: these and similar numeric measures have been routinely employed in administration for decades. Counseling office anecdotal and testing records for individual learners burgeon disproportionately with every uptick in student populations. More drastic and comprehensive (usually electronic) means for obtaining and making use of both behavioral and numerical data are adopted as soon as opportunity permits. Enthusiasts for "information systems management" are as much a part of the education as the business or government scene. Record-keeping for its own sake has become steadily more integral to school administration.[5]

In however underground a fashion, then, and often with no historical awareness on the part of major players themselves, the development of numeric bases for making judgments in regard to both individual students and groups of learners proceeds irreversibly. Despite the ridicule directed at the devotees of numbers in education by critics like Raymond Callahan (in his 1961 book *Education and The Cult of Efficiency*[6]), and by many another writer since, irresistible momentum in this direction continues. It is a road from which, in major respects, there is no turning back.

Meaningful information is the objective of this quest, just as, in general, it must be in the evolution of all human organizations. But what are the real purposes to which these data are put? If we are extracting greater value from such information, why should this not show up as a saving on resource employment in instruction itself, as well as improved learning outcomes? Does this trend in fact not run in contradiction to the continued, almost universal insistence by professionals on the need for more, not less, in the way of human resources to be given over to standard classroom teaching? As might be expected, educators can provide us with no satisfactory response to this line of questioning.

Education remains a highly manpower-intensive profession. It may well continue to be. But how much manpower is really necessary?

The maintenance of large human staffs is in large measure the outcome of a traditional way of looking at education, and not much more. As time and technology advance, some perhaps embarrassing queries are in order: Is that human adult we call a teacher in fact in a given situation serving primarily a babysitting or an instructional function? If we answer automatically "both," what genuine proof can we offer that babysitting has not in fact become the main activity and that the instructional function is still receiving its proper level of attention?

It is possible that the oft-heard, familiar "truth" of pedagogy which requires always more human adults in attendance on the learner, rather than fewer, comes down to no more than another smokescreen thrown up by those who would dupe the public with slanted evidence. In an age of scientific measurement, numerical information is taken for granted as provably meaningful—far beyond other measures. But if this is as true in education as in physics, then why do test scores decline even when teacher-learner ratios are at their historically most optimum levels? Could the process, if its efficiency is the real desideratum, not be in fact carried on with fewer human adults once technology can be brought to bear in some suitable fashion? This is a question even the most advanced national societies will in time have to come to grips with.

"Avoidance thinking" hardly makes the issue happily disappear. A more forthright view might acknowledge the problem head-on: Information *can* be used by men to reach goals which are of adaptive value just as readily as it can be used to push valueless make-work objectives. The problem in school management does not have to do with whether information will continue to be gathered about individuals at an increasing pace or not. We cannot prevent this trend from continuing. The problem, rather, has to do with the nearly total vacuum of *philosophical* supports for the application of information management in instruction.

This has been the situation, indeed, for all of the twentieth-century. As economic constraints more and more hamstring school operations on the old traditional lines, individual learner needs multiply while outmoded instructional practices have increasingly negligible effect. The whole process of internal breakdown has notably accelerated. Yet at the same time schools are pulled forward, like it or not, into the Information Age. Information technology is available and must be used. For better or worse, education systems are accumulating more information per student and per group than ever.

All school personnel are involved in some degree in this formal gathering of student information. The great bulk of such data never goes past the acquisition stage, remaining inert in files and data bases.

At best a maximum of ten percent of all data on students might be actively utilized to facilitate some aspect of instruction. But given technological trends, this drive simply to stockpile mostly unusable information builds with an increasing momentum.

(The school in this respect, one should understand, merely duplicates on its own level what goes on in the larger adult "dossier society." An evolutionary logic of instruction and learning, preferably, would actually require that such data be used purposefully in forwarding the instructional process itself. For now, though, data accumulation, in the perverse logic of all public administration, is somehow thought to shore up the school's image as competent instructional provider—a dubious assumption at best. Adult society, in any case, already so fully accepts similar rationalized information uses in its own sphere that it may pay little heed to the schools' rather excessive—because not applicable for instructional purposes—buildup of information about students.)

These practices, in fact, are already so imbedded in the fabric of adult living that we are mostly not conscious of them. But their presence is nonetheless ubiquitous. From psychiatry to bank lending, data accumulation has become all one with the business concept of "client-centered service." Educational analogs such as counseling and special education already make a fetish of data-gathering in individual cases, contributing only too often to the negative bureaucratic aspects of the schooling process—while doing little or nothing for instruction itself. Yet it is precisely in the individualization of instruction as a means of securing improved learning that better information-processing of the individual's own data will become steadily more of value.

What educators find it convenient not to acknowledge is the similarity of purpose between uses of information in school instruction and information uses in other service professions. Whether in medicine or law, in religion or business consulting, in prison management or psychiatry, the justifying rationale is the same: One practices his profession to aid another individual, and in a manner both direct and informed. This, nonetheless, is something which cannot be done without access to information, including relevant information about the person being served—and the right to discretionary use of that information, within only those basic limits established by privacy laws, statutes protecting human rights, and other purely legal restraints.

Even beyond this, other similarities in approach among all such "helping" professions exist: When asked to explain what his aim for a client may be, a service practitioner today will likely describe himself as a specialist in information—"for benefit of the client." He sees himself, indeed, as no more than the more experienced member of a partnership, an expert helping a non-expert under conditions of mutual cooperation. Banker, doctor, lawyer, diplomat, business consultant, office manager, sales rep, even a politician, all will say when pressed: "Yes, I give service as both a counselor and a teacher. My work, to describe it accurately, is both technical and psychological." And much of the information used must, of necessity, be *about* the client—provided either directly by him or obtained from other sources known to be reliable.

A sometimes but often only vaguely stated second purpose in all "helping" or "service" professions is that of enhancing the ability of the party being assisted to develop his own further capacities: Professionals use information to enhance a client's own information-handling skills. Educators, too, at least verbally ascribe to this principle. After all, the school exists *au fond* to enhance an individual learner's adaptive powers. Yet what educators at present cannot claim is that they use information in any objectively thorough way on behalf of the *vast majority* of school learners.

It becomes more and more difficult to maintain, on the basis of available data, that an exclusively group-oriented method of instructional management allows for very effective use of information gathered about individuals. Indeed the classroom teacher increasingly fails—is bound, in the very nature of her inalterable situation, to fail in ever greater degree—as one who aspires to meet the requirements of comparable adult-serving professions in building the client's own adaptive capabilities. A psychiatrist in practice may have sessions with twelve to fifteen patients a day. A teacher in a US junior high or senior high school with five class periods will probably face a hundred and fifty learners on that same day. How can such a teacher possibly do much in the way of either gathering or using information about her individual students—except by singling out one or two as "special," and thereby shortchanging all the others?

It will be argued that counseling and special education are nevertheless first steps in the direction of individualized use of information in instructional management. These, it will be said, point to a future in which "client-centered" instruction will be the universal norm because there will be enough information available on every learner and—somehow—all of it will be optimally utilized. But such an interpretation assumes a great deal.

While the data-gathering function these programs require surely edges education more directly into the Information Age, since the amount of data collected on a growing number of "special" individuals, or those deemed to be in "special need," is usually extensive, the question remains: Are counseling and special education, focused as they must be on certain individuals, really advance indicators of a genuine shift in fundamentals of instruction for the future? Or do these expensive programs merely reflect administrative recognition of the possibility of a serious system breakdown unless increasing resources are shifted into information-intensive remedial services that more effectively control malcontents and slow learners.

The school must, it seems, remain in the mainstream of social evolution; it cannot bypass its primary role as an agent of all individual development. As British writer Gerald Heard expressed it, in the present era the individual "can be taught to adjust, to make mutual adaptations with his altering society...only if the therapy of psychophysical hygiene that he is given is more than curative, more than preventive. It must be developmental."[7]

But, however true, this generalization ignores the many difficulties of daily administration, of "nuts and bolts" decision-making in both political and professional sectors. It is not merely a question of "how actually does one do it." Individualization done for whatever reason has about it an "all-or-nothing" aspect, in both the doing (for once done, it cannot be undone) and in the social and psychological results it produces. If we provide it for one, but not for another, is this ethical? Is individualization of only the handpicked good in any social sense? Evading such questions, as at present, makes our lives more, not less difficult. Under a regime of scarce resources such as we now endure, one which ignores the fundamental contributions technology, properly used, could make, we must still decide who shall be favored and who shall not be—a losing proposition if there ever was one.

Is there any provable economic benefit to be had from spending relatively disproportionate sums on the individualization of services to juvenile delinquents or the retarded, when at the same time the achievement level of a majority of "normal" students is steeply declining? Is it in any way rational to provide so-called economically disadvantaged learners with greater developmental opportunities via individualization when so many of the less disadvantaged average and below-average cannot qualify for similar special treatment? For how long can society accept as fair, or even afford, the use of information-intensive methods of instruction for a few, while the great majority must do without? An economics of mass adaptation that leaves all but a few without the optimum opportunity for self-development is by definition undemocratic.

"Information Economics" and the Technology of Instruction

The public mind embraces a disturbing contradiction over uses of information in education. We seek some as-yet-indefinable pivotal advantage from information technology applied in instruction, but we give little thought to necessary disadvantages and tradeoffs. On one hand we accept automatically the fact of increasing employment of dossiers and electronic data bases in the conduct of almost every school activity. On the other we maintain an attitude of emphatic distrust for machines and what they can do by way of ordering and interpreting information (including that relating to the individual per se) to serve instructional purposes.

Using information to craft individualized programs of instruction, in any case, is no more than a logical extension of trends already long under way in counseling, special education, and aptitude testing. These trends are simply made more explicit for instruction by recent phenomena such as the Individual Education Plan in public schools and the highly successful Kumon Mathematics Program (popularly called "samurai" math) marketed commercially.[8]

The uses to which any information is put in the education process, of course, depend finally on motives of those who oversee the instruction. If our motives as overseers are in essence to keep adult teachers and administrators employed, and nothing more, then we will go on with group-biased instruction, largely ignoring data on the individual's progress (or lack thereof). Yet this contradicts the whole more general trend toward increased individualization, and to a more comprehensive use of information to serve that purpose. Traditional group bias in instruction for centuries disallowed exploitation of any but a minimum amount of data on the individual learner himself. But for how long into the future can this continue? As other helping professions have already done, education, however belatedly, will surely be obliged to face this problem.

Psychiatry, perhaps the most drastic mode of direct client service so far developed, bores deep into a patient's psychic life to secure and interpret the information needed to enhance his mental health. Instruction of school learners may never require such in-depth involvement, at least with most subjects. Yet the lessons of psychiatry and related professions for instruction are reasonably clear: Information about an individual learner put to use in serving his self-development will inevitably become more significant, as instruction moves from a predominantly group-management mode to a mode stressing a higher level of management for the individual.

Electronic technologies already provide a solid scientific basis for the economic utilization of such information. That is, machines are now emerging which have the potential for processing effectively information of all kinds relating to an individual in his efforts as a learner—machines which will be able to control and direct instruction for an individual efficiently under circumstances found in the common school.   But progress in this direction does not come about automatically. With only the availability of this level of technology and nothing else, there would still remain an unresolved problem of instructional *management* for the individual learner. We lack a concept of how to put such machines to use, both in such a manner that they function in a pedagogically successful way for the learner and at the same time for the benefit of society.

Economic efficiency, then, involves something more than just good hardware and more imaginative and all-comprehending software. More, in a word, than technology *alone* and initially unguided can provide. Those who order the directions of the process of school instruction—in contemporary mass democracies the entire literate adult public—will also have to mandate *why* so innovative a path should finally be taken. In short, a consensus view of what any new approach to instruction via technology will be expected to accomplish must be achieved—a philosophical agreement, on the popular level, as to what *human* goal tomorrow's education should reach.

There is today, unfortunately, no socially acceptable basis in a consensual philosophy for combining already developed machine information-evaluation capabilities with the processes of individual instruction. Nor in a society preoccupied with mass norms of thinking and behavior are even well-educated adults able to give attention to the matter in the necessary depth. School remains school; the classroom and the administrator's office represent the acme of management possibilities for instruction.   We recoil from the demands of a threatening future with the same sense of fear with which prehistoric man burrowed into his cave to escape the unknown terrors of lightning or eclipse. As the poet Goethe once complained in a parallel context,

> "...though Time changes everything, men cling to the form of a thing as they first knew it, even when its nature and function have changed."[9]

It remains indeed characteristic of all mass societies—to this point in history, at least—that they lack an orientation to fundamental philosophic issues, especially those which bear on the more difficult questions of radical social-evolutionary change. Yet this particular underlying problem, that of the philosophic basis of instruction, whether or not we prefer to push it aside, looms steadily larger in any overall vision of the human future. We are obliged to accept limits on what can be done by any society in making advance preparation for so globally threatening, yet so vague and difficult-to-define a dilemma.

Man is condemned to wait in relative ignorance for the convergent forces of evolution to bring him face to face with the inevitable, since to give much thought to the issue now, before the fact, asks too much. The problem, nonetheless, refuses to go away, and will one day—perhaps sooner, rather than later—require to be resolved. The questions of *why* and *how* therefore cannot be permanently evaded.

Chapter 10

Evolution and Information:
Enduring the Vacuum of Philosophy

As a routine undertaking, education on the surface seems a self-sustaining necessity, a function of every society, whose operation needs no theoretical basis beyond the unspoken, consensual admission that without it human progress would cease. Social change goes on, ravaging the cultural landscape, but no one questions the need for systems of basic formal education to continue in place. Still, in the long history of philosophical ideas and theories which support education, disagreement over fundamental issues has been the only constant. If even philosophers speaking to these issues cannot come to a consensus as to the *why* or *what* of education, one might conclude, then control over the method—the *how*—is not likely to be reached either.

And while a problem of the philosophical roots of education remains, men must also face up to the aspects of change over which control could not be exercised in any case—the blind forces of evolution in an alien universe doing what they do irrespective of human needs or desires, even those of a majority. Evolution, a constant process, proceeds in increments of time and space so incomprehensible to the imagination that we fail to appreciate its unfailing presence. Only time reveals its process outcomes with any degree of clarity. Men, it will be claimed, are successful because they are amazingly cooperative, and are becoming ever more so. Civilization has been built over millennia by a cultivation of the arts of cooperation. Yet before cooperation there must be learning. And all learning has an individual, and therefore a competitive, aspect.

The uncooperative child-learner of today is quite possibly willing to learn, but not by competing under rules of play other than those he finds comfortable. The specter of Hobbes "war of all against all," of competition and conflict, of an unending procession of winners and losers, it appears, pervades even the otherwise cooperative world of human learning—an inescapable aspect of the evolutionary process as a whole, and even when specifically manipulated, as in the case of human learning systems, to promote organized cooperation. Learning too, becomes a weapon, a specialization, in the struggle, not just to survive, but along with those others of like mind to survive and *prosper*. Darwin summed up the whole complex process succinctly:

> The inhabitants of the world at each successive period in its history have beaten their predecessors in the race for life, and are, in so far, higher in the scale, and their structure has generally become more specialized; and this may account for the common belief held by so many paleontologists, that organization on the whole has progressed.[1]

Even so, evolution has never come down to mere straight-line development. Specific environmental conditions during some eras affect the length of time testing and weeding-out processes will go on, and the adaptations they will require. It has been widely accepted that the whole family of dinosaurs was wiped out by some sudden cataclysmic event, such as the intersection of earth with a large asteroid. Yet it seems equally evident that the dinosaurs endured as long as they did without adaptations which today would be considered vital to species survival, e.g., large brains, smaller but easier-to-maneuver bodies, warm blood instead of cold, and so on. In their era, however, these adaptations were clearly not necessary, and the dinosaurs remained dominant—so completely dominant, indeed, that insofar as is known they failed to develop any significant new adaptive characteristics, physical or behavioral.

Evolution, though, permits compression as well as elongation of time spans during which dramatic new adaptations must be attained. As a dominant species, possessed of a unique intelligence, man has forced a compression of "adaptive time" hitherto unknown. This has meant a significant change in the environmental "rules of play," for both dominant and other species. In our self-constructed late-industrial environment, the rules of play now require larger and more constantly active brains. Adaptive time has been drastically foreshortened—and entirely by man himself.

This milieu has become one in which intelligence in continual use acts as the knife-edge of successful adaptation—for both individual and collective. But what *kind* of intelligence? Automated machine intelligence has been until now highly limited in the scope of information it can process. Human intelligence has, potentially, no limits, but its disadvantages are numerous: The human mind wanders; it gets itself tied up in emotional circles, bored with straight-line reasoning even when such reasoning is most needed, attempting rational analysis when simple emotion suffices to interpret a situation. British scientist Roger Penrose argues that *thinking* in and of itself, the principal attribute of consciousness, underlies human intelligence, whereas the simulation of intelligence by machines consists solely in their ability to perform complex algorithmically controlled operations—meaning that a "non-algorithmic ingredient" *must* be present with consciousness.[2]

Man's intelligence, this uniquely individual consciousness with its distinct "non-algorithmic" bent, then characteristically yearns for algorithmic solutions, for some all-embracing principle which explains and guides him on his path through the chaos of reality. Traditionally, this has always been the province of the philosopher. Man himself is, as Pope John Paul once described him, by nature a philosopher. And even the non-Christian Bertrand Russell could write (in a mood of foreboding during the dark days of World War Two), that to "understand an age or a nation, we must understand its philosophy, and to understand its philosophy we must ourselves be in some degree philosophers."[3]

But where today do we find a commonly held philosophy, a consensually held world-view of why and how life should be lived? Modern man faces a crossroads: If there is no philosophy, how is life to be comprehended at its very root and core? And is this not the real situation faced by mass man in his late-industrial existence? For can we speak honestly at all today of any credible philosophy of "intelligence," or of education, or of learning, or of society—or even of civilization?

Such philosophy as we see offered today is in fact almost certain to be what Allan Bloom properly described as of the "no-fault" variety, in which "when we speak of the right to choice, we mean that there are no necessary consequences (in individual actions), that disapproval is only prejudice and guilt only a neurosis. Political activism and psychiatry can handle it."[5] The system, in brief, however little or much intelligence animates it as a whole, nevertheless is somehow expected to resolve all problems.

That this solution can never succeed in the long run is a nagging thought which, when they do find time to stop and consider, must leave even the most comfortably situated men and women profoundly discouraged. How can any system, human or machine, prosper when its component units function altogether randomly, following not even a semi-rational algorithm? Still, there is no escaping the need for personal decision-making. So-called relativism (suiting one's behavior as an individual to one's perceptions of a situation, with no reference to norms of conduct) thus only too-often inevitably brings about highly negative outcomes, in both personal life and in that of society.[5]

The failure of man's understanding of himself and of his place in society and the universe can indeed be seen most clearly in the young, and most clearly of all in school settings. As he senses (and resists) limits on his behavior, the child-learner has two routes open to him, that of making a yet stronger show of conformity to a particular group, or conversely of demonstrating a persistence in the quest for self-realization *only* as the individual he is. Yet once he asserts his variability, his self-determination against the lure of group conformity, the individual involves himself in serious risk. In mass school systems the would-be independent youth is particularly vulnerable. The rise of school violence in recent years well demonstrates the extent to which what was once a zone of childish innocence, of mutually understood, cooperative roles to be enacted, has become quite the opposite. The prevalence of "gang cultures" (in some cases virtually supplanting all established authority) in US urban schools is one example. Another must surely be the incidence in contemporary Japanese schools (including even junior high schools) of the various brutal practices of *ijime*—bullying by schoolchildren of any classmate identified as non-conforming or individualistic.[6]

Social and individual development have been partners with philosophy, so to speak, through recorded history, mutually reinforcing each other by providing, on one hand, a thought-through system of beliefs about the world and man's place therein and, on the other, providing an experiential nexus in which fundamental ideas about man's role in the universe could be tested under real-life conditions —that is, until the modern age, the arrival of an era of breakaway technology. Today our adult loss of a sense of certainty in how life should be lived has devolved on a younger generation virtually unable any longer to mature for lack of such a sense. The failure of any one consensual world-view to establish itself in our own times has been in good part a failure of education itself. Educational systems have been less and less successful in beating back the new global floodtide of ignorance which technological advance, paradoxically, has itself brought about. And so far as they depend on philosophers for their directions, such systems are clearly unlikely to find incentives to improve or change at any point in the near-future.

World-views now dominant pay too little attention in any case to the growing list of unfulfilled needs today's outmoded systems of formal education leave unaddressed. Adherents of a currently dominant capitalist democracy as a forever sustainable system reverently fall back on the macroeconomic dogma of Adam Smith, with his "invisible hand," as unassailable guarantor of benevolent long-term effects in man's earthly existence: A working economic system and its underlying philosophy together provide all that is needed for happiness of both individual and collective. (Not much is said of the presumably critical position of education as vehicle in *creating* such a future near-utopia.) But for others just as accurate a description might be found in Hobbes' classic "war of all against all."

In any event, no extant philosophy offers either a world-view capable of demonstrating with clarity individual man's place in a new "order of things" now taking shape, or the nature of an education which would allow him to benefit from the drift of evolutionary development on which he finds himself carried forward. In face of so many harsh realities, man's inventiveness indeed seems to have come to a full stop before the facts of history. Individual mind, since it can neither comprehend nor will away the larger world, as a result takes refuge in illusion. But the illusion gives no relief from the problems of reality, and the individual ends in the grip of a permanent neurosis. Daniel Bell has aptly summed up the universal character of this issue:

(Modernism)…denies the primacy of an outside reality, as given. It seeks either to rearrange that reality, or to retreat to the self's interior, to private experience as the source of its concerns and aesthetic preoccupations. The origins of this change lie in philosophy, primarily in Descartes and in the codification of the new principles by Kant.[7]

If the end-purposes of education and philosophy were not so similar, then perhaps the inability of philosophers to shed a clearer light on these perennial issues might not matter. But the link between educational and philosophical thinking is too close, and the failure of philosophy too obvious, for that: Philosophy and education are, or should be, after all, parallel concerns of the human spirit, mutually reinforcing enterprises in that unavoidable struggle by intelligence against the random universal destruction which is so much a part of the broader process of evolution.

Do this linkage and this failure then mean that the story of philosophy itself as an historical phenomenon contains no lessons whatever for those concerned over the future of formal education? Certainly there are lessons, and they may not even be wholly negative: They simply reflect the vagaries of evolution and species development in general, and in man's case the accompanying adverse pressures that dog his efforts to raise the level of human knowledge. They thus deserve some further, even if not detailed, scrutiny.

The Philosophic Vacuum and its Effects in Education and Society

From pre-Socratic times onwards, philosophers have consistently sought to provide some behavioral "algorithm," some all-embracing concept, that would guide all men in their thinking and behavior, and do so through all of earthly life. The result, by and large, has been the establishment of *virtue* as the goal. Yet no vaguer term has ever been coined. Virtue can mean different things even to different philosophers—for example, knowledge primarily (as with Socrates), or a developed ability to bear up against worldly evil and incomprehensible change (as with the Stoics). (Even the early existentialists, e.g., Kierkegaard and Nietzsche, rebels though they were, in their own way confirm the importance of virtue; their definitions of the term, however, tend toward an idiosyncratic, often anti-social extreme, and too, they differ from the earlier mainstream in their insistence on non-rational thought to define both means and ends.)

At a certain point, nonetheless, most such definitions merge, almost imperceptibly, into a single message, that of the unavoidability of action in spite of the finiteness of human knowledge. A modern philosopher like Bertrand Russell reflects these traditions almost undiluted: "Uncertainty, in the presence of vivid hopes and fears," he writes, "is painful, but must be endured if we wish to live without the support of comforting fairy tales.... To teach how to live without certainty, and yet without being paralyzed by hesitation, is perhaps the chief thing that philosophy, in our age, can still do for those who study it."[8] This rather negative summation expresses only too concisely the psychological dilemma of, among other professions, that of the modern educator.

Conceivably, to be sure, a society sophisticated enough to adopt a single philosophy of modern mass life would most certainly produce a clearer consensus of purpose and action (an "algorithm" to fit if not all, then most behavioral situations). Such a higher-order consensus would, inevitably, provide the enterprise of formal education with a rationale through which instruction could transcend the more destructive features of the present mode. It would more closely unite theory and practice and, while not by any means ending conflict in the larger adult society over aims and ends, offer a foundation in method from which all concerned would attain greater net rewards.

Opponents of change will assert that such a single philosophy in fact already exists—in the system of democratic capitalism which has put down roots globally, and seemingly firmly, in the adult world since the demise of Communist imperialism. But one look at the state of development of average pre-adult minds today quickly dispels this self-serving claim. Before puberty, before he comes to look out on the Information Age with that critical mind that adolescence first brings and which is the precursor of critical adult intelligence, a bright child often seems to assume, and to a high degree, the existence of such a "consensus adult world" as governing reality. (Piaget's studies confirm this for specific age cohorts, and from both a moral and an epistemological standpoint.) But with experience this childish assessment changes radically. The assumption that the adult system is built on total consensus—on a shared certainty as to means and ends, as to techniques and purposes—is gradually, and sometimes (if the randomness of rites of passage so dictate) violently dispelled.

Some will always dispute the point, yet philosophy's failure over historical time plays a part in these by-now inevitable youthful coming-of-age afflictions. The inability of philosophers over three centuries, from Descartes to Buber, to identify a set of common beliefs by which adult society might function in true "organic solidarity" has, as a primary side-effect, undoubtedly served to prevent school instruction from developing any more effective basis in method than it now has. The question of why this fact, however arguable, may yet suggest possibilities and expectations of a positive cast for school instruction of the future deserves consideration—in light of major trends of philosophy itself through the centuries.

Descartes' subjectivism marks a watershed in the entire story of man's efforts to comprehend both himself and the external world. For Descartes, mind was the only objective reality. All things other than the fact of one's own mental existence may or may not be what they seem. Hume soon carried the issue further, raising doubt to the status of an intractable absolute: Is there any real basis whatever for what is called reason? Is there any such thing as cause and effect? Early twentieth century German philosopher Ernest Cassirer interprets the Cartesian-Humean skepticism in these terms:

> The more penetrating our knowledge of the nature of man and the more accurate our description of this nature, the more it loses the appearance of rationality and order. Hume had reached this conclusion even in the realm of theoretical ideas. We usually consider the law of sufficient reason as the principle of all theoretical knowledge.... But sharper analysis of concepts dispels this illusion. For the very concept of cause, which was supposed to stabilize our knowledge, is itself without foundation.[9]

Rousseau and Kant completed the work begun by these pathfinders. The educational implications of their work are a jumble. Both detest anarchy, yet at the same time offer ideas and measures sure to further it. Rousseau, the acknowledged father and intellectual source of modern revolutionary movements, in his hodgepodge of writings offers equal doses of contradiction: adoration of hyper-individualism on one hand and a justification of collective slavery on the other. At one extreme he invents Emile, the ideal youth who must be given a proper education. To this end the philosopher piously provides an all-wise tutor who succeeds, presumably, in forming Emile into an adult who can be at one and the same time both a man and a citizen—something impossible in existing "unnatural" societies. Rousseau praises examples of "natural" morality, such as the love of a man and a woman, and at the same time he condemns the corresponding bourgeois legal form (contractual marriage). His works are permeated by hard-to-interpret contradictions of this kind, unresolved antagonisms between subjective wants and social necessity.[10] At the opposite extreme, Rousseau proclaims the need for a universal social contract based on a "general will." Rousseau's social doctrines, in fact, in the words of Bertrand Russell, "though they pay lip-service to democracy, tend to the justification of the totalitarian State."[11]

Kant brings the contradictions of Enlightenment philosophy to a head. His work has had the effect, perhaps not wholly intended, of wildly enhancing the emphasis on "maximum subjectivity" as the dominant factor in human mental operations. Kant sums up Enlightenment liberalism with his credo "Dare to know," a cry for the individual to use his own understanding in the search for knowledge. But Kant, overpersuaded by his own optimism, adopts (as Dewey phrases it) an eighteenth century "individualistic cosmopolitanism" in which the "full development of private personality is identified with aims of humanity as a whole and with the idea of progress."[12] Kant provides no basis for a practical use of individual intelligence (and much less a basis for formal pedagogy), which could reconcile the individual's intuitive drives and preoccupations with the needs and demands of society. Kant's writings involve, as Santayana commented, a wholly false view of subjectivity as the source of progress. Yet Kantian subjectivity exercised an historical and social-psychological influence which was profound, and which is very much with us still.[13]

Individual action for its own sake, the triumph of the id, is one inevitably negative consequence, for which only a superior education provides any effective antidote. The creed of "Dare to know" has always borne within itself a fatal over-emphasis on the hyper-active self as sole interpreter of reality. Reflection as the real source of information-interpretation, of learning itself, is all too readily shunted into the far background. This excess of action and lack of reflection is only too well mirrored in the conditions of learning of today's average school classroom.

In the circumstances of modern life, how *can* men "know"? Only by "doing," that is the best answer later-day philosophy can give. (It has not yet absorbed the lessons of experimental psychology, which by now—on the basis of empirical evidence—no longer has a choice, and must allow a more serious role to reflection in the decision-making process.) "Activity," says Daniel Bell, "making and doing, (thus) becomes the source of knowledge." In the Kantian revolution, Bell writes, "(individual) mind is the active agent, scanning and selecting experience from the maelstrom of the world, though still within the fixed coordinates of space and time.... (Kant's) categories...were a synthetic a priori, the fixed categories of mind that allowed one to organize experience."[14] Yet how does any mind (in particular a child-mind) organize experience in an optimum fashion today, when it is constantly preoccupied with demands for immediate action from an environment itself out of rational control?

Only pragmatism, paradoxically, among modern philosophies has attempted to deal with this problem of excessive imbalance between active and reflective mind with some success, at least on the theoretical level. But pragmatism also makes a grievous error of curricular emphasis which cancels out its other advantages: It blindly accepts science and technique as the sole educational lodestar. Allan Bloom surely has a point when he comments, almost bitterly, that Dewey's pragmatism, "the method of science as the method of democracy, individual growth without limits, especially natural limits— (unfortunately came to see) the past as radically imperfect and regarded our history as irrelevant ...."[15]

(At the same time, parenthetically, enthusiasts though they might have been, the pragmatists were no fools. In his vision of the school as a microcosm of society, to the extent one can consider it apart from his stubborn insistence on scientific method as the basis of all progress, Dewey presented a not altogether impractical, though typically vague, scheme for instructional policy: Its benefits lay in the fact that it would *combine*—in a balanced fashion, and in a single working nexus—the child's activities of mind with activities of the body, thinking with doing.

Even so, the critics of pragmatism remain on solid ground, for the theory lacks psychological consistency: An intelligence which largely ignores the past and only "instrumentally" operates to realize the future in some desirable shape, and this is pragmatism's major emphasis, may not really be able to function on a basis of genuine science, or even of intelligence itself. Further, the significance of traditional values seems all too likely to be lost sight of—if, indeed, the pragmatists' curriculum has any values at all in the accepted sense, other than those forced on it at the moment of action by powers that be. Only in its insistence on the child being actively involved in the business at hand, that is, involved in learning in both its social and its reflective/cognitive aspects, does pragmatism seem to have one foot planted squarely in the educational camp of tomorrow. As Dewey himself states, "If the living, experiencing being is an intimate participant in the activities of the world to which it belongs, then knowledge is a mode of participation, valuable in the degree in which it is effective. It cannot be the idle view of an unconcerned spectator."[16])

In any event, while the excessive subjectivity that is the heritage of Kant's doctrine may have been justifiably disparaged by the pragmatists, it is still far from being exorcised. The course of two centuries of history since Rousseau and Kant merely confirms that the problems Enlightenment philosophy poses in the practical sphere are with us still. Neither Dewey nor William James (with his theories of "pure experience" and "will to belief") were able (or in James' case was even interested) to alter the radical drift towards unrestrained subjectivity—to the use of individual mind primarily as a seeker after illusion (rather than as a persistent "explicator" of reality), and eventually to what in the late twentieth century Daniel Bell could call the cult of the "imperial individual" and of his "untrammeled self." Thus the disjunction with which a new millennium begins, between strong self-conviction on one hand and weak individual competence in social adaptation on the other. For modern bourgeois democracy, as Bell says, "lacking a culture derived from its empty beliefs and dessicated religions, in turn, adopts as its norm the life-style of a cultural mass that wants to be 'emancipated' or 'liberated,' yet lacks any sure moral or cultural guides as to what worthwhile experiences may be."[17]

(And as for pragmatism's larger effects, both in and beyond formal education, it must be noted, again parenthetically, that at root it remains no more than yet another system inviting abuses, however noble its originators' intentions. Its principles can be and have been made to serve no other discernable purpose than as basis for organizations (including schools) which are vehicles of power for ambitious individuals. Interestingly, in view of Dewey's and James' extreme reticence as theorists, Bertrand Russell ascribes this largely unintended outcome of pragmatic thought to a kind of "cosmic impiety"—of the type common to so many lesser but ambitious men intoxicated with the lure of a role to be played in the seemingly unstoppable progress of modern science and technology.

Russell critiques Dewey in these terms: "His philosophy is a power philosophy, though not, like Nietzsche's, a philosophy of individual power; it is the power of the community...[18] Not, surely, an entirely conflict-moderating, even if an already common, world view—as a new century begins, and in a global environment where the ordinary individual already finds he must seek more and more to find his own way through a growing thicket of information and collective forms of coercion surrounding him literally from birth.)

Can there be Alternatives in School Instruction? Evolution as Driver and the Role of Philosophy

Two and a half millennia of philosophy have actually rendered education a singular benefit: Philosophy has posed the major questions facing man in the universe; it has even allowed men as self-conscious beings to visualize, at least in certain eras, an "algorithm" for consensual adaptation. And because it treats of ethical issues along with those of meaning and being, philosophy reaches where science alone cannot go. Psychology, its later-day offshoot, has aided in interpretation of the mechanics of mind. But only philosophy tells us in any substantial way where man might properly fit in the universal plan of evolution.

All this has meant a great deal historically in education, for it linked the rationale of social life with the rationale for instruction. Many cultures came to possess a common and conscious view of where they expected the process of formal learning to lead. Up to a certain point in Western history, there was a steady relationship between educational concepts, on one hand, and politics, ideology, and economic development on the other—from Plato and Aristotle to Leibniz, roughly. A continuity and a reciprocity existed not only from Greece to Rome and from Rome to later Christian culture; it remained in place right on through the European Dark Ages and beyond, as a tradition of philosophic justification for the diurnal routine of school instruction.

This connection between philosophies and curricula survived until modern power philosophies emerged in the Age of Enlightenment. Then began the massification of learning, and the progressive disappearance of any credible philosophy in support of the educational enterprise. From pre-Socratic Greece to Rousseau and Kant, the expectations of society in general were reflected in the form and direction of school learning, and both were in turn reflections of a largely asecular intellectual environment, whose underlying principles were spelled out in the philosophies of the era. But after the arrival with the Enlightenment of a cosmopolitan, secular world view, a dramatic change came about: After Rousseau and Kant, philosophy became the tool of social reform, and such reforms require above all the power to direct men in the mass. Cut off from its theoretical roots, philosophy could no longer only explain; it had to provide power—or, more precisely, at least an illusion of power. The link between philosophy and education, like that between philosophy and religion, ceased to matter and even to exist. That this absence of a unifying algorithm, a consensus philosophy for the modern industrial era, has created evils for formal education is now one of the great givens of modern history.

Francis Bacon's "knowledge is power" had demonstrated long before Rousseau that philosophy could be infected with a power virus. But only with Rousseau does philosophy cease, for the first time, merely to explain the world abstractly and begin to lay down how it can be positively reformed. In his muddle of sentiment and self-certainty, of radical individualism and social conviction, Rousseau reaches beyond Plato's theorizing about justice and the "just" state. He *prescribes* for the future, expressing not merely personal thoughts and beliefs but laying down rules not (as he says) deduced "from the principles of a high philosophy, but (which come from) the depths of my heart, written by Nature in ineffaceable characters."[19] Instead of analyzing after the fact, summing up experience as the classical philosophers had done, Rousseau lashes out in a fashion which today we could only describe as political, even wildly utopian—in effect banishing philosophy, that "terrifying apparatus," in favor of natural feelings and individual conscience, as the "infallible guide(s) to right action."[20]

Kant did what was possible to shunt Rousseau's contradictions to the metaphysical level, where they could be more readily moderated in tone, setting up reason as the arbiter of morals, the keystone of knowledge. But Kant's own subjective bias has consistently and effectively defeated linkage between philosophic theory and day-to-day affairs—including (conceptually) that of mundane formal instruction in schools. And the post-Kantian dilemma continues. As Russell observes, "Kant's inconsistencies were such as to make it inevitable that philosophers who were influenced by him should develop rapidly either in the empirical or in the absolutist direction."[21] In either case, philosophy descends into a quagmire of arguments more remote from practical life than ever.

Still, can the mind of man not find a more directly objective basis for more effective instructional operations, an "algorithm" for our time and beyond, one which cannot so readily be dissolved into endless metaphysical speculations? Science offers at times its own somewhat contrary yet tantalizing insights. British physicist Jacob Bronowski has offered one possible solution. He acknowledges where all knowledge of human value must inevitably originate: within an individual organism. But where humans are concerned there are two sides to this coin. Each man is biologically both like to, and completely different from, any other member of the species. In the psychic realm, the same situation applies. Variability is one constant, therefore, and similarity another. Similarity, pushed to its limit, leads to the machine. In many respects, man is a machine both biologically and psychically. But in certain other, indeed more crucial aspects he is an individual, whose matter and mind cannot ever have existed before and can never again exist in the future. Each man is both to some degree a machine and to some degree a "self."[22] This line of thought is surely replete with possibilities.

What defines this self which is, intellectually and affectively, different from anything else in nature? The biological functions common to all men, also the functions of mind which involve only mechanical repetitions and are in no sense different when you perform them or I perform them—all these occupy the domain of machine context. They have no inherently original content. What is original in every individual is his accumulated experience, which has an end-effect of creating something wholly different from anything else in the universe. As Bronowski expresses it, "a definition of self hinges on the study of human experience...the self is the process in which all (a man's) experiences, of the body and of the mind, are fixed as knowledge."[23]

Surely this is an insightful metaphor. Bronowski concludes: "Man is a machine by birth but a self by experience." The eminent scientist points out as well that no ethic "is effective which does not link...social duty with the sense of individuality.... (The) knowledge of self does not teach him to act but to be; it steeps him in the human predicament and the predicament of life."[24] What does this then mean for education, and specifically for school instruction?

It remains difficult for the human mind to recognize evolution as a force in itself, a force over which neither culture nor political authority holds more than passing sway. Humanity is, individually and collectively, like it or not, a part of a process of universal evolution. Yet for man, the only self-conscious animal, nothing arrests the arrow of time, the dissolving agent of evolution, so much as the effective application of individual intelligence—a phenomenon depending in high degree on environmental circumstances. These circumstances in turn depend on social and economic developments at given stages.

Modern mass societies increasingly demand a use of intelligence which obliges the individual to acquire knowledge almost without exception in its non-Socratic sense—as a survival instrument. The knowledge needed to make a living, to hold onto a niche in the structure, is ever more consistently part of the machine, not the self, in each of us. The old philosophical phrase "Know thyself" is a good starting point for getting in tune with the universe—but only if we follow through with knowledge about *something else*. Self-knowledge alone might today let one into the bread line, hardly more.

Seen in this light and at first glance, Bronowski's dichotomy seems off the mark of reality, for the modern self, dominant as it may seem today, appears destined progressively to disappear, in time to be swallowed up in mass. And indeed much external evidence points generally more, rather than less, in this direction. The common bottom-rung line employee, along with his harried mid-level manager, the factory hand as well as the highly paid CEO, all decompose into the anonymity of no more than a "formal self"—and fit ever more tightly into their slots in the socioeconomic machine whose workings, as college students still discover, Max Weber was able to dissect with such skill (and not without a certain show of contempt for its "functional rationality" and bureaucratic inflexibility). Yet this unsubtle but already traditional rendering of the modern predicament leaves aside critical questions of the nature of information and knowledge, of human intelligence and human diversity.

It has been argued by a few socioeconomic "convergence" theorists that diversity largely dies out among national, even regional, societies as they rise in the scale of industrialism. As socioeconomic structures everywhere rationalize, societies become homogeneous; gradually they lose those characteristics which over past centuries gave them their uniqueness and variability.[25] This leads in turn, and in the long run, to a single world fabric in which "natural" individualistic traits themselves disappear, and the effort by individuals to compete on the basis of existing rules of play enforces a world-view akin to that of lesser animals: A law of the jungle gradually returns. The things for which civilized man lived are no longer within reach; a light that burned in the darkness is extinguished.

Man's destiny may *be* extinction. But that is not consistent with either ordinary hopes or history. Man has survived, both as species and individual, because he has adapted through technology, has learned to use the machine to augment the inadequate powers of that side of himself which is also machine. True, reduced to this machine-self and nothing more, he may indeed revert to the state of lower animals. But the historical record suggests a different, better fate: His imagination has, at every stage of historical development, produced machines which enlarged his powers of mechanical control over his milieu, machines which permitted him to see and understand more of the universe and thereby adapt to its pressures more successfully.

Now he has no choice in the game of survival, other than to face up to the overriding issue of technique in modern life—not simply to acknowledge verbally that information handling machines are becoming "smarter" than humans in many areas of information processing (for this is well enough known), but to focus on why men have not yet come to agreement as to how this phenomenon will be turned to proper use. It seems likely enough, indeed, at this late stage that a consensus in the more critical process areas, education first and foremost, cannot be put off for too much longer.

Though media have led the way in the mechanization of information handling, their role in the information environment of the middle and later 2000s is surely uncertain. It is clear that mass media in particular yield only an illusory form of direction. They ignore the individual, respecting solely the collective. Most social critics and certainly the psychological professions already agree that a technology grounded in an exclusively mass outlook has gone nearly as far as it can without destroying individual independence of thought altogether. And as an added negative, what mass media, along with most of the other technologically oriented information-producing techniques in modern industrial life, fail to provide—and will never be able to provide—is an automatic, machine-directed means of assistance in personal decision-taking for the *individual*.

The disappearance of Soviet Communism in the last decades of the twentieth century was in one sense a victory over the total rationalization of a centralized information control system by a self-serving ideology. Yet in another sense this momentous historical event was a potent reminder that *all* systems of information control face natural limits. The Soviet demise was a phenomenon replete with warning: for what took place was in fact the breakdown of a vast unitary political system of controls over information-flow, in which the individual was deliberately propagandized instead of educated, the self forced out of a constructive social role, and reliance placed totally on bureaucratic order-giving as the basis for all individual decisions.

(It may be recalled that in earlier decades the USSR as a viable form of government impressed even well-informed and critical observers like C. P. Snow, who assumed it would likely endure for hundreds of years. Today, people in the West continue to claim that the downfall of monolithic Communism was a victory for that ultimate intangible, "human freedom." But it might also be viewed as no more than a preliminary yet inevitable step in man's longer evolutionary trail—one that places the burden for tactical decisions in his own life ever more exclusively upon the individual. The mirror-opposite of a state which controls all information and makes all decisions for the individual can only be one which regards him as an information user capable, if well enough educated, of his own best judgments, and which tends more and more to expect from him decisions authentically his own.)

Can Technology and Philosophy Coexist—in Society or in the School?

Media are, to be sure, only a part, though a significant part, of an information system which, in the normal course of events, comes to restrain excess of diversity in society. Yet how much media control in the handling of information is consistent with society's progress? The individual has "rights" against all media. But in a democracy the reverse must be true as well. Media are organized, a signal point of difference, to be sure. The individual, as a minority of one, will always lack for enough defenders; he must reflexively, often aggressively, perform his self-defensive role as a "unit of diversity." Still, there can be only so much diversity, just as only so much homogeneity, if the information system which supports society is to remain in balance.

From at least the days of Mill and Spencer in any case, a strong liberal lobby, speaking in the name of progress, has insistently drummed away at the need to provide individuals with better means for furthering their own "fitness to survive." Spencer's intellectual heirs have worked hard as well at accommodating evolutionary theory to fundamental issues of human adaptation. In so doing, they make the repeated claim that, despite the evident evils of a collective existence marked by increasing competition for individual survival, a fundamental "law of human progress" nevertheless prevails.   In the operation of this law, a seemingly insurmountable contradiction is bridged: "progressive heterogeneity or differentiation" forces all human energies ultimately into ever more original and creative channels.   With time and however gradually, morality and social justice improve the human condition, through the self-renewing energy of a steadily more liberated "social vitality."[26]

In our age of universal negativism this seems again not philosophy but unprovable dogma.   Yet it is also the more optimistic side of Social Darwinism.   It asks, as Jefferson had asked earlier, the question of whether or not there is any finite limit to the power of individual intelligence, once set free.   In the twentieth century, this view of human possibilities has been argued perhaps more successfully by thinkers steeped in Asian religious traditions—the Buddhists, the Taoists, Sri Aurobindo, or Krishnamurti—than by western thinkers.   Yet these are all no more than counterpart schemes mirroring the dichotomous nature of man's mind—Bronowski's division of man's intelligence into a self and a machine.

There is a further important point made by Bronowski, in which he suggests that science itself accepts—as perhaps society as a whole as yet does not—that a real machine is no more than a "human artifact which mimics and exploits our own understanding of nature."   Yet by contrast, one should keep in mind, it is also true that no one, scientist or layman, can foresee "how radically we may come to change that understanding.... All that we can say...is that we cannot now conceive any kind of law or machine which could formalize the total modes of human knowledge."[27]

Only a human being operates, at this point of time in any event, as both a genuine self *and* a machine.   But evolution has also brought about our increasing dependence on the external machine—the extension of our internal machine—which "mimics and exploits our own understanding."   We have too, in one of those perhaps natural juxtapositions of the space-time continuum, reached a stage in the evolutionary cycle when only advanced technology allows man, as individual, fully to realize himself, to extend and develop his intelligence beyond that which is only potential. Technology, thus, has become the veritable open sesame of his self-realization.   There is nothing else.   In the tenuous balance between self and internal machine—for the individual and, through him, for mass as well—technology is man's key to adaptation.

But what kind of technology, and directed to what ends? The last two-plus centuries have seen technology put to use mainly as an information purveyor tied inextricably to a social culture of perversely utilitarian ends and controls. If there is a problem, it is that this culture, today the culture of mass capitalist democracy, moves forward with no fundamental and consensual ethical underpinnings, while at a further remove from day-to-day reality its origins in Greek thinking and Enlightenment political and social philosophy have been lost sight of, abandoned to the chaos of a blind mass life-surge. Such as it is, the "algorithm" of social progress is concerned today almost solely with the technical control of where and how mass energies will be expended—a negative ethos. Moral development of the individual intelligence has been thereby forced automatically into a lesser role than it should play in a well-educated society.[28]

And as educational measures increasingly reflect the vacuum of philosophic certainty, so too are the results felt, first in the school and then in the changed adult society which successive school-leaving cohorts gradually create. At the extremes there are excesses of either socioeconomic diversity or homogeneity, neither of which resolve the dilemma of an optimum place for individual intelligence in the working-out of a new social fabric. No one as yet knows what the results of a worldwide, steadily expanding diversity might entail. If excess diversity comes to reign entirely, however, we may be sure that social chaos can only follow in its train. Of the opposite ideology of an ultra-conforming humanity we already know a great deal, and this may well be the worse of the two evils. Nor has this philosophic contamination died off with the passing of the USSR and its "new Soviet man." It lurks in the collective mind-set of every contemporary society hypnotized by the lure of economic strength as the be-all and end-all of existence.

Indeed and unfortunately, as the cases of present-day Japan or Singapore rather clearly demonstrate, while this approach may make a society temporarily wealthy and nominally democratic, on one hand it denies the individual self that independence of spirit essential to what is still properly called a full life for the person, while on the other it stands in the way of optimum use of individual intelligence in moving forward the collective business of society as a whole. The mass culture of "doing and knowing," of overemphasizing self as machine, of disengagement from all the world save that of an immediate present and its physical environment, leaving all major decisions in society to those few with both time and authority to reflect adequately on just measures, on long-range possibilities, in the last analysis allows an average human individual only to act, never to be. His experience pushes him only further into mass; his life becomes not one of self-realization, merely one of repetitious, other-directed actions which serve the culture temporarily but contribute nothing to its long-term welfare. He has fallen into this slough of negativism as a psychological naïf, but this outcome was only possible in the first place for lack of an adequate realization of technological and educational necessities.

A true philosophical outlook would, logically, consider any basic human process, just as Aristotle might have, as something in which intelligence and experience should have a permanent hand in not only creating but also in *re*creating over time, and as shifting conditions appeared to require. In particular (as doubtless Aristotle would agree) the enterprise of formal learning fits into this zone of possibility. With formal instruction and learning, since it concerns all citizens, surely the creation of change by man, and in the effort to benefit man, could be viewed as justified not solely by every known philosophy but by the constant flow of practical needs themselves. The current barrier? Indeed, no one need be in doubt on this point: Human culture in its reflex opposition to the manifold uncertainties represented in technology is a frightening, even self-destructive force.

No accepted philosophy guides man in this dilemma. Alternatives are hard to conceive of without some guiding theory, and in the formal education of the child and youth the problem is most acute. For today's child is tomorrow's worker, citizen, leader, decision-maker. Already at an age when the child of yesteryear was innocently playing with his toys, today's neophyte goes about with a real gun and plans adult-type crimes in imitation of his elders—phenomena represented as almost unavoidable (or even normal) by the mass media. It comes as no surprise then to see ever larger masses of human beings, young adults as well as toddlers, yielding to the tactics of individual survival behavior, and not much more. What real choice have they been given?

Without a philosophy, we are left with only the phenomena of reality themselves. Evolution moves the whole. It destroys as it builds, blindly, without consciousness or conscience. Intelligence exists and can make a difference. It could save what in its own eye seems worth saving. But what is it? Where do we find it? How can we develop it? It will be said that intelligence resides only in a knowledge of what other intelligences will accept as suitable thinking or behavior. This is the accepted or at least implicit social interpretation for our times, the democratic bias. But is such an interpretation, bound to a specific cultural and political concept, in consonance with evolution, with the deeper future? More to the point, is it "right" for instructional method?

Like it or not, intelligence itself has a completely individual component as well as its never-to-be-escaped social aspect. The coming century will reveal if intelligence is defined and developed formally in terms of mainly individual or mainly mass perceptions. Science can produce, in time, an instructional technology of diversity balanced to one of conformity, instead of solely, as now, at least in the average school, a bias of convenience towards the latter. Science can achieve a covenant between man in the mass and man as self-cum-machine, or we can continue with the imposition of mass cultural predispositions. Such a test, in any case, inevitably must sooner or later come, as societies are forced by evolutionary pressures to optimize formal development of intelligence in the school and in the process of school instruction.

Some anthropologists have written prophetically (and perhaps too optimistically) of a future time when man will have moved "beyond culture," when the unique self which experience builds has realized itself within the confines of a world no longer antagonistic to the potentially optimum contribution of the individual, when hierarchy for its own sake no longer misdirects individual mind to its own purposes but works to advance the person's self and its mechanistic counterpart simultaneously. In the arena of school instruction, certainly, where the still-unformed psyche is so critically influenced, this would be a task impossible to move forward without advanced technology. It would be a process, also, subject to approval (or disapproval) by the adult majority, which after all constitutes the culture. But above all, it would demand a form of management, a method of process control, which would move beyond the unpondered conventions and basic operating assumptions upon which the largely failed system of today so firmly rests.

Chapter 11

A New Century: Prospects and Possibilities

With or without philosophic supports, the coming century will surely confront evolutionary demands for dynamically new uses of technology to achieve critical human ends. At this point of time Western science and rationality seem to have all the potential answers, and the westernizing trend will evidently continue. What it lacks in spiritual foundations is made up in the enthusiasms of those who design systems of control. Technique is applied in knee-jerk formulae—to whatever can be conceived of as a social, economic, or even psychological problem—by self-confident, ubiquitous scientific and administrative elites.

The range of problems recognized expands almost exponentially. Any process of reform or redirection seen as not threatening to the welfare of established interests receives consideration. "Reform" of education is thus an automatic priority in every advanced industrial nation, and in the primarily administrative sense already discussed. The child is approached as a programmable entity, able to deal with information as would a machine, a mere processor of the symbols of language and number. Yet the child as a *self* remains more ignored than ever in the past—a critical system failure. And this is a dilemma no system can resolve in its present configuration.

To no one's surprise, a poignant reminder of how completely the individual can be swallowed in mass comes from contemporary Japan, the world's most de-individualized large industrial nation. Japanese educators are questioning the very basis of their own supposedly successful system, on the grounds that it is turning out human goldfish, people so attached to work and culture that they are incapable of any sense of self, and lack all ability to generate ideas of their own.[1] The outcome for adult society has been aptly summed up by one US critic of Japanese education: "The well-intentioned teachers and well-behaved students put their efforts to purposes that are ultimately shallow and uninspired. The nation benefits economically. Society is well run. But it is a system without heart."[2]

Nor is it a system likely to find the Information Age a comfortable or automatically fulfilling experience. Professor Jerry Salvaggio of Houston University, who has studied the effects of an increasing information glut on Japanese society, concludes that the Nipponese future, wealthy nation though Japan may be, holds less than unmitigated happiness:

> ...there will clearly be (writes Salvaggio) certain adverse consequences as Japan becomes one vast information network. I...make the case that Japan will lead the world in the development of communications technology. If this turns out to be the case, then it would logically follow that Japan will be the first to experience the social effects of being highly informationalized. The primary side-effects are likely to be in the areas of government censorship, information overload, psychological dependence on video, computer piracy, and invasion of privacy.[3]

How does one educate the individual in such a society? The question is not unique to Japan. As American historian of education Rush Welter suggested years ago, with respect to the US system:

> (A) reaffirmation of the belief in education is likely to sanction unintelligent methods...by making it seem that our only need is to do the job we have always tried to do, but better. The preservation of... democratic institutions depends upon the reality, not the mythology, of democratic education.[4]

When method becomes too unintelligent, then, something better suited to the situation must be found. Encouraging school learners to tinker with computer and communications devices may seem like a change in method to many people, but this simply confuses means with ends. There may be some payoff in random instances from such tinkering, yet how it contributes in any systematic way to sustained intellectual development would be hard to say. There is a real problem of perception here. *How* one achieves the goal of intellectual competence cannot be determined until one has admitted that this *is* the goal.

Mistaking the real burden of an Information Age, it seems, people still tend to devalue fundamental intellectual competence at the very stage in history when the need has never been more critical. And side-stepping the issue today, even admitting current cultural and economic constraints in all the advanced industrial societies, means only more trouble further down the road. Recall Whitehead's somber warning: "In the conditions of modern life the rule is absolute, the race which does not value trained intelligence is doomed."[5]

The larger socioeconomic environment in which contemporary education is carried on can be defined in terms far less ambiguous than in the past. The human world has indeed entered what can rightly be called an Information Age. Such a portentous figure of speech, certainly, has about it a ring of journalistic glibness, a Barnum-like hyperbole and phoniness. But as an expression of what is happening in the mental universe of the five or six billion human inhabitants of this planet, the expression has a considerable validity. We live in an environment increasingly saturated by information in flow. The wonder is not so much that education has not caught up to this fact and undertaken measures by which to harness intelligence to interpretation of information, but that even informed adults in large numbers—like the ostrich who found it more appropriate to stick his head in the sand when trouble approached—refuse to acknowledge the scope—or even presence—of this reality.

Theodore Roszak, American academic and New Age guru, in his book *The Cult of Information*, typifies this reaction. To him and like-minded critics there is neither historic nor evolutionary significance in information. Making an issue of it is just an exercise in journalistic voodoo. Why bother even to think about it, or about the questions that arise regarding uses to which the machines that process it will be put? Unfortunately, such a response does not make the hard reality disappear. It comes down instead, to propaganda, uncritically accepted by many who should know better, against the very truths of daily living.

Arguments of this kind are at this late date already tautological for adults with broad conscious experience of a universal information-rich environment. What other response can one make to such flippant assertions as the following? 1. Information not only does not relate to knowledge, but actually stands in its way. (In which case, upon what basis does knowledge rest? Perhaps D. H. Lawrence's visceral "intelligence" suffices, after all.) 2. No machine can acquire knowledge or values, since these are by definition uniquely human possessions, unable to be transferred to any other entities. 3. Information in the forms accumulated by organizations has no human purpose; it invariably serves to violate individual privacy, promote war, push millions of humans into blindly accepting life under "the system." And so on.[6]

Such half truths, vaguely accurate as assessments of the current situation, might perhaps be significant if incorporated into a philosophical scheme with insights for the future. But this is impossible, for their underlying assumption is that of the fundamental unimportance of information, period. And since the bulk amount of information in today's world continues to grow, never lessen, clearly the only characteristic impression we can have of these stubborn "anti-information" gurus is that they are, like the audience they serve, largely divorced from contemporary reality.

To compound their perverseness, such nay-sayers are also quick to blame others for whatever they find distasteful in a world not made to their express order. "The system," or at least some one of its more consensus-demanding elements, bears direct responsibility for having "created" all problems in question. Critics like Roszak indeed simply dismiss today's mounting and universal information flows and their effects on individual consciousness as an invented journalistic vehicle, one purporting to explain and even justify imposed political and social inequities which should not exist—rather than a basic fact of life inevitable in that ever-more crowded, competitive environment that is today's imperfect human world. On this point ordinary people who daily face the milieu of organizations and public opinion, of markets and their enigmatic nature, of human social and economic discontents, of mass and individual expectations and persuasions, are less poorly informed about the global significance of information than the cognoscenti.

Yet this instinctive sense of the value of information in ordinary man fails to jibe with his unsophisticated and in fact still nonchalant attitude to the school instructional process. Non-professionals, angry as they may be over lack of suitable outcomes in school instruction, still view instruction as something in which it is unwise in any way to interfere, a fixed process in which only that intangible called individual effort (and never the method imposed by the system) is the significant variable.

Adults, though passively for the most part, continue with the comforting assumption that "people are so much alike, therefore they must learn in very similar ways." These typically traditional reactions seem implicitly self-serving. They reflect a private belief, also widely held, that systematic learning, carried too far, produces useless eggheads, of which society already has an excess. In turn this belief bolsters a common refusal to face the more general challenge of the information-rich future. (It probably also suggests, as well, a common subliminal fear of the future and its terrors among the many who see themselves unprepared for what might come.) Thus no one questions *how* instruction is conducted, only what its content might be. The consequences for formal education of this popular view of instruction are highly negative, at least for the short-term.

Experts and laymen are thus alike in finding it hard to grasp the highly unique nature of individual mental operations. They find it extraordinarily difficult to come abreast of the unavoidable role of individualization in education of the future. Yet when adults drive their imaginations beyond the current technocratic rigidities they readily discern, even if only dimly in its details, an emerging "education in the future tense"—a process, at least in terms of management, which will have to be very different from what today passes as instruction.

The Intellectual Dropout Syndrome and the Issue of Control in Effective School Instruction

Once we concede the immediate problem of instruction—that of managing the individual learner's development in handling information with critical intelligence—ways and means can be found for reorganizing the use of school resources to that end. But it is important not to lose sight of the underlying basis of any systematic innovative change in this direction: the idiosyncratic character of each individual mind. The very nature of psychological individuality argues against process-enhancement in a context where machine intelligence is denied a role consistent with its capabilities. The machine must, finally, play its part. To expect the human teacher alone, in contention with thirty or forty different minds always leaning in as many different directions, to succeed in harnessing the energies of every individual learner in some genuinely effective way in a twenty-first-century learning environment is patent nonsense.

Neither a lower pupil-teacher ratio nor an increase in the amount of raw data on the individual student available to teachers will make a difference. Only a system in which decisions of educational consequence for *that* individual can be made by an informed mechanical entity will signify a genuine breakthrough. Unfortunately, therefore, little of consequence in the way of real innovation is to be expected in the short term, given the laggard scientific interest in human learning problems, along with the traditions of educational technomanagement as well as its built-in position in the general economy. (In an era of global economic retrenchment, how other than negatively would the loss of hundreds of thousands of educators' jobs over a brief time-span, for example, impact developed societies?)

Thus it is only too easy to misread the role of technology in school instruction of the deeper future. Many people either dread or ridicule the emergence of machine aids to instruction; they make the false assumption that the learner will spend his time "talking" to a computer and end by being cut off from human interactions. This simplistic view seriously misinterprets the direction technology will take in the instructional arena. The future of educational technology involves machine intelligence working in the background primarily, but in a more powerful and independent way than is currently imagined.

What is lacking in every average classroom situation today, without exception, is a challenge not so much to the social conscience of the child as to his intellectual direction of interest. Too much about the lockstep classroom system is both banal and predictable. Indeed, its banality, produced through the unfortuitous combination of familiarity and outright didacticism, makes the whole routine over-predictable; such a routine then, with today's child, brings on early boredom and contempt—and a growing sense of the uselessness of it all. Everything else matters more; the process of formal learning, unchanged in its mode of delivery since Roman times, cannot compete in an external environment of myriad flashing visions focused on novelty, diversion without cease, and the thousand and one stimuli of escapism our advanced adult milieu of telecommunications provides.

In many respects the simple, repetitive routines of "school days, happy golden rule days" exercised certain beneficial effects on school learners, even through the early post-1945 era. A growth of self-assurance, a sense of being, if not happy, at least modestly satisfied with the regularity and seeming coherence of a learning environment confined to the traditional age-cohort-determined classroom could be claimed even for the average and below-average child (often the gifted one as well) until about the 1960s. But then the psychological backwash of a maladapting mass society, smothered in its own unexamined materialistic urges, took absolute root in the classroom. The power of individual mind to chart its own course unaided slipped a notch, first in the adult sphere, then inevitably in the child's also.

The mass medium became the self-anointed spokesman for this only half-comprehended social-psychological sea-change, and the unprepared child-mind was increasingly its victim. The outcome for the individual can best be summed up as a pervasive bias against systematic intellectual effort among the great majority. Since no fundamental change in the method of instruction was possible, the child psyche drew away ever further, with passing years, from both substance and form of standard instruction. The motivation of the mass of learners to perform "academic work" as traditionally defined and in the traditional format evaporated. The trend continues and accelerates with each new age-group and in all developed countries.

It is instructive to ponder Bronowski's dichotomy as a non-metaphysical explanation for the phenomenon of this progressively self-destructive "intellectual dropout" syndrome. The child's self, one may accurately say, responds to information buildup with only a fraction of the powers of discrimination already available to a competent adult mind. The difference lies in accumulation of experience. Freud's categories have simply formalized certain distinctions between the pure animal and "higher" motivations in all humans, and while a few otherwise normal people "may never really grow up," a basic difference grounded in greater experience exists de facto between one generation of men and its still-unformed successor on the variable of "intelligently crafted behavior." The human id arrives with birth; the ego and superego must be constructed.

The mechanical side of a human mind, like it or not, is guided by the non-mechanical self; the emotional self must commit itself to the use of its mechanical alter ego for action to take place. But the child-self has no experiential background of developed self-control, of power to restrain its own emotional drives. Our adult refusal to accept this fundamental condition of childhood for what it is may be understandable; but it does not reflect reality. With no agent of external control over this childish self and its direction of interest—over its very most basic patterns of attention and motivation—what can be expected other than a period of relative psychological chaos, however brief or prolonged in duration?

Thus control over the neophyte's environment must always matter. This control can never be taken for granted, at least in any formal educational sense. Some identifiable agency must provide, invariably, both the rationale for and the power of control. Men have accorded the state the role of control agent for formal education. But what forms of control have resulted, and with what results for instruction of the individual?

Enormous administrative and legal machinery has been set in motion to insure adherence to established norms of pro forma behavior. New and always more costly mass measures are sought to bring about desired results. Mandatory attendance laws provide the ultimate instance of this "enforcement" approach. But in all this a confusion between concepts of control and method persists. More than ever, the situation is what William Ernest Hocking described many years ago: "The assumption has been that the modern state can educate not alone the mental person but the volitional person as well. The state by itself can do neither."[7]

It would be better to admit that society, through its unwillingness to criticize what traditional leadership has prescribed over past decades and centuries, *has* (in however negative a sense) been the true agent of control in education. The problem is that a hands-off approach, which is what the uncritical acceptance of technocratic management clearly dictates, leads finally to wholesale stasis. This is where we are today. The modern state, acting on behalf of the social culture, imposes control only in a physical sense. It controls the child's body; but the child's mind is elsewhere. The essential issue of method—permitting a sufficient measure of process-control so as to enforce an adequate level of attention and maintenance of the individual's direction of interest—gets addressed in its technocratic context only: the individual self who is the unique child-learner remains ignored. All this could go on indefinitely into the future except for one thing—the unstoppable thrust of science and technology into the domain of human learning.

Advance or Retrogression in Method—Finding the Process Key

Poets and essayists employ a metaphor in which human life is compared to that of a moth circling a flaming candle: Self-realization is the organism's aim. But it exists within a web of conflicts, often potentially mortal. To venture too near the flame risks premature immolation. On the other hand, a retreat into the further darkness lessens expectation of self-realization, and hastens death equally. Somewhere there is an optimum point of vantage, a niche neither too high nor too low, neither too distant nor too close, where for a while self-realization seems possible. In pursuit of this niche the moth flutters, never quite finding the perfect location, yet in using its array of sensors time and again coming close.

The moth in some degree, clearly, operates on a basis of intelligent response to observed conditions. It seeks homeostasis, if not exactly self-realization, by interpreting information from without. It may even react in preeminently sensible ways to larger forces in its environment—wind, heat, the presence of other organisms. This is all characteristic of biological existence. Such a moth image is of course rife with imprecision. But man too must act in response to information as the price of adaptation. He must also deal with information not just passively, as an uninvolved observer; no process of learning to cope is automatic. The organism is obliged to *interpret* what is "out there"—and do so intelligently.

The unique environment of humans becomes at the same time more global and more demanding of individual intelligence. Doing involves consequences less and less to be taken for granted, either for the individual or the collective. A global society brings increased interdependence. What one unit does or does not do affects the welfare of all others. There is no alternative to intelligence applied by the individual—as he acts—with increasingly discreet thought. Yet of all living creatures, man (thanks to the very level of intelligence with which he is initially endowed) has the longest, most difficult road to travel in attaining optimum use of his power of thought. Technology brings us the artifacts which "mimic and exploit our own understanding," but it also allows us with ever-growing power to select the paths that understanding might follow. In the era of intelligent machines, how can we use this power to best advantage, especially for those in the first two decades of life—the critical period for development of intelligence?

The work of what for want of any better name we may call an AI instructional tutor will be of a consequential character, for the mechanical system which can be of real use in an instructional milieu will not have the function of a "learning toy." Rather its task will be that of "manager of the learning environment." This denouement will frighten more timid souls, tied as they have been to a tradition of process for its own sake. But machine direction of formal learning *for the individual* is as inevitable as any other major development of a high tech future.

The results can mean for the first time in history a genuine individualization for every student. This will be a more completely individualized instruction than ever before possible, yet not in the sense that a child does nothing but "talk" with a mechanical tutor. He may go for days and weeks without a one-on-one interaction with any machine. Rather, his program *in general* will be managed and monitored individually; he will be the beneficiary of what an advanced "thinking machine" can do by way of resolving *his* individual problems as a learner. The coming era will thus be one of instruction managed for the *individual*—and not (as now) for the group alone.

What will come about eventually, I believe, and only after much painful trial and error, is a combination of management of the individual's instruction by a mature artificial intelligence and an actual maximization of interaction among individual learners—as well as between learners and more experienced adults, either on site or through electronic media. The AI will come to "know" so much more than today's administrator or teacher about what is needed psychologically by the individual learner that it can expertly schedule both interactive and non-interactive experiences. This will in fact be possible for every learner, regardless of student numbers in a given environment. Once each learner has his own AI tutor-manager, the various AI units will be in continuous contact with one another and will share whatever information may be required to facilitate and optimize all interactions.

Nonetheless, there should be no mistaking the key issue here: the mechanical aid in question, while artificial, will also have to be intelligent. A computer and an artificial intelligence are two distinct and different entities. A computer is an artifact circumscribed by its lack of any genuine intellectual scope; it can be used for learning by drill or by inquiry, even for unfocused and intellectually stimulating play without a specific immediate goal; but it can never in and of itself determine what is of the most crucial importance: the conditions and needs of a specific individual human's learning environment.

One can state with confidence that no computer alone can "manage" a learner's instruction in any acceptable sense today. Nor is there any reason why even a machine which a clear majority in the scientific community would deem sufficiently "intelligent" for that purpose should be allowed to fill this role in the near-term future. The real question, and one which society itself alone can answer (and probably only well into the future of which we can yet see so little), is "just how intelligent" a machine will have to be to control from behind the scenes an individual learner's general program and progress.

Advocates for the computer in classroom instruction remain studiously silent on this whole issue. To them it is a non-issue, in fact, because they admit neither the seriously limited value of high tech as presently employed in instructional practice nor the growing unsuitability of the universal classroom method of instruction itself in the management of individual instruction. Professional optimists who conveniently ignore the mainline questions of instruction—how to manage the individual's sequence of instruction optimally and how to control sufficiently his environment for formal learning—must content themselves with songs of praise for current technological baubles: popular but unproven phenomena like the classroom PC for every learner, "distance learning" via satellite video courses, cable TV instruction (such as that provided in the US by Channel One or CNN Newsroom), and computer networks linking several schools.[8] But introduction of gadgetry ad nauseam without a clear concept of purpose remains a typical case of putting the educational cart before the horse.

Understandably progress with technology in school instruction is slow. How can it be otherwise? Science in this domain moves slowly, for one thing. For another, our contemporary social consciousness is simply not prepared for the drastic shift in cultural outlook the ultimate step to AI management of instruction will entail. We believe in the value, indeed the efficacy, of human interaction. And in good measure we should. Without question every child and youth ought to experience fruitful human contacts every day of his school life. The likelihood is that, by its ability to plan and manage instruction in advance, an AI tutor would enhance and fructify, rather than inhibit, the learner's social relations. Even so, the complaint that an AI management system will "mechanize" unduly the child's environment for learning, that it must necessarily dehumanize him and cut him off from his fellow learners, will nevertheless be voiced loudly—even with no advance indication that this must invariably be the case.

This is not, unfortunately, even the immediate practical issue, which is a related but still very different matter: whether or not a single overworked human manager, the classroom teacher, can continue, with some acceptable minimum of efficiency, to direct the learning programs of ever larger numbers of school learners who are also, alas, ever more unable or disinclined to pursue in systematic fashion school work as presently ordered. Today the system may still "work," in some sense of minimal effect, but will it be possible for us to go on making even this half-nugatory claim by, say, 2010 or 2020?

We cannot be complacent about the growing manpower problem in quality education. As a recent Brookings Institution study remarks, the number one problem even for the near term remains the growing shortage of enough human teachers who possess superior abilities for coping with the present system.[9] It is no exaggeration to say that the psychological and nervous-system demands teachers face in the majority of high schools, and even in many elementary ones, as a mounting psychological warfare between the uninitiated but also disaffected young and the established adult order runs its course, are truly overwhelming. This is not a problem limited to any one country or region of the world. Universally, the typical environment for instruction already demands more in the way of psychological skills and charismatic presence than the average teacher or candidate for a teaching position could possibly possess.

Not surprisingly, though, many of the same characteristics which eventually must be embodied in an AI manager-tutor are those possessed by the best teachers today: broad academic and general background in social and scientific areas of knowledge; possession of techniques for handling information with psychological expertness; a power of independent and objective judgment in creating a sequence of learning experiences; and above all the sense of and ability to communicate individual human values.

We will be told that none of these global characteristics can ever be "built into" the mental wiring of any machine. But this view assumes a condition of unlimited and permanent "noise" in human-to-machine communication processes—a questionable assumption, especially where the potential for comprehensive control of the individual's learning environment becomes more than ever technically possible. (Witness the relatively successful "holding power" exerted over children by present-day TV, despite its (for adults) mawkish and almost unfailingly tiresome content. And TV as a mass technology, it should also be stated emphatically, can use its "control powers" to destroy rather than build individual learning capacity—as has already been shown in studies which show an inverse relationship between TV watching and development of children as readers.)

The issues I am discussing here are not so much effects as symptoms. The increasing shortage of good human teachers and their inability to cope any longer with the straitjacket classroom milieu are results of a social catalepsis typical of a gridlock culture. As with government itself, caught in the vise of countervailing forces representing conflicting interests of society at large, democratic education becomes mired in inaction. Without supports in any consensual philosophy, the culture of egalitarian democracy moves forward through time with no orientation to what must come; it responds only to what has been, to the ineffable preference of people in the mass for repetition of past processes as the only bulwark against overly rapid change.

Still, no culture is as a matter of expressed intent maladaptive. All human culture is an effort by a congregate to adapt, successful in some ways, unsuccessful in others. Acceptance of change may be nonetheless often reflexively delayed, shut out of the collective consciousness, by cultural and institutional forces not yet capable of facing up to underlying realities. Eventually, though, the need for change must be faced. That such delayed change will then be doubly difficult to endure seems self-evident. This is more than likely to prove the case when at last a genuinely new pedagogical theory has generated the momentum needed to attract broad social interest. As early as the 1970s Jerome Bruner commented:

> Pedagogical theory…is not only technical but cultural, ideological, and political. If it is to have its impact, it must be self-consciously all of these. The technical task, indeed, is more formidable than ever we suspected, and we may now be operating close to the scale where we can begin to do the appropriate engineering to realize the implications of even utopian theories.[10]

In the competitive global society of tomorrow, the person's early years and what he does with them will count more meaningfully than ever in determining his life chances. It is implicit in the concept of mass democracy that "giving the individual the best education we can" should become more than just another piece of empty political verbiage. Even as the technical task, thanks to scientific advances, becomes progressively less formidable, society will still find itself up against the cultural, ideological, and political negatives of an information-drenched milieu whose effects cannot but reach with steadily increasing influence into the domain of school instruction. A look, however brief, at the range of disadvantageous options twenty-first-century instruction will face makes clear how exposed and open to ruin is tomorrow's learner—if, as now, he has no source of instructional direction available to him other than the traditional classroom system.

Individual and Group—The Continuing Contradictions of School Instruction

The need for a more specifically clinical approach to the individual learner and his problems already, as earlier mentioned, indicates the extent to which the *how* of instruction is undergoing an evolutionary modification. Any truly client-centered service remains a difficult concept to assimilate to the school classroom method, however: the client is an individual and only part of his group as an accident of birth, residence, and legal requirements. Within the barrier-ringed technocratic process, alternative and less expensive or system-threatening approaches must, in the nature of things, be given a chance to show how much (or how little) they can contribute to the child's progress as a learner.

What has not yet sunk into public thought in any country, and has not even in any degree penetrated the thinking of professionals, has been the extent to which even typically administrative or politically inspired programs for reform of instruction already bear within them the seeds of a radical individualization of method. This may even be seen in the proposed scheme for US schools called goal-based education. Here set objectives are laid down by states for hundreds of thousands of students pursuing certain courses of study. The general goal for each learner is the same, but a *different* pattern or sequence of instructional experiences—as a few sponsors of such programs themselves admit—will be needed to accommodate any single learner's unique needs and interests. Unimpressive as such occasional admissions may seem to us now, they are nonetheless straws in the wind; they speak to a future in which a more failure-proof instruction crafted to the individual child will have to be made available by the schools—with the help of science and technology.

In an unwitting acknowledgement of Information Age demands, we already in fact cater to individual learner needs for specialized instruction (with or without the use of advanced technology), when we employ any of the currently available innovative individual methods and/or more daring interactive arrangements permitted under existing rules of operation. A movement is afoot here, though as yet it is barely in its earliest stage of development and operates only on a small scale. In an evolutionary sense of educational progress, what is one to make of such phenomena as, for example, the Individual Education Program (IEP); the various CAI schemes that steadily expand the individualized components of personal instruction; cooperative group learning intermixing several grade levels (but with different yet predetermined goals for each participating member); promotions on a basis of contract performance alone; or the many other special schemes for individualization already in use in alternative schools and commercial tutoring firms catering to ambitious parents and their offspring?

Do these varied and also modestly innovative means for reaching the individual learner have promise? Certainly in the short run they do, if in judging them we admit that by their use the lockstep mass system can, in some individual cases, be bypassed to beneficial effect. But whether or not any of these schemes is of long-term usefulness—and whether or not it can be integrated meaningfully into a long-range future form of instruction based on socially acceptable principles—remains a far more open question.

Tinkering at the fringes of any process involving constant and direct human interactions should be considered in light of the ideal of a still admittedly nebulous Information Society, in which participation becomes increasingly more intellectual in character, even for the youngest members. To be sure, there are many as-yet untapped possibilities inherent in, say, the mixed-group principle or the concept of an IEP. These need to be reflected upon by concerned adults, but not without a sense of both historical experience and human limits.

Mixed-age interactions, as a case in point, are nothing new in classroom instruction. The monitorial system of the nineteenth century, through which older children were given instruction in some basic subject matter and then made to "teach" these lessons in turn to small groups of younger children, was hardly an unqualified success. Yet for the time, in early industrial England and America, it served a certain purpose. Monitorial schools, though a mere historical curiosity to us now, indeed "helped to show that class instruction could not only be reasonably efficient in handling large numbers of children but that discipline through rewards and social punishment could replace corporal punishment."[11]

In a similar way, today's concept of mixing children of different ages and backgrounds in the same learning group possesses certain pedagogic possibilities. The shifting-about of mixed-age or -grade groups provides one more means for avoiding the trap of boredom, which arises with ever-greater frequency and at ever-earlier ages with today's action-obsessed children. Too, the practice involves possible psychological advantages: Older students are at times more tractable and interested when (as the Monitorialists apparently understood instinctively) they take on roles they see as of a more leading character, and younger learners themselves may well relish some relief from the everyday boredom of always "the same faces and same room." But the pedagogic limits of such a practice should also be recognized.

A need exists in all cases to keep individual minds focused. At times this can best be achieved (as with mixed-age group work) in a shifting social milieu, at other times in a more routine class setting, and on yet other occasions (as the Kumon program seems so obviously to demonstrate) in a complete social vacuum. The logic of pedagogy involves a balance of social and individual experiences if learning is to be carried forward optimally. The first only too readily destroys the second. This danger indeed lurks behind the otherwise only too obvious allure of mixed-age and -grade grouping today.

Combinatorial mathematics allows us to estimate, for example, the extent to which such a practice could be carried even in a small population. In a non-graded community school serving, say, four hundred students, with thirty teachers and twenty available classrooms, the number of different groupings possible becomes literally an unimaginable set of contingencies.[12] It will be readily apparent that even over a span of several years' attendance for the ordinary student, daily or perhaps even hourly shifting of group makeup would turn into a sad joke for all concerned.

No student exposed to such a constantly fluctuating social milieu for instruction would be expected to prosper intellectually. Yet in saying this one cannot overlook another truth—the clear-cut capability which a computer management system able to delineate possibilities in such scope at the same time possesses: If the system can compute and specify details of this entire range of interaction combinations itself, then, with sufficient additional information for making qualitative judgments as to instructional effect, that system can also identify the few useful "real possibilities" for mixed-group makeup—and far better than human administrators and teachers operating within their traditionally separate technomanagerial compartments.

This example shows perhaps better than others one might choose how technology may serve contradictory purposes. It provides too much or misleading information just as easily as it provides information that is too little and thus equally misleading. It can guide toward good or evil. Technology affects mental life at every moment, yet its outcomes in society can only be measured after the fact. For this reason, the direction technology takes in the process of instruction must be to a maximum degree predetermined if education is to make sense in terms either of economics or of social justice.

For a culture pervaded by long-held concepts of individual freedom, free will, and rights of individual choice, this creates a grave problem of reaching consensus on educational purposes. For now, traditional forces of control dominate the uses of information technology in education—as in society at large. This is not simply a matter of the power-holders exercising an unhealthy dominance over uses of a vital universal commodity. It also comes from a failure of both producers and consumers to alter a shared mind-set: from one which asks only "What can the machine do?" to one which specifically demands "What can the machine do for the human individual?" That this mind-set cannot soon be eradicated—in fact, that it for the time being may become even more fixed among the many frustrated adults who can visualize no alternative—is evident to anyone carefully following trends in information technology.

The Coming Challenge—Gearing Instruction to Confront an Advancing Infoglut

Manufacturers of computer and communications equipment and software rightly foresee on the horizon of the new century a vast educational market for their products. These industries control a growing commerce of information creation and distribution. Information and its interpretation are already recognized by every alert adult as central to the twenty-first-century education enterprise. This is true not only in the developed nations but also in the populous Third World, whose persisting turmoils—without some amelioration of the massive ignorance existing there—will undoubtedly bring serious consequences to the world system as a whole.

Fortunately, both computer and communications industries recognize that, at base, they are engaged not simply in a hardware or sales contest but in a long-range teaching and learning project in which they have a vital role to play. Even profit for the business and its shareholders is no longer seen as the sole raison d'être of operation. Manufacturing and selling are recognized as having a social component. Like many education professionals, industrialists themselves acknowledge the great significance of education for humanity's future, agreeing with H. G. Wells' dictum that civilization has become a race between education and disaster.

All the same, evolution is not ordinarily a matter of sudden miracles. Catalytic development is far from automatic. Business has no choice other than to be primarily concerned with profitable market products, the creation and sale of technology useful to those with the heaviest information-processing needs. It is no surprise that until the recent advent of lower-cost PC technology, organizations, especially large ones, and not individuals, were the primary target of the information industries.

The seemingly remote question of school instruction *for the individual learner* has thus not yet really surfaced in the work of these industries. This is the case not only among hardware and software producers (and for probably both technical and cultural reasons). It holds true even more in the educational information development field itself (instructional materials; curriculum management; urban school curricula), where understandable prejudice against drastic change will persist regardless of the timing of arrival of new resources for individualization of instruction.

The true role of technology in an Information Age has yet to be acknowledged—and not solely by the industrialist or education professional: The political mentality, eager as it normally is to seize new opportunities for integrating emerging developments in science and technology into current policy, has also failed so far to grasp the slow but subtle drift towards a technology whose mandate is to fulfill primarily individual thinking needs. This gap in political thinking was clearly borne out by such reactions as those of the incoming US federal administration of 1993, in its blanket declarations of support for various Porter-type projects—educational multiuser visual interaction networks, multimedia, and the several emerging cinematic technologies for instruction. The short-term political gain in making such pronouncements may be considerable, but the long-term value of such technologies applied only in the context of standard technocratic management of instruction remains open to serious question.

What seems a politically expedient commitment may, in fact, fail ever more abjectly than have past so-called enrichment schemes in resolving that up-to-now most difficult of all pedagogical questions: How will these technologies be made use of in instruction of the individual? Clearly, with all the new computing and communications technologies pouring an increasing load of information upon the relatively defenseless child-mind, school will soon enough become an even less comfortable place than before for the average unmotivated learner. And the unmotivated will constitute an ever-growing majority. Infoglut is a disease with no ready cure, especially for the affected mental apparatus which is immature, impressionable, and already biased against any effort to participate in its own learning.

Whatever their ideologies or political preferences, hard-thinking adults know that a child who must live out his years in a twenty-first-century world will need in his formative years all the help he can get as a user and interpreter of information, for he will be dealing with little else in his later decades. And nothing can automatically "explain" it for him. The age of philosophy has passed without yielding up any algorithm that comprehends the world. To paraphrase Hegel, "What is rational is what is real"—and the reality is information, in quantity. The child too must coexist with this reality.

Education as a new millennium begins is caught in a quagmire of conflicting interests, mainly those of organizations, all shaped to control individual thought and behavior to some advantage, to identify, lead, and in various ways exploit the individual from an early age (and through the school if need be). These collectives' concern in formal education is only too often not so much cultivation of individual minds as it is that of governing *what* is taught—and *how* as well. The automatic acceptance of this as a normal state of affairs continues. But with the advent of ever-more-intelligent machines, this equation seems bound to shift. Could that shift occur too soon, arousing too much social ire and bringing the necessary experimental work to an untimely early end? Could it be too long delayed, making impossible the experimenter's vital role, as some new regime of cultural retrogression destroys public confidence? Socrates is no longer here to provide an opinion. We can only guess what his thoughts might be. But technology moves ever forward. Even the expectations that, for current lack of a technology, are impossible of fulfillment today become routine tomorrow.

AFTERWORD

In the Wake of Darwin: A Speculation on the 2000s

I return to the question with which this book began: Is American education different? In the short term and given surface characteristics, there seems undeniable evidence that across the developed world the industrial system has, relatively speaking, flourished with (or in spite of) measurable differences between major nations in modes of educational administration and philosophy. Yet it would be only too easy to overstate the importance of these variations and understate similarities of direction and process.

Democracy takes different forms in different societies; so too does the form of education provided. But resources become more constrained with increase of population and demand. Access is the critical factor in every system of formal education. As Freeman Butts said in the 1970s, "Where the egalitarian outlook begins to criticize highly selective institutions as closed preserves for an aristocratic elite, it also begins to push toward a more comprehensive institution freer of the stigma of inferiority on one side and the stigma of academic snobbery on the other."[1]

We speak today, almost automatically, of education as an instrument of "empowerment" of the individual. Empowerment for what? Over what or whom? The basic contradictions of Enlightenment philosophic thought remain unresolved, but we have nothing else as yet on which to go forward. The later philosophies of utilitarianism, Bergsonism, Existentialism, and pragmatism, like Eastern mysticism—none have given modern man a sense of his rightful place in an alien universe. As Robert Nisbet remarked of the century and a half before 1900, so might we one now say of the twentieth century: There has been a flow, in and out, of "new doctrines of nationalism and statism, along with utopianism and racism. In each of these we find power linked with the perspective of progress—always of course in the name of some kind of liberation, some kind of redemption or salvation on earth."[2] But for the individual, this release into power remains a myth, an illusion: He cannot escape the collective and its expectations.

Perhaps the Japanese have been the first to comprehend as a nation the true implications of this plight. They are taking advantage of it by first and foremost accepting it as *the* fact of collective life. Cooperation

189

brings power, nothing else. If the individual gains something in this process, well and good. But the process itself is what matters, for without cooperation from all the survival of any individual can no longer be guaranteed. This is the realpolitik of Japanese society. As American science writers Ed Feigenbaum and Pamela McCorduck explain:

> The Japanese talk to each other...(they) share one language—and that is meant in the metaphorical as well as the literal sense. Their cultural homogeneity is precious to them and is fostered actively by everything from the government to the mass media.[3]

If this constitutes empowerment of the individual pushed to its furthest rational limits, given the strength of Western traditions American and European culture can only resist. The homogenization of all humanity on the Japanese model would therefore seem, fortunately, to be still a long way off. However, as Japan's restrictive immigration policy and its approach to world politics and commerce in general demonstrate so well, this ethos can take on a highly effective racial and ultra-national character which grossly distorts the perceived function of anyone not "inside the system." Indeed the outsider exists, conceptually, only as an object of exploitation.

Yet it also must be admitted that *within* the Japanese system's confines, access to opportunity is universally available—albeit under a harsh condition. The rules of play are absolute: Empowerment comes to the individual solely as a consequence of his own effort, applied within the system nexus. This effort is ever more primarily intellectual in character, and as the well-known "examination hell" of the hyper-rationalized Japanese school system so clearly reveals, formalized competition between or among individuals largely determines whatever "empowerment" of individuals does in fact ensue.

Individual success in such a society, as in the other wealthy workshop societies of East Asia, comes to have only one meaning, that most concisely described by Max Weber for the last phase of his "iron cage" sequence: Those who must live their lives in this kind of system become "specialists without spirit, sensualists without heart; (yet) this nullity imagines that it has attained a level of civilization never before achieved."[4] If by the term civilization is meant an efficient, busy bee socioeconomic order and nothing more, then the Japanese model cannot be improved upon. But the net effect of any "civilization" in which the individual has no genuine role to play, in which mass and only mass matters, comes down simply to a case in which human thought has turned its back upon itself, helpless any longer to devise a means of progress in human terms. Albert Schweitzer put it thus:

> Our world will not get upon its feet again till it lets the truth come home to it that salvation is not to be found in active measures but in new ways of thinking. But new ways of thinking can arise only if a true and valuable conception of life casts its spell upon individuals.[5]

Nonetheless, it would be a grave error to dismiss the Japanese system as irrelevant to world development. Japanese education well prepares the individual for a fast-spreading nightmare adult culture of wholly rule-based competition; it is in fact itself the most loyal agent of that kind of culture now extant (and, understandably, to the evident discomfiture of Western liberal thinkers). Still, it is often said, such an education like the socioeconomic system it sustains, while suitable for Asians would never be tolerated by more individualistic cultures of the Western tradition, in particular the free-swinging Americans. Perhaps—and again, perhaps not.

Be this as it may, it is all too easy to lose sight of formal education's fundamental effects in the development of any society. No national system for educating the young fails to reflect in some degree the felt needs of its adult society. The questions most needing to be asked then should not be the wholly commonplace ones: "What are the differences between this and that national tradition of education which we can specifically pinpoint as influential in the course of national development? Which among these differences have given each national culture its distinct contemporary character?" Rather, our question should be a more future-oriented, "What are the common directions formal education will take in due time in all countries at a similar level of development—as part of a global process governed by universal evolution, and in which existing national traditions are only a reflection of natural idiosyncrasies of social experience of time and place?"

The Japanese model then provides as an obvious end-result something not all that much different from the American, though the human costs in what is achieved are indeed of a different order and magnitude. Both systems aspire to a socioeconomic utopia, while approaching their goal by somewhat opposite means. This common goal is best described as the balanced industrial state, an outcome made possible only when the driving forces of capitalism and egalitarian democracy jointly recognize that the nation's educational system and natural resource base are the essential limiting factors in the developmental process.

The nature of industrial success as a national goal, in short, and seen in hindsight, itself has dictated the different modes of development any national player would take (and hence in a high degree has also predetermined its educational needs). To understand this dynamic fully, one must go back to the vision that unites industrialism and utopia (itself of fairly recent vintage), and the conditions of development sustaining that concept. The widespread acceptance of the view that man in the mass would at last be both master and main beneficiary of the cornucopia of good things scientific research has been creating, especially since the late seventeenth century, traces to a single inexorable development: the advance of what H. G. Wells called the mechanical revolution.

An industrial revolution, Wells held, had been under way, with long start-stop periods since Roman days. Roman civilization, though, was built on a base of cheap, abundant manpower, largely enslaved. Modern civilization is built, instead, on cheap mechanical power. The distinction is important, though not always well recognized: Machine power, of whatever kind and however scientifically complex, is less expensive than manpower, and the human input, except where it reaches a level of sophistication or originality critical to socioeconomic well-being, ends as a glut on the market.[6]

Today at the millennium, indeed, the net effects of history and dwindling resources are catching up with everybody. Even Americans must compete and cooperate. They are hoist on the same petard as every other advanced national economic unit. This is clearly reflected in the predicament of those who would shift the balance of forces in school instruction to serve the learner as a person more effectively. It is no exaggeration to observe that the Americans are facing in even greater measure than others, and earlier, the universal problem described by Butts as "the ambivalence between achievement-oriented and learner-oriented pedagogy."[7] Like every other function in an integrated economic system, that of formal instruction and learning has for a long time been excessively focused on test scores and diplomas, ignoring the learner as an individual. Yet individuals who are apt at lifelong learning and have learned how to learn as children and youth, and the more of them the better, remain the basis of any successful industrial society. "Each of the Western nations has found this out in its own way, some sooner, some later," writes Butts.[8] There is, like it or not, clearly more ground to make up here for the rich than the not-so-rich.

But what Americans, like their Japanese counterparts, face is only the earliest thunderbolt in a great worldwide storm now brewing, and whose final resolution none can yet foresee. The old method is flawed, not because people want it to be but because it is. School instruction on the existing lines becomes for a majority of learners ever more a losing proposition, whether one looks at it from a cognitive, affective, or even solely moral point of view. If no mainline change in operations comes about in the interval, fifty years down the road the system—worldwide—will have been reduced to a mere shell of a process, to what in outline it has already revealed itself to be: a mechanism for exposing children to information in the most ineffectual and haphazard ways, doing nothing to lead them to the essential knowledge and development of self that is the only real business of education.

In this sense America's situation and educational prognosis and those of its seeming antithesis in Japan thus both resemble each other and emulate the situation and general outlook of the world at large, rather more than differing from them. And any North American who has visited schools in the less affluent districts of such cities as London or Paris will have recognized the aggravating similarities in learner mind-set and behavior between those settings and ours. The average and even above-average individual is no longer being reached intellectually (and all too often also morally) the world over. Below-average learners opt out quickly everywhere, headed, and all too hurriedly and prematurely, for the back streets of adult life. In sheer numerical terms at least, failure of mass education slowly but surely overtakes every national society. The process and its forms remain intact; the substance is lost. Though we realize this is in the longer term an impossibility, institutional education seems the latest universal concept condemned to certain death in the turmoil of a mass global civilization.

***   ***   ***

It may then with some accuracy be stated that, in the domain of school instruction one sees in microcosm the struggle of mankind at large to adapt to an alien universe. Alien, because it demands learning as the price of survival, and learning must keep up with the times. Since primitive days it has been consciously recognized that if the process of self-instruction is too slow, too haphazard, then assistance to the learner must be provided. What has *not* been achieved in this effort can hardly be ignored in the happier task of tallying up what has in fact been achieved. Though man would be nothing without the gift of education over the centuries, he cannot make do today and tomorrow with what was already yesterday insufficient. The negative trends, viewed historically, are increasingly and universally evident.

Those who lament the disappearance of old-style discipline have a point, for example, though its full implications may elude them. A school *is* a center for discipline. This is its fundamental raison d'etre. But discipline of what kind? The reality of school and the discipline it imposes today are of a particular character: We prattle about the school encouraging individual self-discipline, yet experience tells us that school involves first and last an *institutional* discipline, in which hierarchy and physical constraint come before everything else, in which any more liberal historical rationale for establishment of *that* building in *that* community has long since been superseded by a legally mandated confinement rationale—a system whereby social discipline and oversight of bodily activity take on a more and more exclusively supervisory and surveillance character. The key guideline is that of fail-safe central control; this demands above all a power of observation by authority of everything that transpires in a physical sense. Other concerns are secondary. Contemporary French writer Michel Foucault has described how even architecture must be considered in providing such militarization of control:

> The perfect disciplinary apparatus would make it possible for a single gaze to see everything constantly. A central point would be both the source of light illuminating everything and a locus of convergence for everything that must be known: a perfect eye that nothing would escape and a center toward which all gazes would be turned.... The perpetual penalty that traverses all points and supervises every instant in the disciplinary institutions compares, differentiates, hierarchizes, homogenizes, excludes. In short, it normalizes.[9]

Successive generations of children and youth in even the developed nations, raised on TV with its obsessive concern for the commonalities of culture, thus find what meaning life can give not behind school walls and the closed doors of school classrooms, but on the streets. As they experience it, school simply inhibits the search for other-directed pleasures for a given number of hours over a period of days and weeks in the year—all for reasons unknown, but which have been determined by adult society. The basis for this strange state of affairs is some abstract desire to induce uniformities of behavior among the young to match those required of mature adults. The prison metaphor thus becomes increasingly less far-fetched from the learner's point of view. What school instruction could be, what it will in time have to be, is well understood—at this point of time—neither by those who must attend nor by those who demand attendance.

We see in fact in the continuing emergence of new mechanical systems which enhance control of human activities the growing ineffectuality of cultural means alone for guiding behavior. Development of surveillance technologies for adult-world use by institutions and organizations has moved forward rapidly in recent years; to safeguard valuable property or information, the human functionary, a traditional security guard or alert clerk or doorman, can no longer be depended on singlehandedly to contain the aquisitiveness or hostility of a myriad of anti-social, mainly young adult individuals. All activity of the client, inmate, recruit, visitor, or whatever else one must label the individual caught up in the network of behavioral constraints, is now comprehensively monitored by hidden cameras, wiretaps, electric eyes, encoding mechanisms, a host of devices for centralized oversight. But the very rapidity of advance of this trend to automatism of surveillance of adult behavior yields an insight into what has come before in the individual's earlier life—into that blind alley down which failure of our pre-adult educational measures itself leads.

In adult society this automated surveillance has become an accepted phenomenon of existence. Small mechanical "brains" are the guardians of an entire spectrum of the socioeconomic order. Everyone complains about the invasiveness involved, but all are well aware of the practical necessity for it. Knowledge of the presence of these mechanical "guardians" restrains even the non-criminal person's irrational anti-system urges, and in probably uncounted instances. No one at this point can say how, or even *if*, an adult society in late-industrial times could function adequately without these useful machines of control.

Over the generations this approach to maintenance of order in the adult environment has taken ever surer hold in the educator's psyche, too, despite (and as much as anything confirmed by) increasingly strident pronunciamentos from the education establishment claiming exactly the opposite. Today's inner-city schools, with their high wire fences and metal detectors, their costly hired policemen or administrators wielding baseball bats to maintain order, serve as signposts of the educational future. In the only existing social institution where a future adult's character could be formed free of the shadow of an encroaching "prison mentality," this attitude of those in charge becomes instead security-conscious to a fault—and, as might be expected, at the same time ever more educationally negative. Should it be wondered at that no one can see a clear road forward—either for pedagogical science itself, or for the optimum use of technology in school instruction?

If there were any clear alternative to the present system of mass formal schooling, society might exercise its rights of choice. But the matter is hardly that simple. Time and further scientific advance are needed for the evolutionary crux of the matter—and true options for choice—to become sufficiently clear. But instructional method will never again be reducible for future learners solely to a supposedly complete-in-itself process of transmitting, as basic knowledge, something that, however widely accepted it may be as valid "cultural knowledge," yet remains by rules of the game still presentable *only* in a single, largely unworkable group format.

Even if for, say, two or perhaps three decades more, technologies of potential use specifically for management of individual instruction seem to progress only at half speed, there will still come into being over those same decades and the ones beyond a continuously growing availability of computer and communications technologies in the service of individual users. As a consequence, a plethora of purely technical resources for a wholly individualized instruction will, in the fullness of time, be available in schools—and to parents and homes as well. This new pattern of possibilities can only serve to alter attitudes of both learners and adult public towards the instructional process, and regardless of the persistence of a general ignorance of matters educational. But since there will then be a real choice to make, how will its terms be put?

Some limits must apply. Man cannot abandon the common school, even if every child were to have available to him at home the full range of tools for a managed program of individualized instruction. Sociality is never so important as in childhood, as a century of primate research with deprivation subjects has made abundantly clear. No child is a loner by or of his own volition, nor wishes to be. Childhood is a time for cooperation par excellence, and not solely with those family adults upon whom an average child comes primarily to depend. Piaget rightly speaks of an organic solidarity in child society itself, which takes on a less egocentric and a clearer moral tone as the children age.[10]

Nor can home as a sole source of childhood socialization ever replace school for a variety of reasons, some eminently and obviously practical. The quirkish habit of some parents who insist on teaching their children at home will always remain a rarity, for interaction with real age-mates remains a sine qua non of full personal development. Denial of this social opportunity for the child strikes at the fundamental concept of adult democratic society itself—as a body of interacting, equally capable minds. But if a different type of instructional management *in school* can enhance, rather than inhibit, the genuine impulse of childhood sociality, can it be forever resisted?

Society will be faced, finally, with a choice evolutionary in both its scope and its dangers. A persistently growing, indeed already universal democratic ethos demands opportunity for all on an equal basis. Taking the term in its broadest sense, opportunity in every individual's life begins, as I have sought to make clear, and historically especially in the past two-plus centuries of modern mass industrial life, with the individual's formal education—or lack thereof. A handful of autodidacts, the Eric Hoffers of today or yesterday, are the exceptions proving the rule. Formal education increasingly provides the only route for achievement of any given individual's ambitions, however narrow they turn out to be.

There can also be no evading the energizing force of technology in creating substantive change in society and in moving its processes forward. Man cannot escape his history, but neither can he escape evolution, and in the human context the products of both history and evolution are increasingly attributes of the dynamism of science and technology. At this point man is then caught in a web of pressures which place ever greater demands on his individual intelligence as the tool of species adaptation. Technology offers him the needed extensions of his natural endowment of intelligence. How this technology is to be used, what its consensual rationale will be—these are the salient questions for tomorrow.

On at least a technical level, a level of potentiality (though not of concrete realization), technologies of communication and information control push the human world ever more steadily toward a stage of development called by Father Teilhard de Chardin the level of "super-organization." Because super-organization will make man more personalized and human, Father Teilhard reasoned, the "very fact of our becoming aware of this profound ordering of things will enable human collectivisation to pass beyond the *enforced* phase, where it now is, into the *free* phase...in which a natural union of affinity and sympathy will supersede the forces of compulsion."[11] But what, it may be asked, must man himself do to reach this new, higher plane in the evolution of his species?

***   ***   ***

If technology is the one constant in a world scene otherwise dominated by unpredictable change, then why, it will still be asked, and in a serious study of education, dwell on a concept of artificial mind as *the* future facilitator of instruction? And why, to compound the felony, link it so unequivocally to the further concept of Socratic method? Yet worse, why depict an AI agent of individual instruction not as another mere "aid" but as a "manager," an entity preempting what have been sacred human functions for millennia? And beyond all this, why give the appearance of promoting something that almost seems a science fiction adventure out of what, after all, remains a profoundly human problem—one with only an essentially human solution?

The only response to these seemingly intractable riddles would seem to lie in the underlying nature of the Socratic approach to man and knowledge, and its continued relevance. Socrates refused to accept that knowledge (or virtue) was directly teachable. The teacher's role, to Socrates, was not to instruct directly, on the premise that through mere exposure to the information of instruction a learner must automatically improve and gain virtue. Learning instead, he believed, was an inner occupation, dependent on the condition of mind of the learner himself. The learner, not someone else, must "take hold of his own mind" before learning can occur. As educational historian Henry Perkinson has expressed it, in the Socratic mode "all that a teacher can do is to help a student become aware of his errors, his mistakes, his limitations. It is up to the student to bring about the improvement."[12]

Whether or not he pondered the question of teaching method, with this line of reasoning Socrates was driving to the heart of the economics of instruction: There is no point in carrying on the process if no change in the learner's thinking is brought about. The learner must be able, as an individual, to concentrate, to confront abstraction, yet at the same time never lose sight of who he is and the value to himself of the stimuli presented. Once his sense either of his own individuality or of those stimuli ceases to have value in his eyes, the cause of instruction in his case is lost.

The psychological conditions for formal learning are at base, then, quite immutable. While his imagination must be challenged, the child cannot in fact succeed as a learner when persistently dreaming of non-contextual pursuits; he cannot exclude wholly those matters of thought placed before him in the instructional sequence—if he is to succeed in learning. All this is implicit in the Socratic principle. Can Socratic management then really make a difference? Without experiment nothing will be known. We are in fact likely to go on for several decades more, traversing an orbit of circular reasoning in which we are unable, or unwilling, to face up to the evolutionary demands the future will place on human intelligence.

Yet the question of how our increasingly ineffective system of non-Socratic mass management of instruction could be changed to provide a more effective Socratic management of individual instruction is hardly as remote from present-day realities as we might think. Industrial society is undergoing a new, more swiftly moving phase of the mechanical revolution—one in which microintelligence as a comprehensive process-manager succeeds machines intended for heavy lifting alone as the dominant element in socioeconomic development. And the time-scale shortens.

Even in the lower tech world of a few decades ago, it would have been absurd to call for experiment with a Socratic method for individual instructional management, using what was then at hand in technology—an obviously unsophisticated device like the teaching machine. The dedicated mechanical mind whose task it will be to direct and manage future individualized Socratic instruction was not so much unimaginable as plainly far out of reach in the *Weltanschauung* of that time. Today, as a new century begins, by contrast, we already inhabit a shadowy, uncertain realm of alternative modes of intelligence. Not many people—even informed observers, inclined by nature to write off the wild claims of futurists, or of industry insiders who readily see in current technology powers of mind akin to those of its human analog—are really sure of what artificial intelligence *can* do, though all agree its development is rapidly going forward.

As tomorrow's high tech world slowly but surely takes on a more discernable shape, the distinction between Socratic and traditional methods for managing instruction becomes increasingly meaningful. Soon enough we may expect, however belatedly, to hear calls for "more focused" experiment to "get at" the individual learner. But even then will those who demand action still have the old purposes in mind? Will they be willing to engage with the new, essentially moral challenge advanced technology brings in its train? And of most importance, will they find a way to reduce the vagueness of theory to a praxis which can in fact make a difference for every individual learner?

Between theory and practice the gap remains wide. As a case in point, seemingly already taking shape around us is a universal system of mind-to-mind communication. How can this radical departure from the conditions of personal communication through all of history become or be made of genuine use to the individual school learners? One must first ponder a deeper question: In what way does such a system derive from any philosophical theory? Perhaps it represents no more than science, as usual, following paths of least resistance and accomplishing something men must thereafter live with in spite of themselves. It has no pertinence for the immature learner—without still other products of science to help him along the way.

Seeing the philosophic reality in the physical realities surrounding us is not a simple matter in any event. Father Teilhard's global communications constructs (super-organization; enforced phase; free phase), for example, however accurate as metaphors or philosophical constructs for identifiable stages of human social evolution, nevertheless still lack any concrete reference in the microprocesses of daily life. They are examples of what Poincaré termed the "necessary preconceived ideas" out of which scientific certainty can develop (and that certainty then turned into technological reality); but in Teilhard's idealized formulation they do not yet form a system which could in any way be mirrored in the facts of practical use. AI as a manager of individual instruction *could* clearly make the difference here, in determining a learner's optimum mode of use for on-line communication. Yet it too remains in a conceptual stage, a potential Socratic "electronic midwife of the mind" but no more.

Individual learning all the same depends as much now as in Socrates' time on instruction that develops the person's powers of intelligent thought, heightens the value of his experience, and allows him to interact with a measurable degree of success with the world—a world now already more difficult to confront or understand (even at the immediate local level) than it was a mere decade or two ago. So that forever nagging question remains: How *is* a childish intelligence, a mind in formation rather than an intact adult entity, a being without experience or any real sense of self as distinct from, yet always a part of, the culture which surrounds him, to be instructed in an optimum manner?

The role of technology is inescapable. Technology in the modern world has a presence which, for better or worse, already shapes every individual's personality, and beginning with childhood. We can on one hand think of a human neophyte as a Bronowskian combination, a self and a machine functioning in tandem, a unique human system, which must be tuned finely for character development—to achieve perhaps the classical synthesis (a sound mind in a sound body). On the other we can use some less positivist, more commonplace psychological schema (e.g., the Freudian categories, in which the balancing agent of an individual ego must regulate the excesses of a volatile id and superego). Whatever our theory of human development, it must recognize childhood as the critical period for formation of what will become standard adult patterns of learning and response: However much a nature-nurtue controversy still rages, the adult person becomes, in increasing measure, a product of his early experiences. And today's child's environment is primarily one of character-forming mass-information flows.

This overwhelming truth of our times is almost too obvious. We find it difficult to absorb its full implications. It is painful to imagine ourselves in the youthful learner's situation. Even so, some aspects of that situation we cannot force from consciousness, if only as a matter of empathy. Traditional societies, with their slower-functioning information networks, could never have subjected the young to such conflicting pressures as they face today from a myriad of well-organized, behavior-demanding information purveyors. For today's unformed child intellect, there is a daunting necessity to confront, relatively unaided, an ever-present information stream against which there can be few genetically invoked psychological defenses, and against which accumulated experience cannot yet be employed to advantage. Formal education must subsist, willy nilly, in the same culture with these pressures. Education's proper role in the cycle of human development and the *how* of an optimum method for individual instruction are therefore matters more than ever open to question. Nor is the problem limited to industrially developed nations or cultures.

The excesses of contemporary fundamentalist movements around the world remind us all too often that the "ideals" of a hyper-traditional, anti-modern way of life are still a force to be reckoned with. Many political regimes even today completely deny the new, freer role of information in mass life; they require total adherence to their behavior-restricting doctrines, on pain of excommunication or worse. Mind control, on which such movements depend, is an ugly term, with its distinctly Orwellian connotations; yet its presence in history has never been as limited as we may think: All history's religious wars come down to a conflict of absolute doctrinal values as between one cult and another. And in practical terms, political movements in industrial countries, especially in the twentieth century, have been just as committed to such means.

Older people today readily recall the era of ideological extremism and its political propaganda enforced at gunpoint, its Gulags and torture chambers. Yet we easily forget the extent to which children were as much targets as adults. The *Hitlerjugend* or Stalinist creche and Young Pioneers were schemes that in retrospect inspire only our after-the-fact repugnance. We are justifiably revulsed by such deliberate efforts to subject children en masse to radically totalitarian systems of thought and behavior control. Looking back, indeed, such mass-mind-forming campaigns of the twentieth century's fascists and Communists now seem altogether too heavy-handed and simple-minded ever to have been taken seriously. But they were. As case studies in history they demonstrate a simple truth: that mass societies of any kind, totalitarian or otherwise, can destroy human individuality by breaking individual habits of thought-taking early enough in the life cycle. That a similar denouement can be prevented any more tomorrow than yesterday, democratic traditions notwithstanding, without education of a distinctively person-oriented nature, seems an excessive leap of faith.

All this should therefore provide ample warning of the dangers, as well as the promise, of any system of technologically managed "individualized" instruction in schools. Compared to the low tech but distinctly high pressure methods of fascism or Communism, in the wrong hands such a system could also eventually (though rather by more subtle means) enslave youthful minds in an equal degree. How this outcome can be avoided, and how the common school itself can be rescued, worldwide, from sliding steadily further down the present slope of inutility (from which there seems to be, under the current technomanagerial dispensation, no possible path of escape) constitutes a challenge of profound scope.

In the development of AI and of a variety of more advanced communications systems, scientists and technologists are moving resolutely, even if not swiftly, towards significant new breakthroughs. But they too are haunted by questions of the same kind that bother the man on the street: Again, on what human basis do we apply the emerging technology? From what theories do we create experiment? From what point in time and in the course of our political development do we *consciously* begin this new evolutionary cycle? It is appropriate to return here to a concern earlier expressed in this book but not fully elaborated: We must briefly complete our examination of the shadowy character of Socrates, and not so much the philosopher so lightheartedly parodied by Aristophanes in *The Clouds* as the teacher, whose method and its implications for us today, and for twenty-first-century technology—indeed for twenty-first-century humanity as well—have not yet been fully explored.

***　　***　　***

Socrates the philosopher, as presented to us by Plato, stands for certain core principles. These most later philosophers have found it necessary, thanks to their central place in philosophic thought, either to confirm or reject: Socrates held knowledge, or the objective search for it, rather than blind action alone, to be superior. Knowledge as well, he claimed, has always an ethical basis. Knowledge is, when attained, in fact, the equivalent of virtue, and thought to this end is clearest and knowledge surest when the "barriers" of sense perception play no part in the acquisition process. These are not easy topics, even for the professional philosopher. They raise questions for which simple answers really do not exist. Yet fortunately, they are not vital to the understanding of Socratic *method.*

For a comprehension of Socrates the teacher, we find ourselves on firmer ground. The dialogues offer a revealing picture of how the sage went about his business. Oddly, the wide-ranging discussions he seems to have led often end with no conclusion reached—in itself a key to his method. Socrates did not "instruct" directly, this seems apparent. His role was, and by his own admission, to act as "midwife"—for the birth of counter-thoughts and new ideas, for further self-examination by the participant, and in the search for tenable definitions of such generalities as justice or truth. In his role as teacher he acted not invariably or even primarily as a philosopher, but by serving as what we today would describe as an objective and ethical guide. This kind of role has strategic pedagogic advantages; in the instructional discourse it allows a relative separation of all parties from the realm of the obvious, of what is immediately to hand, of the minutiae of one's culture as be-all and end-all of learning; it encourages and even demands an exercise of "wider thought" in the individual participant's response—and in this respect it carries over dramatically into our own age of evolving AI instructional management.

AI-managed instruction will come to do a better job, it now seems self-evident, precisely because it carries a smaller load of human cultural baggage. It will represent not only the Socrates who pioneered dialectic reasoning and theorized on the just state; it will also represent the practical man of independent mind who accepted society and culture, was in and of it and yet was somehow "different," listening to his "voices," performing the functions of a gadfly rather than those of a citizen in any accepted sense. It asks for the extraordinary in thought and response, in place of the ordinary, an ever-available purveyor of universal thoughts as against a mere sophist or drillmaster. (As Socrates stated at his trial: "...if anyone desires to hear me speaking and doing my business, whether he be young or old, I have never grudged it to any.... I offer myself both to rich and poor for questioning, and if a man likes, he may hear what I say and answer."[13])

In our age of mass-managed information flows, what Socrates aimed at is thus difficult for the ordinary citizen to appreciate. Who needs or wants the assistance of a gadfly, at least on a continuous basis? We are used to "the world as it is," even when that world is rapidly changing. Whatever clues are needed for what we should think and do, we believe, are always right there in front of us. Yielding to old, culturally ingrained patterns, we find our leads to action in "established" information sources. Typically, we see no need for assistance in comprehending the world, because we are so constantly told we do *not* need it, and we find the argument credible. Yet all this illogically contradicts a future in which ever newer and more onerous information-processing burdens will inevitably be placed on individual mind—and, if formal school learning continues as now, will depend for their resolution on the experience of not much more than a randomly effective self-help process through age eighteen or so, a process which can only leave the supposed adult mind in a tragically underdeveloped state.

It cannot be denied, in any event, that there is a revolutionary aspect in any scheme of "machine assistance" for carrying out critical human processes. Success in the Industrial Revolution has demonstrated this principle at work in society at large over several centuries. The term revolution is thus well chosen. But the *mechanical* revolution drives the whole trend one giant step further. It does not stop with the broadly social and economic effects of cheap power and increasingly self-driven, self-regulating machines. It now brings the machine, in microminiaturized form, to the exclusive service of an individual human acting solely on his own initiative—but in need of "informed assistance" at levels which, logically, can extend from that of the pocket calculator at a lower limit to that of the AI manager of an individual learner's instruction at a higher.

At a certain point on the spectrum of intelligence, then, a machine comes into existence with powers of information-assessment rivaling those of a mature human being. Such a truly intelligent machine of course is an assistant like none other before known. A sharer of our human niche in the domain of intelligence, it will like us primarily interpret information at high rates of speed. But (also like us as individual intelligences) it will tend to act on its own in making decisions. In assisting a learner, it will (like Socrates) make him "take hold of his own mind." Thus a genuine AI Socratic manager without question has the attributes of a gadfly: It would replace hierarchic control of instruction with individual control—that of the intelligent machine acting on its own initiative. In its appointed role, such an intelligence would also have, literally, no financial or economic ax to grind; it would be neither "anti-culture" nor "pro-culture." Its stance would be rather that of a neutral. Are men yet ready for such a momentous turn of events?

It is then this stubborn fact of "machine objectivity" which poses such vast difficulties. The intelligent machine has no ambition, other than to fulfill the mission assigned to it. It aspires to no possession of worldly goods, demands no lifestyle. It is content with "speaking" and "doing its business." Indeed, in all this it puts us in mind of nothing so much as the Socrates who is known on occasion to have remarked, "There are so many things of which I have no need." How strangely remote, indeed, yet also how appropriate to the times, does such a statement seem when heard again in our day!

So it is that Socrates, this twenty-three-century-old phantom being, who out of what seems nothing less than evolutionary necessity itself, comes to symbolize two vital and continuing strands in the human learning cycle: On one hand the continuing force and power of individual mind; on the other, the logic of informed opposition to blind worship of culture as source of all certainty and wisdom. As Allan Bloom has expressed it, "one should never forget that Socrates was not a professor, that he was put to death, and that the love of wisdom survived, partly because of his *individual* example."[14]

Socrates' importance to education has therefore deep but largely unrecognized historical roots. His contribution is to have understood the absolute significance of individual mind in both the learning and teaching processes. That this was part and parcel of the ethos of his age may be readily admitted. But it cannot diminish the originality of his legacy. If the AI instructional manager of tomorrow has any identifiable historic ancestor, that person must be Socrates—the gadfly who, living before books, newspapers, broadcasting networks, or any centrally controlled media, acted as critic to whoever sought him out, gave spirit to the Greek search for learning, for the means of distinguishing in all things truth from falsehood, right from wrong, good from bad.

***   ***   ***

Perhaps the concept of a Socratic AI as the remarkable catalyst it will eventually be can be properly understood only if seen within the context of world history itself. The era of Greek city-states, to be sure, stands out in recorded history as exceptional, not solely for its experiments with political democracy, but for its practicing acceptance of the individual. We easily forget the extent to which both earlier and later history is a lopsided affair from the point of view of ordinary individuals living it. World history begins with mere tribes, true, but all too early these become social juggernauts. The successive appearance of massive empires soon becomes the norm, and as history continues, remains so. Nor have most national states, from then until now, been in any consistent sense *democratic* societies.[15]

Until the late eighteenth century, in fact, human history reads as little more than a succession of largely despotic social pyramids, governments of the powerful, by which the individual was progressively reduced to an exploitable unit and little more. Thus the phenomenon of Socratic pedagogy was like the brief flash of a brilliant and prophetic comet across an historical sky otherwise darkened by successive overlapping oligarchies—with their insistence on conformity in matters both behavioral and intellectual. Plato himself surrendered to the conception of a rigid class society, in so doing vitiating the very Socratic ideal of the self-motivated individual he had embraced as Socrates' pupil.

While Plato had (in Dewey's words) a clear comprehension of "the function of education in discovering and developing personal capacities, and training them so that they would connect with the activities of others,"[16] at the same time he espoused a highly anti-democratic society: Plato's solution was the regime of philosopher-kings (which, with or without good reason, he has originate with Socrates—in Book III of *The Republic*). But over the long term history has moved in essentially another direction, recognizing the inadequacy of a division of mankind into three discrete classes (workers; soldiers; philosophers), each performing largely unrelated tasks. For better or worse, this historical rejection of philosopher-kings has been made possible, not so much by the freeing-up of democratic sentiments among the masses, as by the development of technologies which allow the individual a measure of self-determination not otherwise available—a means of holding at arm's length the vast organizational systems that would otherwise more freely exploit him.

Today, however, this same advancing technology also places man at the edge of a new abyss, the crossing of which will require critical and conscious (indeed, mass-conscious) decisions, not solely regarding the activities of organizations and uses or abuses of organizational power, but also about the role of intelligent mind in the processes of society itself. The post-Soviet world may seem unified behind what is thought to be a common democratic ideology, but it lacks both the common

ethos and the concrete institutional framework that held older major
civilizations together. Organizational arrangements effective in the
past are today losing ground, while definitive new modes for
organization of human energies have yet to appear. Political, religious,
and even long-established commercial systems continue to be gradually
undermined by innumerable fragmented and shifting smaller
constituencies, which reveal in their very fragmentation and
transitoriness the changing patterns of thought of individuals
comprising them. The pressures of a global Information Society, in
short, now threaten every existing "empire," and by the same token and
simultaneously the old formulas, the "absolute" hierarchical model.

Free exercise of informed individual intelligence cannot any longer
be downgraded if an industrial society expects to maintain itself and in
some sense to thrive. Rather is the opposite true. On this point the
evidence of history provides a formidable argument: Not one historical
kingdom or imperial regime (whether European, Middle Eastern,
Oriental, or Mesoamerican) found it possible to endure for long in a
literate but still totalitarian form once it had reached its evolutionary
peak; from the pre-Christian Jewish state to the British Empire of only
yesterday, as soon as any such regime began to commit the masses to
systematic formal learning, it found itself progressively less and less
able to fall back on collective initiatives to maintain its grip. In our
own era, the similar fate of modern totalitarianisms like Fascism and
Leninist Communism, even with all their far more refined means for
destroying the individual spirit, again demonstrated the same
fundamental principle at work: A purely ideological framework cannot
survive the rigors of an education sufficient to free the person from his
shackles of cultural ignorance.

Education, indeed, is a term without meaning apart from the
individual person and his development as a rational being. We may
have many forms of training. We may force upon older youth and even
upon mature adults training exercises in which we employ the same
rote and repetitive methods traditionally used with small
children—perhaps even with some success. Yet while training and
education are both needed, they are never one and the same. Training,
reaching only the "machine side" of the individual learner, is of
severely limited pedagogical use. We are wrong to suppose that we
educate solely for the purpose of inculcating performance skills,
regardless of their cash value. By letting education, like everything
else, be swamped in what Santayana rightly called "the horrors of

materialistic democracy," we destroy its foundation in human reason—the person both able and willing actually to think for himself.

Technology alone nevertheless cannot be the sole answer in education any more than in training. But this negative hardly outweighs its multiple positives: As it pushes man the learner toward a more consistently individual and less culturally preprogrammed thinking process, technology becomes inseparably linked to progress in instructional development. And this fact, fortunately, while it often exacerbates instructional problems, demands broad social attention and action, and sooner rather than later. The issue of who or what provides an effective instructional AI with its reasons for decision-taking—its original sources of cognition—has to be faced. Human culture *must* decide.

A deliberate but necessary gamble, and on a global scale, is involved here: If a machine which can think is to become the catalyst for a more effective instruction, what real basis will it have for its thoughts? If in fact an independent intellect, to what or whom will it be held accountable, as indeed it must be? What aims will it have for those humans to whom it must be of service? These are the difficult questions, the fundamental issues of formal education, which twenty-first-century man will unavoidably confront.

In outlining his laws of robotics, science fiction writer Isaac Azimov asserted that no artificial intelligence should ever do harm (or even be permitted to have harm done) to a human. On a longer-range view, this seems a rather negative approach to the problem. Should we not be asking instead: What will an AI always and under all circumstances do to *advance* the adaptive powers of the human? But this line of thought, it is true, only opens the door even more widely to the problem of final responsibility: Once an AI reaches this level of competence, it must operate not only to optimize cognitive outcomes but to achieve the inculcation of greater moral understanding as well. In that case from what source then does its own understanding of moral principles come? Do these reside in social and historical man or in some identifiable individual mind? In information the AI has been literally "fed", or in what conclusions it has itself reached in the course of its own reasoning processes?

This conundrum is not likely to be quickly resolved. One cannot speak of any immediately available alternatives for school instruction, at least while both social culture and developing technologies of mind remain at their present levels. But the twenty-first century promises a radical foreshortening of development time, for both technology and social consciousness. It will see if not sooner, then later, a necessary shift of forces, a converging of technological development with by-then self-evident social needs—beginning with a growing recognition of developed individual intelligence as the basis of species survival.

The combination of machine intelligence with Socratic method as the foundation for school instruction may for a long time provide no perfect solution. But as experiment should progressively demonstrate, it will come far nearer than any other to doing so. Why? Because it alone drives toward the Socratic ideal of both an objective tutor and a willing learner, a learner who, however reluctantly to begin with, in time gives himself over wholeheartedly to the cause of truth. Even today, objections to this approach are based far more on wishful thinking than on realities of the situation: Once Socrates' rational individualism and its modern machine incarnation are in fact rejected, then what conceivable practical alternative for optimum intellectual development do we have?

Machine intelligence, indeed, moves forward with an inevitable momentum all its own. The mechanical revolution seems now, in hindsight, to have been leading, almost as if supremely fated, to this one end-point—the so-called "thinking machine." Science continues building ever more efficient models (though none as yet comparable in overall scope to the human machine). Still, so far we find no real place for them in education—in great part because we are afraid of the unforeseeable consequences of their use. Social and management prejudices are without question a major inhibiting element. We are left with a temporary backwardness in the development of our pedagogy. But can a demonstrated inefficiency of process remain the basis of policy in an ever more intelligence-demanding world of tomorrow?

Surely the element of threat from thinking machines in instruction has been overreacted to. It may be human nature to pinpoint this or that technology as a convenient scapegoat for our inability to comprehend the pace and drive of global change. Yet there can be little excuse for non-recognition of the fact that transformation of an institution and its processes is never a matter of destruction pure and simple. Except in rare cases, societies do not replace an institution; they improve it. So it must be with the school. There is no substitute for school. If it did not exist, it would have to be invented. It provides what is unavoidably necessary—a local gathering-point of minds and bodies, a physical and psychological site for both social interaction and the child's individual intellectual development.

So we cannot do without schools in the future any more than we can now. This is the one limit no one can ignore. In the information-rich world of a more distant tomorrow, all institutions of society will perhaps little resemble their counterparts of today. Nonetheless they will in most cases remain securely in place—those dedicated to serious learning, given the increasing need for their product, visibly so. But the school, like other institutions, will have no choice but to move with the tides of change. Effective adaptation demands rising above the ever-present drag of archaic custom. Sooner or later decisions of substance must be made about methods of education. No one loves risk; but there are times in the cycle of human evolution when only risk makes sense, and we are approaching one of those times with greater rapidity than we may care to admit.

School instruction remains the most critical of all formative processes imposed by society on the child. Instruction cannot continue to deteriorate if nations and the individuals who comprise them are to improve their chances in an unpredictable and dangerous future. Intelligence, an individual gift, is readily degraded. In a twenty-first-century global Information Society, competition—between and among individuals as well as organized entities—will take on a steadily more intellectual and moral character, but it will be competition just the same, probably more unforgiving than even that which we know today.

Childhood itself is of course a realm of necessary fantasy and play. At the same time it is also the one most vital period for concentrated learning. The child cannot be chained to an unreasonable task, and in many ways the learning which he must accomplish to live out his life adequately in the twenty-first century will be just that. So neither can he be allowed to forego its stresses altogether. A steady direction of interest, not psychological or physical force, would seem the educator's, and the tutor's, most elemental guiding principle.

To match rationally the child's inchoate but still unrealistic sense of direction in life with his open-ended diffusion of energy in no direction at all, this is a task that adults alone have been unable to master. Nor will they be, for it lies beyond their immediate scope of power. It requires a power which can best be exercised behind the scenes, even to some extent out of the immediate sight and consciousness of other humans. Only the extension of our own intelligence in artificial mind can manage this harnessing of the seemingly negative combination of self-contradicting forces in the immature human. In the new century only just begun, we will discover how far and how well the art and science of pedagogy can travel on this road never before trod.

NOTES TO THE CHAPTERS

INTRODUCTION

1.   Quoted in *Time*, June 16, 1986, p. 53.

2.   From remarks to Conference on American Education, Del Coronado Hotel, San Diego, May, 1986. Reported in *Oakland Tribune*, May 18, 1986.

3.   **Paul Goodman**, "The Universal Trap," reprinted from Daniel Schreiber, ed., *The School Dropout*. NEA (School Dropout Project), 1964. In Stan Dropkin, et al, eds., *Contemporary American Education*. New York: Macmillan, 1970, p. 375.

4.   **John Kenneth Galbraith**, *The New Industrial State*. New York: Signet/New American Library, 1968, p. 255.

5.   **Margaret Mead**, *The School in American Culture*. Cambridge, MA.: Harvard University Press, 1959, pp. 39-40.

6.   See **Harold W. Stevenson**, "Learning From Asian Schools," *Scientific American*, December, 1992, pp. 70-76. Psychologist Stevenson presents the thesis that, on the basis of extant studies, Asian students outperform US students for a variety of reasons, including superior family motivation, strong discipline imposed by both school and society, and parental help with homework. Asians do view hard work as just as essential for children as adults. While Japanese and other Asian students are expected to show actual achievement as the outcome of instruction, American parents and teachers are satisfied with the knowledge that their learners possess the intelligence to "move on" in the world. But this line of interpretation, which lays stress on cultural differences as basis for contrasts in learning performance, carries an implicit, though largely hidden message: that the less diligent culture had better reform itself on the model of the more diligent. On the surface, given the primacy of competition as mainspring of evolution in every era, this reasoning makes a certain sense. But it also ignores both the differential effects that history has already brought about and the directions evolution seems poised to enforce in the future. Asia enjoys what no other cultures have historically had: a tradition of four or five millennia of Confucian ethics and an equally long-enduring legacy of Buddhist self-discipline. It also is privileged—so far—through the means of its adult culture of anti-individualist conformism, its collective expertise and devotion to hard work in and for itself, to ignore the rapidly developing and seemingly unalterably individualistic nature of work in a future full-scale Information Society. Conformity alone cannot be the answer to a twenty-first-century environmental challenge in

which socioeconomic progress will depend on the ability of all individuals not only to acquire knowledge but also to employ that knowledge in adaptive ways—using intelligence with originality in response to ever-shifting information flows and new demands for psychological flexibility in patterns of response. In such a globally competitive environment, if a traditional method of instruction had once seemed better suited to a given culture and its children, must that method necessarily prove equally adequate when the real demand is for ever greater individual flexibility and information-processing skill across the whole socioeconomic spectrum of decision making? As one Japanese critic himself, while admitting that schoolchildren in his culture are hard workers and superior achievers, put it in regard to the present generation of entry-level Japanese workers: "They can't come up with new solutions and ideas...they are like goldfish. They open their mouths and you feed them information." (Quoted in Joel Kotkin and Yoriko Kishimoto, "Theory F," *INC.*, April, 1986, p. 60.)

7.   **Bertrand Russell**, *Political Ideals*. New York: Simon and Schuster, 1964, p. 89. (First published in 1917.)

CHAPTER 1

1.   **Michael Marien**, "Some Questions for the Information Society," in Tom Forester, ed., *The Information Technology Revolution*. Cambridge, MA.: MIT Press, 1985, p. 656.

2.   **R. Freeman Butts**, *The Education of t h e West*. New York: McGraw-Hill, 1973, pp. 436-37.

3.   **Christopher Dede**, "Educational and Social Implications," in T. Forester, ed., op. cit., p. 244.

4.   **Philip H. Coombs**, *The World Crisis in Education*. New York: Oxford University Press, 1985, p. 133.

5.   Ibid. Even by 1998 the "miracle cure" technology was supposed to accomplish seemed to be further than ever from realization—in some measure, surely, given the lack of a rationale for its use. Diane Ravitch wrote in *Forbes*, March 23, 1998, for example, that there is "no evidence that use of computers or the Internet improves student achievement. Yet the billions spent on technology represent money not spent on music, art, libraries, maintenance, and other essential functions."

6.   **J. J. Servan-Schreiber**, *The World Challenge*. New York: Simon and Schuster, 1980.

7.   **Freeman Butts**, op. cit., p. 567.

8. **Norbert Wiener**, *The Human Use of Human Beings*. Boston: Houghton Mifflin, 1954, p. 166.

9. **Aristotle**, *The Politics*. Trans. T. A. Sinclair. New York: Penguin, 1962. Book VIII, Part iii.

10. Ibid., Book VIII, Part ii.

11. Ibid., Book VIII, Part iii.

12. See National Endowment for the Humanities, "Report on 1989 Poll of College Seniors (Conducted for the Endowment by the Gallup Organization)." Washington, D. C., 1989. As a typical instance of reports from the 1980s on lower schools and the problem of teaching fundamental knowledge, see the Education Report, "Losing the War of Letters," *Time*, May 5, 1986, p. 68.

13. **Robert M. Gagné**, *The Conditions of Learning*. New York: Holt, 1966, p. 247.

14. **David Riesman,** *Individualism Reconsidered and Other Essays*. New York: Free Press, 1965, p. 38.

15. Ibid., p. 37.

16. **Herbert Kohl**, *Basic Skills*. Boston: Little Brown, 1982, p. 5.

CHAPTER 2

1. **Van Cleve Morris**, *Philosophy and the American School*. Boston: Houghton Mifflin, 1961, p. 306.

2. **Martin Buber**, "Education," in N. N. Glatzer, ed., *The Way of Response: Martin Buber. Selections From His Writings*. New York: Schocken, 1966, p. 93.

3. **Harry Broudy**, *The Real World of the Public Schools*. New York: Harcourt Brace, 1971, p. 248.

4. **Lucien Gerardin**, *Bionics*. Translated by P. Priban. New York: McGraw-Hill, 1968, p. 224.

5. **Arnold Kauffman**, *The Science of Decision Making*. New York: McGraw-Hill, 1968, p. 230.

CHAPTER 3

1. **S. P. Marland**, "The School's Role in Career Development." *Educational Leadership*, December, 1972, pp. 203-05.

2. **Gilbert Highet**, *The Art of Teaching*. New York: Vintage, 1950, p. 247.

3.   **Mortimer J. Adler**, "The Paideia Proposal," Chap. 19, in Beatrice and Ronald Gross, eds., *The Great School Debate*. New York: Simon and Schuster Touchstone, 1985, p. 191.

4.   Ibid., pp. 192-93.

5.   **Thomas Lickona**, *Education For Character*. New York: Bantam, 1991, p. 183.

6.   Ibid.

7.   **Gilbert Highet**, *The Art of Teaching*, op. cit., p. 108.

8.   **Thomas Molnar**, *The Future of Education*. New York: Fleet Academic Editions, 1970, p. 135.

9.   **Bertrand Russell**, *History of Western Philosophy*. London: Allen and Unwin, 1957, p. 112.

10.   **Jacques Barzun**, "What Any Schoolboy Knows," Chapter 10, in *Of Human Freedom*. Philadelphia: Lippincott, 1964, p. 156.

11.   **Peter Brimelow**, "Competition For Public Schools," Chapter 43, in B. and R. Gross, eds., *The Great School Debate*, op cit., p. 349.

12.   **John Ralston Saul**, *Voltaire's Bastards*. New York: Free Press, 1992.

13.   **Henri I. Marrou**, *A History of Education in Antiquity*. Translated by George Lamb. New York: Mentor/NAL, 1964, p. 203.

14.   See **William Boyd**, *The History of Western Education*. New York: Barnes and Noble, 1966, pp. 38-39.

15.   **Roger Penrose**, *The Emperor's New Mind*. New York: Penguin, 1989, p. 411.

16.   **John Dewey**, *Democracy and Education*. New York: Macmillan, 1916, p. 89.

17.   **Jerome S. Bruner**, *The Process of Education*. New York: Vintage, 1960, p. 12.

18.   See **Claude E. Shannon** and **Warren Weaver**, *The Mathematical Theory of Communication*. Urbana, Ill.: University of Illinois Press, 1949. This book contains in its later segments an exposition of the theory (first presented by Shannon in a highly technical 1949 article) in reasonably comprehensible layman's terms.

19.   Historian of Greek education Werner Jaeger observes that in Plato's scheme "the doctor is the man who recognizes the sickness because of his knowledge of its opposite, health, and can therefore find ways and means to bring that which is sick back to its normal condition. That is his model for the philosopher, who is to do the same for the soul of man and its health." W.

Jaeger, *Paideia*, Vol. III. Translated by Gilbert Highet. New York: Oxford University Press, 1971, pp. 21-22.

20. **E. M. Forster,** *Two Cheers For Democracy.* New York: Harcourt Brace, 1951, p. 70.

CHAPTER 4

1. **Jacques Ellul,** *The Technological Society.* Translated by John Wilkinson. New York: Vintage/Knopf, 1967, p. 348.

2. **Aldous Huxley,** "Knowledge and Understanding," in *Adonis and the Alphabet.* London: Chatto and Windus, 1956, p. 48.

3. See the essay by Professors Fred Newman and Thomas Kelley, "Excellence and the Dignity of Students," in Bertram and Beatrice Gross, eds., *The Great School Debate.* New York: Simon and Schuster Touchstone, 1985, pp. 222-28.

4. **Joseph Adelson,** "Educators Are Stuck in the '60s," in Gross and Gross, eds., op. cit., p. 320.

5. **Allan Bloom,** *The Closing of the American Mind.* New York: Simon and Schuster, 1987, p. 276.

6. Ibid., p. 275.

7. **Hans Moravec,** *Mind Children: The Future of Robot and Human Intelligence.* Cambridge, MA.: Harvard University Press, 1988, p, 100.

8. Ibid.

CHAPTER 5

1. **Christopher Evans,** *The Micromillennium.* New York: Washington Square Press, 1981, p. 127.

2. Ibid., pp. 128-30.

3. Ibid., pp. 130-31.

4. **Stanley Rothman** and **Charles Mosmann,** *Computer Uses and Issues.* Chicago: SRA, 1985, pp. 290-92.

5. **PLATO** *User's Guide.* St. Paul, MN.: Control Data Corporation, 1981, p. 1-1.

6. **Rothman** and **Mosmann,** op. cit., pp. 292-93.

7. Ibid., p. 294.

8. Ibid.

9. Ibid., pp. 297-99.

10.   The inadequacy of much instructional software, in both concept and detail, is well known. As one disgruntled newspaper columnist long ago put it, educators seem to have bequeathed to software publishers a catalog of situations that make learning difficult if not impossible and they "are cranking out programs to incorporate almost every negative listed." Jean Bennett, "Educational Software: A Loss for Learning," *San Jose Mercury News*, July 15, 1984.

11.   See "Reports of the Research Briefing Panels, 1984," in NAS, *New Pathways in Science and Technology: Collected Research Briefings, 1982-84.* New York: Vintage, 1985, pp. 303-04.

12.   **Alan Porter**, "Work in the New Information Age," *The Futurist*, September-October, 1986, p. 13.

13.   **John Stuart Mill**, *On Liberty*. In *The Six Great Humanistic Essays*. New York: Washington Square Press, 1963, pp. 230-31.

14.   I see no reason to alter the remarks I made over two decades ago on the subject of teacher qualities (in effect, that we are mistaken to think that a pleasant personality and a compliant attitude are the prime requisites for employment in teaching, when dynamic qualities of mind and openness to new experience are far more significant). See my *Environment and Learning: The Prior Issues*. Cranbury, N. J. and London: Associated University Presses, 1977, pp. 106-14.

15.   **Ernest R. House**, *The Politics of Educational Innovation*. Berkeley, CA.: McCutchan, 1974, p. 184.

16.   **Robert Jastrow**, *The Enchanted Loom*. New York: Simon and Schuster, 1981, pp. 164-65. (Italics added.) Deliberate efforts to create artificial intelligence on a basis of how the human being learns (and not simply on a basis of language structure) have been for some time going forward under the general designation of "connectionism" (what is "connected" to learning per se, rather than what is feasible or desirable as programming alone).

17.   **Norbert Wiener**, excerpt from *God and Golem*, reprinted in John Diebold, ed., *The World of the Computer*. New York, Random House, 1973, pp. 455-56.

18.   **Patrick Suppes**, "The Future of Computers in Education," in Robert P. Taylor, ed., *The Computer in the School*. New York: Teachers College Press, 1980, p. 260.

19.   Ibid., p. 259.

20.   Ibid.

CHAPTER 6

1.   **Bill Honig**, *Last Chance For Our Children*. Reading, Mass.: Addison-Wesley, 1985, pp. 141-42.

2.   Ibid.

3.   **George Leonard**, *Education and Ecstasy*. New York: Delacorte Press, 1968, p. 127.

4.   **Bill Honig**, op. cit., pp. 185-86.

5.   Ibid., p. 186.

6.   Ibid., p. 187.

7.   Ibid.

8.   **John I. Goodlad**, *A Place Called School: Prospects For the Future*. New York: McGraw-Hill, 1984, pp. 359-60.

9.   **Douglas McGregor**, *The Human Side of the Enterprise*. New York: McGraw-Hill, 1960.

10.   Perhaps the most influential force in the field of psychology emphasizing the significance of personality-forming early childhood experiences was Erik Erikson. See his *Childhood and Society*. New York: Norton, 1963.

11.   As long ago as the February, 1987, Washington conference on early childhood education, a meeting sponsored by the NAEYC and the National Association of Elementary School Principals, the Elkind group urged a reduction in the academic content of pre-school programs across the board. This position meets heavy opposition from a variety of experts, among whom the belief is strong that the very young can and should be "pushed" intellectually, both for their own and society's future good (e.g., Glenn Dorman, of the Better Baby Institute, who has no hesitation in asking three-year-olds to delve into formal math and foreign language study).

12.   Between such extreme positions as those mentioned in the previous footnote, there lie myriad intermediate points of view. One approach is that espoused by Stanford University Professor Henry Levin, who has pinpointed tracking, especially into normal and remedial groups, as psychologically unsound. Levin's group at Stanford has found that avoidance of language study in the elementary school links up with the experience of tracking as a major indicator of a child's future prospects for becoming an academic failure or dropping out in the later stages of the K-12 sequence.

13.   **John Goodlad**, op. cit., p. 236 and pp. 231-32.

14.   In his *Crisis in the Classroom* (New York: Random House, 1970), Silberman provided a remarkably comprehensive documentation of

"exceptions"—those school classroom programs, wherever they would be found on the American scene, which through innovative practices enhanced either learner morale or achievement (or both) in significant ways. One has the inclination now, more than three decades later, to wonder not merely about the subsequent fate of such programs but also, since so few are discussed any longer in educational literature, whether or not they were to begin with excessively unique to their time and place. Coming so much later to deal with this same issue, Goodlad simply referred to certain schools and their programs as "the same but different," an acknowledgement that unusual success of this or that innovation in a particular set of instructional circumstances can hardly signify anything absolute with regard to later use of that innovation elsewhere and under different circumstances. See Goodlad's Chapter 8 ("The Same But Different"), pp. 246-70.

15. See especially Goodlad's summation of what goes on in typical classroom sessions, op. cit., pp. 123-29.

16. See "First Math-test Standards Adopted for US Students." *Washington Post*, May 10, 1991.

17. **Daniel Bell,** *The Coming of the Post-Industrial Society.* New York: Basic Books, 1973, p. 349, footnote 8. A more recent coinage is "technopoly," apparently the invention of Professor Neil Postman. In his book *Technopoly: The Surrender of Culture to Technology* (New York: Knopf, 1992), Postman, much like Ellul before him, espouses the view that by its very nature technology and human culture are antithetical and that the former must inevitably destroy subjective values historically present in the latter. Thus to Postman today's America has become a matured version of earlier technocracy, something to be termed "totalitarian technocracy." That technology itself (and even some aspects of technocratic management) might be made to serve legitimate human purposes seems to be implicitly denied by Postman—probably, one suspects, because he limits his thinking to the megarelations in a mass society, between the Scylla of culture and the Charybdis of technology, thus leaving to one side and forgotten the lone individual who in his uniqueness remains enigmatically both part of yet apart from the mainstream trend-flows of technomanagement and human culture.

CHAPTER 7

1. The Indiana city's program claims success in large measure due to the fact that it found the resources to individualize instruction for a considerable number of underachievers, no small accomplishment in the 1980s in a grimy

industrial city with an increasingly minority population. Other large urban districts with similar populations and problems, however, seem for the most part unable to create the conditions even for meaningful discussion of educational reform or change of direction. Such districts as Boston, Jersey City, and Oakland (Calif.) seem so mired in politics and even outright corruption that initiative for change there can find no spokesman and a frustrated, fragmented public tends to wash its hands of school affairs by accepting frequent changes of school administration and constant wrangling at school board meetings as no longer worthy even of contempt. Even larger districts (New York; Chicago; the two in Los Angeles, i.e., city and county) are equally burdened by bureaucratic overhead, population over-diversity, political squabbling, and public apathy. Only Rochester, N. Y., among larger districts has developed a program for cooperation among schools, businesspeople, community leaders, and university advisers which may perhaps inject new life and hope into a system also in serious difficulties. As of the time of writing of this footnote, Chicago's neighborhood control program was still new enough so that it was premature to attempt passing judgment on its possibilities for the longer term.

2.   See *Encyclopedia Britannica*, Vol. 3, pp. 861-62. (15th Edition, 1985.)

3.   The Winnetka Plan of Mastery Learning was developed in the 1920s. It involved reducing a subject to a number of learning units, complete mastery of the objectives of which, in sequential order, was required for learner mastery of the subject itself. Diagnostic testing on an individual basis determined the amount of time a given learner had to spend with a particular unit. A somewhat similar plan developed at the same time at the University of Chicago Laboratory School was named the Morrison Plan after the professor who guided it. These plans emphasized the learning sequence within any subject area and broke down instructional units into smaller and prerequisite elements. Thus both the Winnetka and Morrison Plans contributed to the eventual emergence of programmed learning—which actually had its inception in the work of the psychologist S. L. Pressey, intellectual father of the teaching machine, also active as early as the 1920s. See James H. Block, "Introduction to Mastery Learning: Theory and Practice," in J. H. Block, ed., *Mastery Learning: Theory and Practice*. New York: Holt, 1971, pp. 2-12.

4.   Programmed instruction developed gradually on the basis of the principle of mastery of sub-component learning enunciated in the earlier theories. As codified by Skinner in the 1950s and presented to the public through a device called a "teaching machine," the practice required mechanical

presentation of sequence items to an individual learner, the usual pattern involving reduction of a text to single "frames," to each of which the learner must respond successfully before proceeding. Essential elements of programmed instruction are: a) sequentially ordered input (frames); b) desired response; c) immediate feedback which can correct a wrong answer and reinforce the right one. See B. F. Skinner's seminal article, "Teaching Machines," in *Science*, Vol. 128, 1958, pp. 969-77.

5.   Mastery Learning is a modernized and integrative development of all the earlier strategies for individualizing and rationalizing learning. Developed by, among others, John B. Carroll and Benjamin S. Bloom in the 1960s, mainly at the University of Chicago, it is a holistic and inclusive approach to the problems of individual learning and takes into account affective as well as cognitive factors, requiring diagnosis of each learner's levels of subject matter interest and general interest, his attitudes toward school and school tasks, his self-concept, and his state of mental health. See Benjamin Bloom, "Affective Consequences of School Achievement," in James H. Block, ed., *Mastery Learning*, op. cit., pp. 13-28.

6.   In its mainline operational scheme Mastery Learning actually implements several non-traditional assumptions regarding individual learning: Aptitude is measured not by a score on an aptitude test but as the time required by the individual to master a given learning task; quality of instruction is defined as an ordering of elements in the instruction to correspond with a standard optimum outcome for "normal" learning; ability to understand and profit from instruction depends on an individual's experience and abilities and, hence, modification of stereotypical patterns for group instruction is frequently necessary if mastery is required as the end-result; adequate time must be available for each individual learner; evaluation of learning must be diagnostic in character, that is, aimed at providing feedback to both learner and teacher as an integral element in a continuous process and not simply a final grading procedure. See Bloom's article, "Mastery Learning," in Block, ed., op. cit., pp. 47-63. The main problem with Mastery Learning as developed by theorists seems to have been its unsuitability for classroom deployment. As computers become more common in schools and the need for individual tuition increases, it is likely that school administrators and teachers may find the concept of greater interest, if for no other reason than that in its very fundamentals Mastery Learning so comprehensively incorporates the "basics" for successful individualization of learning.

7.   **Benjamin S. Bloom**, "Mastery Learning," in Block, ed., op. cit., pp. 51-52.

8. **Richard Hofstadter**, *Anti-Intellectualism in American Life*. New York: Random House, 1963, pp. 350-53.

9. For background on cooperative groups in education see Robert Slavin, "The Cooperative Revolution in Education," *School Administrator*, XLV, January, 1988, pp. 9-13. Interesting possibilities may surface from programs aimed at increasing the independence of judgment of fairly young children in their study of the basic school subjects and for more on this aspect see Harold L. Herber and Joan Nelson-Herber, "Helping Students Become Independent Learners," *Journal of Reading*, XXX, April, 1987, pp. 584-88.

10. See Robert M. Gagné, *The Conditions of Learning*, op. cit. 1966, pp. 59-61 and 285-94.

11. **PLATO** *User's Guide*. Op. cit. See Appendix C, p. 7. And even more promising perhaps might be the individualized instruction programs falling under the heading of ICAI (Intelligent Computer-Assisted Instruction). Work in this area has been going on for a long time at Stanford University and at Bolt, Beranek and Newman in Massachusetts, among other centers. ICAI applications utilize a three-pronged approach, in which a knowledge base provides expertise in the area of individual study, a "student model" allows for analysis of the learner's performance in light of standard reasoning patterns ordinarily associated with that subject, and a "tutoring module" ends up with the task of devising a comprehensive strategy for insuring that learning is completed. See Avron Barr and E. A. Feigenbaum, *Handbook of Artificial Intelligence*. Los Altos Hills, CA.: William Kaufmann, 1982, Vol. 2, pp. 230-35. Nevertheless, development of CAI learning systems remains a slow, pervasively uncertain affair even in this first decade of the new millennium. The wide gap which exists between theory and development in CAI is not yet even near being closed; the question was first explored in some depth in articles appearing as the mid-1980s in the *Phi Delta Kappan*. (June, 1986. Recommended in that issue: Julie S. Vargas, "Instructional Design Flaws in Computer-Assisted Instruction" and Richard P. Niemiec, et al, "CAI Can Be Doubly Effective.") In re. the varying views of the larger problem of a machine's ability to "think," see George Johnson, *Machinery of the Mind: Inside the New Science of Artificial Intelligence*. Redmond, Wash., 1988: Microsoft Press. (Johnson aims to show how close science had already come, and well before the end of the twentieth century, to creating a machine that, by any reasonable definition, does "think" and, indeed, can also work creatively.)

12. **Gilbert Highet**, *The Art of Teaching*. New York: Random House/Vintage, 1950, p. 108.

13. **Robert M. Hutchins,** *The Learning Society.* New York: Praeger, 1968, p. 74.

14. Ibid., p. 83.

15. Ibid., pp. 87-88.

16. Ibid., p. 91.

CHAPTER 8

1. **Robert M. Gagné,** *The Conditions of Learning,* op. cit., p. 8.

2. **Milton Schwebel,** "The Other School System," in B. and R. Gross, eds., *The Great School Debate,* op. cit., p. 238.

3. Ibid., p. 242.

4. Ibid., p. 241.

5. This would meet one of the conditions laid down by educational critics Fred Newman and Thomas Kelly for "maintaining the dignity" of those many school learners otherwise threatened by any regime demanding greater effort in the pursuit of academic excellence without provision for special forms of assistance: Resources are to be directed to both disadvantaged and slower students in more substantial amounts. Nothing is implied, nevertheless, about either holding back or speeding the pace of achievement among learners who are then not blessed with these additional resources. Since equity can only be defined in this scheme in terms antipathetic to those who will be unable to benefit from such a diversion of resources, it is hard to see anything but further unfairness as an outcome. See F. M. Newman and T. E. Kelly, "Excellence and the Dignity of Students," in Gross and Gross, eds., op. cit., pp. 222-28.

6. See for detail, Alan Porter, op. cit., "Work in the New Information Age," *The Futurist,* Sept.-Oct., 1986, p. 13.

7. **Gilbert Highet,** *The Art of Teaching,* op. cit., p. 108 and p. 111. See also Henry J. Perkinson, *Since Socrates.* New York: Longmans, 1980, pp. 7-13 and 213-17. Perkinson emphasizes an unevadable point in pedagogy: Only Socratic method is clearly nonauthoritarian in both intent and organization of the instructional environment. It proceeds from an assumption that knowledge and wisdom are the product of individual "encounter" rather than results of some process of automatic transmission.

8. Consider MIT scientist Joe Weizenbaum's concerns over misuse of computer management schemes in general and of experimental "semantic analysis" programs in the psychological domain specifically. See "On the Impact of the Computer on Society," *Science,* May, 1972, Vol. 176, pp. 609-14. Among schemes which purport to manage through a mix of appropriate

instructional techniques, the Paideia program admits three basic modes of instruction—didactic, coaching, and Socratic—with the last most needed and the first most prevalent. See Mortimer Adler, "The Paideia Proposal," in Gross and Gross, eds., op. cit., pp. 188-94, especially p. 192. What this fails to confront in dealing with the instructional issue is the psychological-situational dimension: How can maieutic or Socratic instruction be used effectively in an environment (the classroom) so continually dominated by momentary social and cultural concerns antagonistic to systematic individual learning? How can the individual's psychological directions and typical mental road-blocks be identified and made use of pedagogically in such an environment—unless he can initially be communicated with as an individual and the classroom processes and activities in which he thereafter engages be themselves prepared and adjusted to take into account his specifically individual line of mental development?

9. **Emile Durkheim**, *The Division of Labor in Society*. Translated by George Simpson. New York: Free Press, 1965, p. 372.

10. Ibid., pp. 374, ff.

11. **Daniel Bell**, *The Cultural Contradictions of Capitalism*. New York: Basic Books, 1976, pp. 99-100.

12. Already in the pre-World War One era Durkheim could complain that the division of labor "has often been accused of degrading the individual by making him a machine. And truly, if he does not know whither the operations he performs are tending, if he relates them to no end, he can only continue to work through routine…he repeats the same movements with monotonous regularity, but without being interested in them, and without understanding them." This description is surely as apt for a distressingly large number of today's school learners as it continues to be for adult assembly line factory workers. See Durkheim, *The Division of Labor in Society,* op. cit., p. 371.

13. **Baron Montesquieu**, *Spirit of the Laws*. Thomas Nugent translation. Chicago: EB Great Books, 1952, Vol. 38, p. 15.

CHAPTER 9

1. **John E. Chubb** and **Terry M. Moe**, *Politics, Markets, and America's Schools*. Washington, D. C.: Brookings Institution, 1990, p. 216.

2. Ibid., pp. 216-17.

3. **Charles R. Reid**, "Choice in Education: What Will It Mean For Instruction?," *Perspectives*, Vol. 19, No. 2, Summer, 1989, pp. 43-46.

4. **Paul Geisert** and **Mynga Futrell**, *Teachers, Computers, and Curriculum.* Needham Heights, MA.: Allyn and Bacon, 1990, p. 319.

5. At an MIT experimental school in the Boston area, for example, author Stewart Brand found that "the computers promote the students…and demote the teachers from the main event to appreciated assistants. More learning, less teaching." Stewart Brand, *The Media Lab: Inventing the Future at MIT.* New York: Viking Press, 1987, p. 151.

6. **Raymond A. Callahan**, *Education and the Cult of Efficiency.* Chicago: University of Chicago Press, 1961.

7. **Gerald Heard**, *The Five Ages of Man.* New York: Julian Press, 1963, p. 310.

8. It should be noted that the Kumon method, which has been used effectively as a method for individualized instruction in math in many countries since its development in Japan in the mid-1950s, emphasizes work with a series of some 4,000 sequential work sheets which lead the learner from the very earliest math concepts to calculus and is signally successful in its mixture of modes of instruction and learning required: sheer repetition until mastery is achieved; self-instruction with adult aid available as needed; short daily periods of work on the subject; no pressure to compete with peers; drill and practice as a means of comprehending concepts (rather than the reverse). See the review of Kumon by Chester E. Finn: "Made in Japan: Low-Tech Method For Math Success," *Wall Street Journal*, July 12, 1989.

9. **J. W. von Goethe**, *Italian Journey.* Translated by W. H. Auden and Elizabeth Mayer. London: Wm. Collins, 1962, p. 113.

CHAPTER 10

1. **Charles Darwin**, *The Origin of Species.* New York: Collier Harvard Classics Edition, 1937. Vol. 11, p. 377.

2. **Roger Penrose**, *The Emperor's New Mind,* op. cit., p. 407.

3. **Bertrand Russell**, *A History of Western Philosophy,* op. cit., p. 11.

4. **Allan Bloom**, *The Closing of the American Mind.* New York: Simon and Schuster, 1987, p. 228.

5. For one interpretation of Bloom's analysis of the problems of relativism and rationalism in contemporary US education, see my article on the reform debate in America: Charles R. Reid, "Educational Reform: Critiquing the Critics," *Urban Education*, Vol. 25, No. 3, October, 1990, pp. 370-74.

6. A series of cases of group violence against individual students in Japanese schools (including the instance of a murder of a 13-year-old non-

conforming boy in the gymnasium of his junior high school in Shinjo City) was detailed by Colin Nickerson, "Deadly Bullying Hammers the 'Odd' Student in Japan," *Boston Globe*, January 29, 1993.

7.   **Daniel Bell**, *The Cultural Contradictions of Capitalism*, op. cit., p. 110.

8.   **Bertrand Russell**, op. cit., p. 11.

9.   **Ernest Cassirer**, *The Philosophy of the Enlightenment*. Translated by Fritz C. A. Koelln and James P. Pettegrove. Princeton, N. J.:   Princeton University Press, 1979, p. 179.

10.   See Allan Bloom, op. cit., pp. 115-17 and pp. 185, ff., for a discussion of the influence of Rousseau's thinking on human relationships and culture in modern philosophy and sociology.

11.   **Bertrand Russell**, op. cit., p. 721. Russell cites Hegel's critique of Rousseau's theory of the general will by pointing out that, while Hegel selected for special praise the fact that Rousseau did in passing distinguish between a general will as an abstraction per se and the perhaps less abstract "will of all," Hegel remarked in his Logic, section 163, that Rousseau "would have made a sounder contribution towards a theory of the State, if he had always kept this distinction in sight." (Russell, op. cit., p. 727) Ernest Cassirer has explored the historical background of this and other theories of social contract in his post-World War Two book *The Myth of the State*.

12.   **John Dewey**, *Democracy and Education*. New York: Macmillan, 1916, p. 96.

13.   As Santayana puts the matter: "(Kant) wished to blast as insignificant, because 'subjective,' the whole structure of human intelligence, with all the lessons of experience and all the triumphs of human skill, and to attach absolute validity instead to certain echoes of his rigoristic religious education. These notions were surely just as subjective, and far more local and transitory, than the common machinery of thought; and it was actually proclaimed to be an evidence of their sublimity that they remained entirely without practical sanction in the form of success or happiness." George Santayana, *The Life of Reason*. Vol. One, "Reason in Common Sense." New York: Dover, 1980, p. 96.

14.   **Daniel Bell**, *The Cultural Contradictions of Capitalism*, op. cit., pp. 110-11.

15.   **Allan Bloom**, *The Closing of the American Mind*, op. cit., p. 56.

16.   **John Dewey**, op. cit., p. 338.

17.   **Daniel Bell**, op. cit., p. 145.

18.   **Bertrand Russell**, op. cit., p. 855.

19.   Quoted in Ibid., p. 719.

20.   Ibid. E. M. Forster's acid denunciation of the craft sums up the plight of modern philosophy: "As things are, the poor creature (man) presents a sorry spectacle to the philosopher—or, rather, he would do so if philosophers existed, but we have realised since the days of Voltaire and Rousseau that they do not exist. There is no such person as a philosopher; no one is detached; the observer, like the observed, is in chains." E. M. Forster, *Two Cheers for Democracy*. New York: Harcourt Brace, 1951, p. 10. In a parallel context Albert Schweitzer points out that philosophy has sought with a persistence bordering on mania to create a wholly theoretical view of the universe, neglecting the nature of the structure already in development. "No effort should have been spared to direct the attention of the cultured and the uncultured alike to the problem of the ideals of civilization. But philosophy philosophized about everything except civilization...she did not even notice that she herself and the age along with her were losing more and more of it." Albert Schweitzer, *The Philosophy of Civilization*. Translated by C. T. Campion. Buffalo, New York: Prometheus Books, 1987, p. 8. Marx had complained that the task of philosophy was not to explain the world but rather to change it. In hindsight how difficult, indeed impossible, that prescription would prove to be in implementation seems now only too evident in an era when, patently, not philosophy but sheer evolutionary pressures alone drive forward the process of human development.

21.   **Bertrand Russell**, op. cit., p. 744.

22.   For the complete discussion of his proposed epistemological ground for the hypothesis of man as jointly machine and self, see the author's essay "A Machine or a Self," in J. Bronowski, *The Identity of Man*. Garden City, NY: Natural History Press, 1965, pp. 2-23.

23.   Ibid., pp. 17-18.

24.   Ibid., pp. 106-07.

25.   An exposition of pros and cons of this argument is given in Clark Kerr, *The Future of Industrial Societies: Convergence or Continuing Diversity*. Cambridge, Mass.: Harvard University Press, 1983.

26.   For a complete discussion of Spencer's beliefs and influence in this area see Robert Nisbet, *History of the Idea of Progress*. New York: Basic Books, 1980, pp. 232-36.

27.   **J. Bronowski**, op. cit., p. 22.

28.   Belaboring the decline of morals and social standards as an inevitable consequence of capitalist development is a time-honored occupation among both sociologists and some economists. Taking cues from Max Weber and

Schumpeter, as Robert Nisbet has pointed out, are such contemporary writers as economists E. J. Mishan and Fred Hirsch. See Nisbet, op. cit., pp. 334-38.

CHAPTER 11

1.   See Kotkin and Kishimoto, op. cit. See also Thomas P. Rohlen, *Japan's High Schools.* Berkeley: University of California Press, 1983, p. 279.

2.   **Thomas Rohlen**, op. cit., p. 279.

3.   **Jerry L. Salvaggio**, "An Assessment of Japan as an Information Society in the 1980s," in Howard F. Didsbury, ed., *Communications and the Future.* Washington/Bethesda, MD.: World Future Society, 1982, p. 93.

4.   **Rush Welter**, *Popular Education and Democratic Thought in America.* New York: Columbia University Press, 1962, p. 335.

5.   **Alfred North Whitehead**, *The Aims of Education and Other Essays.* New York: Free Press, 1957, p. 14.

6.   **Theodore Roszak**, *The Cult of Information.* New York: Pantheon, 1986.

7.   **William Ernest Hocking**, *The Coming World Civilization.* New York: Harper, 1956, p. 8.

8.   See for example Marvin Cetron and Margaret Gayle, *Educational Renaissance.* New York: St. Martin's Press, 1991, Chapter 8, "Desktop Learning," pp. 103-14.

9.   See **Richard J. Murnane**, "Education and the Productivity of the Work Force: Looking Ahead," in Robert Liten, et al, eds., *American Living Standards.* Washington, D. C.: Brookings Institution, 1988, pp. 215-45. See especially pp. 233-34 for Murnane's critical remarks on use of computers in US schools.

10.   **Jerome S. Bruner**, *The Relevance of Education.* New York: Norton, 1971, p. 106.

11.   **R. Freeman Butts**, *The Education of the West*, op. cit., p. 428.

12.   For those concerned for mathematical certainties, the number of possible groupings for the school described (non-graded, 400 students, 30 teachers, and 20 rooms) takes the following form in combinatorial notation:

$$(\text{Unknown}) = 30 \times 29 \times 28 \times \ldots \times 11 \times \frac{400}{(20!) \quad 20}$$

AFTERWORD

1   **R. Freeman Butts,** *The Education of the West,* op. cit., p. 556.

2.   **Robert Nisbet,** *History of the Idea of Progress,* op. cit., p. 237.

3.   **Edward A. Feigenbaum** and **Pamela McCorduck,** *The Fifth Generation.* New York: NAL, 1984, p. 231.

4.   **Max Weber,** *The Protestant Ethic and the Spirit of Capitalism.* Translated by Talcott Parsons. New York: Scribner, 1958, p. 182.

5.   **Albert Schweitzer,** *The Philosophy of Civilization,* op. cit., p. 271.

6.   **H. G. Wells,** *The Outline of History.* New York: Macmillan, 1921, pp. 931-33.

7.   Butts, op. cit., p. 327.

8.   Ibid., p. 328.

9.   **Michel Foucault,** *The Foucault Reader.* Paul Rabinow, ed. New York: Pantheon Books, 1984, pp. 191-92 and p. 195. (Excerpt from Foucault's book *Discipline and Punish.* Translated by Alan Sheridan. New York: Pantheon, 1977.)

10.   **Jean Piaget,** et al, *The Moral Judgment of the Child.* Translated by Marjorie Gabain. New York: Free Press, 1965, p. 320.

11.   **Pierre Teilhard de Chardin,** *The Future of Man.* Translated by Norman Denny. New York: Harper, 1964, p. 125.

12.   **Henry Perkinson,** *Since Socrates,* op. cit., p. 10.

13.   Plato, "The Apology" (Defence of Socrates). In *The Great Dialogues of Plato.* Translated by W. H. D. Rouse. New York: Mentor, 1956, pp. 438-39.

14.   **Allan Bloom,** *The Closing of the American Mind,* op. cit., p. 382.

15.   Modern historians of the Roman Republic as diverse as 19th Century Mommsen and 20th Century Arthur Boak agree that corruption in pre-Christian Rome of the Republic was endemic, so that revolts such as that of the Gracchi were justified in a high degree; in Mommsen's flowery phrase, "though an absolute monarchy is an absolute misfortune for a nation, it is a less misfortune than an absolute oligarchy." Theodore Mommsen, *History of Rome* (Abridged). New York: Scribner, 1890, p. 238. The depth of Roman corruption in those times in well documented also in Arthur E. A. Boak, *History of Rome to 565 A. D.* New York: Macmillan, 1943, pp. 177-83.

16.   **John Dewey,** *Democracy and Education,* op. cit., p. 89.

Index

PLATO instructional system 67-
70, 72-73, 120, 127 (See also
Computers, Instruction)
Poincaré, Henri 200
Political leadership in education
(US) xiv-xv, 15, 91-92, 104
Politics (Aristotle) 10
Popper, Karl, Sir 18
Porter, Allan 71-72, 187
Postman, Neil 220
Pragmatism, philosophy of 156-
157
Praxeology (Science of Action)
25
Pressey, S. L. 99, 107-108, 221
Prison mentality (in schools)
194-196
Private schools (US) 116
Process (and Processes):
educational viii-ix, 47-48, 80-
81, 86 ff, 95-96, 100-101,
166; social xviii-xix, 155,
163-164; historical (US) vii-
ix; information 7 (See also
Educational method,
Instruction, Social change,
Society)
Professions, similarities of 140-
141
Programmed learning/instruction
99-100
Progressive education 36-37, 47
Propaganda, effects of 202
Proposition 13 (California) 46
Psychiatry, practice of 141, 143
Psychology, educational: and
learning 11-12, 109-111;
behaviorist 99, 106-107; US
traditions in 116 (See also
Experiment, Instruction,
Learner)

Ravitch, Diane 214
Reading skills 73
Reality, denial of 151
Record-keeping, school 138 ff
Reflection, as source of learning
155
Reform, of education (See
Educational reform)
Reid, Charles 218, 226, 227
Relativism, moral-behavioral
150, 159
Religious sects, and education 9-
10
Remedial instruction 62, 103-
104, 142
Republic, The (Plato) 207
Research and Development (R &
D) (See Experiment,
Instruction)
Resources, educational 138, 142
Riesman, David 13-14
Robotics 63; "laws of" 209
Rochester, NY, schools of 221
Rohlen, Thomas 229
Roszak, Theodore 171-172
Rousseau, J. J. 100, 120, 154-
155, 157-159, 227
Russell, Bertrand 33, 36, 41,
149, 153, 155, 157, 159, 227
Salvaggio, Jerry 170
Santayana, George 155, 208,
227
Saul, John R. 37
School: as learning center 14-
15, 210-211; as locus of future
change 211; as mass
enterprise xiii-xiv; as
microcosm of society 156; as
social investment 51; as
social unit 37; as source of
public concerns 14-15; as

ABOUT THE AUTHOR

Charles Reid is a native of southeastern Wisconsin, descended from pioneer farmers and entrepreneurs long settled in that area. Among his forebears were men who as Scottish immigrants worked their way to the upper Midwest with jobs on the Erie Canal, and a 49er who not only survived a trek to the California gold fields but also returned to Wisconsin—via Cape Horn—with a small bonanza of nuggets with which to begin a second life as a gentleman farmer.

The author attended the University of Wisconsin, where he studied mainly fine arts and social science. He served in the US Army Signal Corps as a photographer during the Korean War and then spent a few years travelling and studying in Europe before settling down to a teaching career in California. He worked in public schools there and later took a doctorate in education at Berkeley, after which he served as professor in teacher education programs at colleges in Iowa and North Carolina. Sidelined professionally for a time by illness, he resumed teaching as adjunct professor of computer science at Ohlone College in California. He recently retired after two decades at Ohlone; he still lives in the San Jose-Silicon Valley area. Besides his earlier book *Environment and Learning*, the author has published articles in many education journals, including *Educational Leadership* and *Urban Education*. Though an avid user of (and believer in) the computer, Dr. Reid remains as yet uncommitted to the communications industry's current foray into the Internet's world of wonders. "The jury is still out on these trends," he comments, "and at this point we should probably be asking the question: Will humanity be better for this new power given it, or has technology once again called the tune for man, who must dance with this music until a more profound experience becomes possible?"